COCA
YES,
COCAINE
NO

THOMAS GRISAFFI

COCA
YES,
COCAINE
NO

How Bolivia's Coca Growers
Reshaped Democracy

Duke University Press   Durham and London   2019

© 2019 Duke University Press. All rights reserved
Printed and bound by CPI Group (UK) Ltd, Croydon, CR0 4YY
Designed by Courtney Leigh Baker
Typeset in Whitman by Westchester Publishing Services

Library of Congress Cataloging-in-Publication Data
Names: Grisaffi, Thomas, [date—] author.
Title: Coca yes, cocaine no : how Bolivia's coca growers reshaped
democracy / Thomas Grisaffi.
Description: Durham : Duke University Press, 2019. | Includes
bibliographical references and index.
Identifiers: LCCN 2018027122 (print) | LCCN 2018028969 (ebook)
ISBN 9781478004332 (ebook)
ISBN 9781478001713 (hardcover : alk. paper)
ISBN 9781478002970 (pbk. : alk. paper)
Subjects: LCSH: Coca industry—Bolivia—Chapare. | Cocaine
industry—Bolivia—Chapare. | Coca industry—Government policy—
Bolivia. | Movimiento al Socialismo (Bolivia) | Agricultural
laborers—Labor unions—Bolivia—Chapare. | Bolivia—Politics
and government—2006– | Bolivia—Politics and
government—1982–2006. Classification: LCC HD9019.C632 (ebook) |
LCC HD9019.C632 B535 2019 (print) | DDC 338.1/737—dc23
LC record available at https://lccn.loc.gov/2018027122

Cover art: Chapare Mural (*top*) and coca growers attend a
rally in support of the MAS government (*bottom*).
Both courtesy of the author.

CONTENTS

ACKNOWLEDGMENTS

Many people have helped me to write this book. Most of all I would like to thank the people who live in Aurora (which is not the real name of the village). It is hard for me to express the debt that I owe them in kindness, acceptance, and generosity. For reasons of confidentiality I have not named individuals here. I am very grateful to the Federación Especial de Trabajadores Campesinos del Trópico de Cochabamba (FETCTC), Radio Aurora (an alias), the Seis Federaciones del Trópico de Cochabamba, the Gobierno Autónomo Municipal de Villa Tunari, and the Mancomunidad de Municipios del Trópico de Cochabamba. Once more, I have not named individuals who work in these organizations. I am indebted to Kathryn Ledebur at the Andean Information Network for her advice, recommendations, and knowledge. Great thanks also to Dr. Godofredo Reinicke for my first introduction to the Chapare. Linda Farthing read several drafts of this book and provided detailed edits and expert feedback; thank you.

I began my anthropology career as a student at Manchester University. I am especially grateful to my supervisors Penny Harvey, John Gledhill, and Maggie Bolton. I would also like to thank Peter Wade, Hannah Brown, Sarah Green, Orlando Einsiedel, Julian Fenner, Mick Matthews, Tim Rangecroft, Joceny Pinheiro, Michael Kent, Valentina Bonifacio, Pablo Jaramillo, Keir Martin, Hannah Knox, and Priscilla Clarissou. In London I have benefited from discussions with a great many colleagues and friends at the London School of Economics and University College London. I would like to thank Deborah James, Hans Steinmuller, Amit Desai, George St. Clair, Charles Stafford, Yanina Hinrichsen, Maxim Bolt, Mathijs Pelkmans, Andrew Sanchez, Jonah Lipton, Jason Hickel, Lucia Michelutti, Alice Tilche, Matt Wilde, Anna Gutierrez, Charlotte Bruckermann, Tom Hinrichsen, Paulo Drinot, and Juan Grigera. A special thank you to Sian Lazar for her support and guidance. I am grateful to the students whom I had the good fortune to teach and the participants at the LSE Friday seminar.

There are many people whom I have met along the way at conferences, workshops, and in Bolivia. I would like to thank Alice Soares Guimarães, with whom I spent a lot of time with during fieldwork in the Chapare, as well as Carmen Soliz, Amy Kennemore, Jorge Derpic, Zoe Pearson, Jessie Robinson, Desmond Arias, Andrew Canessa, Leonidas Oikonomakis, Cleia Nolte, Ana Meg Rama, and the fellows on the Drugs, Security, and Democracy program. Paul Gootenberg provided valuable insights. Thanks as well to the editorial and production team at Duke University Press, especially Gisela Fosado, Susan Albury, Nancy Zibman, Courtney Baker, and Lydia Rose Rapport-Hankins. Finally, I want to say a massive thank you to all of my friends and family in Newcastle, Brittany, and Grantham. The greatest thanks must, however, go to Insa Koch, who has read and commented on many drafts of this book and supported me with patience and humor throughout. It goes without saying that all errors are my own.

Finally, I would like to gratefully acknowledge the support of the funding organizations that made this book possible, including the Leverhulme Trust (Early Career Fellowship: ECF-2013–014), the Social Science Research Council/Open Society Foundations (Drugs, Security, and Democracy Fellowship), and the Economic and Social Research Council (PTA 031200400011). Thanks are also due to the UCL Institute of the Americas for housing me during my postdoctoral research and the Geography Department at the University of Reading for providing me with a new intellectual home.

Map FM.1. Map of Bolivia showing major cities and roads.

INTRODUCTION. To Lead by Obeying

The convoy of over twenty cars and pickup trucks sped past fruit plantations, markets, houses, mechanics, and karaoke bars. Each car was festooned with the blue, white, and black flag of the ruling Movement Toward Socialism party (Movimiento al Socialismo or MAS by its Spanish acronym). Grover Munachi, a reporter from a local radio station, caught sight of something out of the window: "Look, it's the president!" he shouted. A small jet gradually came into view. The plane flew low over the convoy before climbing up and out of sight, only to return once more from the opposite direction. The car passengers laughed in admiration; one shouted out, "Way to go, Evo!"

When the convoy arrived at its destination, a military base located on the banks of a wide, muddy-brown river, the guards snapped to attention and lifted the barrier to allow the cars through. A man sitting in the car's front seat joked, "Last time I was here these guys locked me up . . . and now look, they are saluting us!" The cars snaked through the base; to the right was the United States–run Drug Enforcement Administration (DEA) compound, and on the left dozens of rusting cars, barrels of gasoline, and sacks of coca, all of which had been confiscated from drug traffickers. Ahead, three Vietnam-era helicopters, UH-1s or Hueys, donated by the United States, stood ready for antinarcotics missions.

Evo Morales disembarked from the plane, followed by the ambassadors from Cuba and Venezuela. The trio strolled across the hot tarmac to where the eighty-strong delegation of union leaders and local government officials waited patiently in an orderly line. Morales shared jokes and warmly embraced old friends. It was October 2006, Morales had only been in office for ten months, and as yet no one could get their head around the fact that the man who they knew as "*compañero* Evo" (comrade Evo), the leader of their agricultural union, was now the president of Bolivia.

The amazement the union leaders expressed on entering the military base and greeting the president reflects a deeper issue that goes to the very heart of this book: namely, the shift from being an agricultural union criminalized as a result of U.S.-led drug war policies, to a ruling party responsible for governing a country. Morales's initial support base was the coca growers' union of the Chapare, a tropical agricultural zone located at the eastern foot of the Bolivian Andes. Here peasant farmers are primarily dedicated to the production of coca leaf, a perennial shrub native to the Andean region. Indigenous peoples in the Andes have consumed coca for millennia; they either chew it or prepare it as a tea, and it is present at every ritual from birth to death. But while many people regard the leaf to be special, if not sacred, according to local farmers a great deal of their crop is used to manufacture cocaine, and Bolivia is the world's third largest producer of the illegal drug. Coca leaf is internationally outlawed; UN conventions list coca, alongside cocaine and heroin, as a dangerous substance that is subject to strict controls. For over twenty years successive governments denounced the coca growers as criminals, drug traffickers, and terrorists, and yet they now had a president in power—one who claimed to represent their interests.

When Evo Morales assumed the presidency in January 2006, he broke with the U.S.-financed and U.S.-designed war on drugs. Bolivia's new program is referred to as "Coca Yes, Cocaine No" because of the distinction it makes between coca leaf, a plant with significant local value, and cocaine, the illegal drug. The new policy permits farmers to cultivate a small plot of coca and encourages them to self-police with respect to these limits. The Morales government has prioritized development assistance to coca-growing areas, improving educational, health, and road infrastructure, as well as developing alternative uses for coca, using it to manufacture everything from cakes to toothpaste. The approach stands in marked contrast to the previous U.S.-led strategy, which focused on the forcible eradication of coca crops by local security forces, leading to two decades of violent confrontation without reducing coca production or the flow of drugs reaching the United States.

Drawing on over ten years of participant observation and interviews with coca union leaders, peasant farmers, drug traffickers, as well as top-level politicians, this book traces a powerful ethnographic narrative from Morales's inauguration and the political hope that accompanied it to the contemporary moment when increasingly critical voices can be heard from within the ranks. The study departs from the premise that in order to understand the mounting disillusion, we need to comprehend the operating logic of the agricultural unions and the expectations for governance that this logic created.

The first objective of this book is to analyze how the coca growers built the MAS and put it into power. The book explains the organization of the base-level unions and the way their vernacular democratic practices were scaled up and projected onto the idea of a nation. The book identifies the central role played by the trope of the coca leaf as a means for collective identification: Given the criminalized nature of coca, the farmers had to find a legitimate language to frame their demands. They achieved this by emphasizing coca's cultural and symbolic significance. In the context of a growing global indigenous rights movement, the ethnic discourse gained domestic and international support.

And yet grassroots movements have not always succeeded in getting what they wanted; hence the second objective is to understand the disappointments and internal conflicts that have persisted since the MAS came to power. The book analyzes how grassroots ideas of democracy and accountability have been corrupted as Morales and his aides have directly intervened in the union organization. It also describes how some grassroots union members have come to feel that Morales has fallen short of his initial promises to protect their livelihoods. Conflict stems from the fact that, in accordance with its obligations to the international community, the MAS government has had to stem coca cultivation, which represents the coca growers' main source of income, and attack drug production, which some growers are involved with. Many farmers whom I interviewed were acutely aware that Morales has distanced himself from the unions, and this in turn has led to claims of betrayal.

Over the past ten years there has been an unprecedented interest in Bolivia, Evo Morales, and the movements that support him. What makes this book unique is that it is the first full-length monograph about the Chapare coca growers' unions and their relationship to the MAS. This book tells the inside story, the one the union leaders, politicians, and academics have so far been reluctant to tell—namely, how the coca growers are tied to the international cocaine trade through the production and selling of coca leaf and the processing of coca paste (a first step to processing refined cocaine). The aim of the book is not to highlight the illegal activities of the coca growers, but rather to theorize the contradictions in Bolivia's claim to be an indigenous-led and grassroots-oriented democracy.

I argue that tensions between the coca union and its party (the MAS) stem from the impossibility of reconciling claims to national sovereignty with the constraints imposed by policies that have been skewed by the U.S.-led war on drugs. Through this case study, the book raises important analytical questions—questions about the problems of scaling up grassroots democratic practices, whether trade unions can ever be reconciled with projects of state making, and more broadly, what the implications of such tensions are for social movements beyond the Bolivian case. This book reveals the difficulties of reinvigorating democracy when the policies constraining it go beyond the mandate of popular sovereignty. In this way, it brings to anthropology a transnational perspective in understanding how national and local-level governance is realized.

This chapter opens by setting out the coca growers' vision of democracy and the delight of union members at the potential for new forms of political participation that the MAS's rise to power promised. It then considers debates that emphasize the difference between vernacular politics, which acknowledges the importance of local cultural norms in political mobilizing, and institutional politics. This sets up a framework for understanding the challenges generated when the vernacular becomes institutional, as was the case for the MAS. The chapter subsequently introduces the field site and considers the specific drug control policies that have impacted the lives of coca farming families in Bolivia. This serves to introduce the core dilemma at the center of the book—namely, the challenge Morales faced in satisfying the material demands of the rank and file in a context where their livelihoods are internationally outlawed.

A Government of Social Movements

In 2005, against a backdrop of political turmoil and widespread disenchantment with democracy[1] (popular uprisings had forced two presidents from office in 2003 and 2005), Evo Morales, the left-wing leader of the six Chapare coca growers' unions, was elected as president of Bolivia with 54 percent of the vote. This was the first time any political party had won a majority since the return to democracy in 1982. Morales and the MAS scored equally resounding victories in the 2009 (64 percent) and 2014 (61 percent) national elections, and a 2008 recall referendum (when Morales took 67 percent of the vote).

The 2005 MAS victory marked a sea change in Bolivian history; until then politics had been dominated by a small group of white *creoles*, and was very much seen as "the private business of elites" (Alvarez, Dagnino, and Escobar 1998: 9). By contrast, the MAS was established by a confederation of agricultural unions (led by the coca growers' union); as such it was composed of outsiders with few links to the political establishment. The rise of Morales (who was born to an Aymara family) was also symbolic, marking an end to the white elite control of the state apparatus, in a country where 63 percent of the population self-identify as indigenous (INE 2003: 157). When the MAS came to power, there was a palpable sense of hope that substantive change was now possible (Madrid 2011: 254).

The day before his official swearing-in as president in January 2006, Morales was honored with a ceremony of investiture at Tiwanaku, the ruins of an ancient Aymara temple located close to the capital city, La Paz. During the ceremony, Morales was dressed in a replica of a tunic worn by pre-Incan priests; he accepted a traditional staff of authority and the blessing from a *Yatiri* (an Aymara healer and priest). Standing barefoot in front of the Kalasasaya temple, Morales addressed tens of thousands of supporters, many wearing T-shirts that read "500 years of indigenous and popular resistance." Morales proclaimed that he would found the nation anew, but this time with and for the indigenous majority. He told the crowd, "For the first time in Bolivian history, Aymaras, Quechuas, and Mojeños, *we are presidents*. Not only Evo is the president, sisters and brothers" (Morales 2006: 13). The following day, at his official inauguration in La Paz, Morales reiterated this commitment: "I will fulfill my duty, as Subcommander Marcos[2] says, to command by obeying the people. *I will lead Bolivia obeying the Bolivian people*" (*Pagina Doce* 2006).

At the behest of the social movements, Morales made efforts to reconfigure state–society relations by following some of the tenets of direct democracy practiced by grassroots organizations. The MAS administration introduced new participatory mechanisms, including frequent elections and plebiscites, new consultative bodies,[3] the recall of representatives, and innovative methods for *social control*[4] at every state level (Anria 2016a). During the first MAS administration, a handful of social movement leaders (who were selected by grassroots movements) were given cabinet positions and other posts, partly as spoils but also as a way to transform the state as a colonial institution. Morales held regular popular consultations with social

Figure I.1. Morales attends a celebration in the Chapare, February 2006.
Photo by author.

movement actors, and he frequently traveled all over the country to attend grassroots meetings.

Significantly for this book, Morales has continued in his role as the executive general secretary of the coca growers' unions.[5] As a result, Morales regularly travels to the Chapare region to attend union meetings, sports events, cultural events, and celebrations (which mostly revolve around the inauguration of government-sponsored infrastructure) (see figure I.1). At union meetings in the Chapare, Morales invariably opens his speeches by stating that his job is to follow the will of the grassroots and that he will "lead by obeying." Morales invites the rank and file to treat him as if he were nothing more than another union member, using phrases such as "tell me when I make a mistake," "please guide me," "this is not the government of Evo Morales alone, this is our government."[6]

Ever since Morales came to power, debates have raged about the role that Bolivia's social movements play in government. On the one hand, supporters have held up Morales and the MAS as an example of popular democracy that works. They argue that it is only right that "the people" are empowered to participate in politics and to rewrite constitutions to transform society (Escárzaga 2012b; García Linera, Tapia, and Prada 2007). Sociologist (and vice president of Bolivia) Alvaro García Linera goes further than most, arguing that the MAS functions as an extension of the social movements from which it emerged. For him, the MAS represents a new form of government, one that is run by and for its social movement base[7] (see García Linera 2006, 2014). In his own words: "Evo-ism as a political and ideological current is a form of political self-representation of the plebeian society, which makes it possible for the social movements to access the highest levels of state decision making" (García Linera, cited in Mayorga 2009: 110). García Linera (2006: 30) has argued that MAS's approach to democracy and state building has regional and global resonance.

On the other hand, there are those who characterize Morales and the MAS as a dangerous and antidemocratic force. Observers have pointed out that Morales continues to act as if he is a union leader, employing anti-institutional and confrontational strategies to get his way (Farah 2009; Laserna 2010).[8] Some have characterized Morales as a *caudillo*,[9] a populist strong man, who eliminates his rivals and rewards those who are loyal to him (Laserna 2007; Molina 2013: 11; Zuazo 2010). Far from empowering social movements, Gaya Makaran (2016) argues that Morales and the MAS have co-opted them through ties of clientelism and patronage (the distribution of jobs and economic resources), both long-standing features of Bolivian political culture (Albro 2007; Lapegna and Auyero 2012; Lazar 2004). The coca growers have received sharp criticism from the national press (building in part from their demonization during the 1990s war on drugs), but also from academics. Eduardo Gamarra (2007: 12) has argued that the coca farmers have been bought off with the legalization of coca leaf and now represent a "praetorian guard" that Morales "can mobilize to obtain specific gains." Political scientists have typified Bolivia under Morales variously as a "competitive authoritarian" regime (Levitsky and Loxton 2013; Weyland 2013), a "semi-democracy" (Mainwaring and Pérez-Liñán 2015), and even a "full-blown authoritarian regime" (Mayorga 2017: 66).

What is interesting is that both those in favor and those against Morales implicitly acknowledge that there is an alternative to the liberal (read: Western) political system and that somehow the MAS is enacting it. Scholars who occupy the middle ground have been more skeptical, however. They point out that the MAS represents neither the revolt of the masses nor autonomous constituent power; rather, they argue that the MAS works within the preexisting liberal framework, but is nevertheless committed to instituting a substantive new state model that can more effectively engage its citizens. These scholars have contested the characterization of Morales and the MAS as authoritarian, arguing that while the institutional base has been partially undermined, democracy overall has benefited from the expansion of political participation under the current government (Anria 2016b; Barrios Suvelza 2017; Cameron 2014; Postero 2010; Wolff 2013).

While there has been a great deal of scholarship on the role of Bolivia's social movements in government, there has been relatively little research on how these enhanced forms of direct democracy play out at the grassroots, particularly among Morales's core support base. At the time of the 2005 election, I was carrying out fieldwork in the Chapare with the coca growers' unions. In the months following the historic victory, echoing Morales's words, coca growers told me, "all of us are presidents," "with Evo in power it's just as if we are governing," and "there are lots of Evos here." But with ten years' hindsight, it appears as if Morales's initial promises have faltered. On follow-up fieldwork in 2015, union members no longer spoke of bottom-up control. Instead, they complained that when Morales visits the Chapare they cannot get close to him,[10] that he is not available to assist with their problems, and that he has abandoned them. In the words of one older female coca grower: "Before Evo was really valued here, he was so well received. He often used to stay here [at her house]. But now he seldom comes, he has forgotten about us." Even high-ranking leaders told me that now that Morales is president he does not answer their phone calls, and when he does, he has no time to talk or will immediately reject their proposals. One male coca grower in his fifties put it this way: "These are not the principles of the political instrument [the MAS], this is not what we set out to do."

The objective of this book is to explore what the coca growers hoped to achieve in government and the extent to which these expectations were met. The main empirical questions driving the study are: What does democracy mean to the coca growers? How have these ideas been scaled up to shape expectations of how the MAS should act once in power? What was promised, and what has Morales been unable to deliver? What reactions has this provoked on the part of the rank and file? How has Morales responded to challenges to his authority? And, more broadly, what happens to the political potential of a union when it blurs with the government? To answer these questions, it is first necessary to take a theoretical detour. In what follows I explain how anthropologists have seen democracy as a culturally specific and historically contingent concept, one that lacks a stable reference point, even if people have very clear ideas about what democracy might mean to them.

One of the most influential definitions of democracy comes from Joseph Schumpeter, who reduced it to a set of procedures and forms. For Schumpeter, democracy is a system "for arriving at political decisions in which individuals acquire the power to decide by means of a competitive struggle for the people's vote" (Green and Gallery 2016: 46). In this reading, voting is the defining feature of democracy. Departing from this, political scientists have argued that once countries develop a certain level of wealth, a robust civil society, and a constitutional framework that safeguards basic political rights, then their (representative) democracy is secure (Diamond 1994; Schedler 1998); it becomes, in the words of Linz and Stepan (1996: 15), "the only game in town."

For decades global events largely supported this hypothesis. The "third wave of democratization" began when, at the close of the Cold War, Eastern European countries became electoral democracies, as did parts of Asia, Africa, and Latin America (Huntington 1993). By 1999, 119 of a possible 192 countries could be described as electoral democracies, totaling almost 60 percent of the world's population, leading the research organization Freedom House to denote the twentieth century as the "democratic century" (Freedom House 1999). Nobel Prize winner Amartya Sen (1999) even referred to democracy as a "universal value."

But these gains have not been as secure as once thought, and today democracy seems to be in poor shape. Signs of democratic malaise are everywhere, from Athens to Washington (Bermeo 2016; Diamond 2015). In the United States, voter turnout in 2016 dipped to its lowest point in two decades (Wallace 2016), confidence ratings for the Supreme Court and the presidency are well below their historical average, and trust in Congress is scraping the bottom of the barrel (Jones 2015). There is evidence that increasing numbers of people are open to populist alternatives with an authoritarian tinge, as the rise of Donald Trump attests (Foa and Mounk 2016; MacWilliams 2016). Discontent has spread to other Western, supposedly liberal democracies. In Europe support for antisystem (right-wing) populist parties is on the rise (Berezin 2009), and the United Kingdom's decision to leave the European Union has been read by some as a sign not only of dissatisfaction with government, but with democracy itself (Koch 2017b).

Latin America's democratic transition began in 1978 with the end of military dictatorships and the restoration of basic civil and political rights to most counties in the region (this happened in Bolivia in 1982). But even here, opinion surveys conducted at the turn of the millennium revealed a growing dissatisfaction with democracy (Valenzuela 2004: 6). Academics have explored the contradictions of democratic politics on the continent, which in many places means little more than the right to vote while poverty deepens under economic neoliberalism (Auyero and Swistun 2009; Holston 2008; Paley 2001). Civil rights have been undermined by endemic racism, corruption, police violence, and crime (Caldeira 2000; Goldstein 2012; Zeiderman 2016), giving rise to what Teresa Caldeira and James Holston (1999) have referred to as "disjunctive democracy." Since 2000 popular uprisings, military actions, and legislative deposals have ousted democratically elected presidents from Argentina to Venezuela.[11]

Political theorists have sought to explain both the genesis of and responses to the growing malaise. Academics have pointed the finger at the way politics in Europe and the United States has been taken over by a technocratic elite (Mair 2013), the dissolution of left and right distinctions (Kalb 2009), the undue influence of corporate lobbyists (Crouch 2004), and the power of the mass media (Manin 1997: 218–26). Combined, these factors have corrupted or "hollowed out" politics (Mair 2013), giving rise to what some scholars have referred to as a "post-democratic" (Crouch 2004) or "post-political" moment (Rancière 1995). But for others, this is only the tip of the iceberg, reflecting a deeper crisis of representation that can be traced to the neoliberal polices advanced in the 1980s, which saw the state's redistributive capacity undermined, the privatization of public goods, and the strengthening of the state's ability to police disorder (Brown 2009: 37–59, 2015; Wacquant 2012).

Cook, Long, and Moore (2016) argue that such macropolitical and economic narratives of disenchantment are very useful, but they tell only part of the story. In order to understand the reasons why people have turned their backs on democracy as an ideal, we have to look more closely at social relationships, affect, and ethical subjectivities. Insa Koch (2016) further argues that from citizens' own perspectives, while macro changes to the economy and politics (such as neoliberalism and technocratic governance) might well have had an impact, their own experiences of betrayal and abandonment do not correspond one-to-one with a retreat form the democratic project (see also Koch 2017c). Anthropology's key contribution in this regard, then, is to connect cultural elements and issues of governance more broadly to understand how one is mediated through the other.

Anthropologists have moved away from the focus on the ballot box to consider citizens' own criteria for evaluating democracy, and the way these vernacular ideas are rooted in deeper social processes (Hickel 2015; Koch 2018; Michelutti 2008; Spencer 1997). For example, Sian Lazar (2008: 91–117) challenges the standard reading of elections as merely formal procedures, showing how they are a way to establish personalized relationships with politicians. In this sense, voting is not just about the electoral moment; rather, it is about everything else that comes before and after (see also Auyero 2001; Gay 2010; Jaffe 2015; Koch 2016). Researchers have also worked with a range of social movements, from indigenous peasant activists to Occupy Wall Street protestors, to examine how they have articulated alternative visions of democracy to those offered by the formal political system (Graeber 2014; Maeckelbergh 2009; Nash 1997a; Nugent 2010; Razsa and Kurnik 2012).

While acknowledging that subaltern groups forge their own political cultures, it is important to recognize that alternative and dominant practices are never entirely divorced from one another (Roseberry 1994). Thus, when considering vernacular forms of politics we need to ask where their inspiration and practices are drawn from and acknowledge some overlap. For example, Orin Starn (1999: 105–54) shows how self-governing peasant communities in the Peruvian highlands emulate features of state bureaucracy in their internal organization (see also Colloredo-Mansfeld 2009), and even apparently "age old" democratic traditions, such as "building consensus," might turn out to be quite recent inventions (Nader 1990).

Drawing inspiration from this work, it is argued here that, for the Chapare coca growers, democracy really has nothing to do with what are often taken to be the core elements of the liberal system, including competitive elections, individual liberties, universal suffrage, and the secret ballot— what David Nugent (2008: 24–27) refers to as "normative democracy." Rather, in their unions, they pursue a form of direct participatory democracy in which all members of the community meet to debate, decide, and enact their laws. Most importantly, there are strong pressures for leadership to remain deferential and collective; in the local vernacular they must "lead by obeying." The fact that the coca growers practice a form of democracy that clashes with the Western liberal ideal is not in and of itself that extraordinary; alternative democratic practices are actually quite widespread (Comaroff and Comaroff 1997; Conzelman 2007; Feuchtwang 2003; Rayner 2014). What makes this case stand out is that the coca growers' political party (the MAS) has transformed into an organization responsible for building a government and therefore for ruling a country.

When the MAS came to power in 2006, status quo views of the nation, the state, and democracy were brought into question. For the coca growers, the state went from being thought of as negligent or, worse still, an enemy, to something that they could now reach, and even control. When they said "all of us are presidents," they were laying claim to a new form of citizenship, one that is modeled on the forms of self-governance found at the grassroots, including continuous deliberation and compliant leaders (Grisaffi 2013). However, as we will see, once voted into government, the principle of "leading by obeying" becomes difficult to enforce as the idea of "the people" becomes abstracted from the concrete into an "imagined community" to be governed.

The challenges presented by the shift from movement to government is nowhere better illustrated than in the case of coca, which transformed from being a means of safeguarding livelihoods for the local agricultural unions to becoming a potentially illegal threat that the government had to control from the top down. The tension stems from the fact that while the MAS government has stressed its desire to free Bolivia of U.S. imperialism, the country exists in a global context where powerful actors place limits on change, and thus courses of action are not always set domestically (Postero 2017: 33). Let us now take a step back to consider the international context of drug war politics and the implication this has for the possibilities of grassroots politics. We will see that Morales was never going to be able to fully satisfy the material demands emanating from the bases, which revolve around the right to grow unlimited coca.

The Drug War in the Andes

"America's public enemy number one in the United States is drug abuse," Nixon declared in June 1971. "In order to fight and defeat this enemy, it is necessary to wage a new, all-out offensive" (Becket 2017). Two years later he declared, "This Administration has declared all-out, global war on the drug menace" (Nixon 1973). Policy makers came to focus on cocaine, which by the mid-1980s had affected the lives of up to twenty-two million users in the United States. The violence associated with its use (particularly related to crack cocaine)[12] transformed the drug into the number-one priority for

U.S. "drug warriors" and led to the dramatic militarization of the overseas drug war (Gootenberg 2012: 166).

Over the past thirty years, the United States has channeled billions of dollars to Latin American military and police forces to enable them to undertake counter-narcotics operations. The logic underlying source-country enforcement is that by reducing supply, the street price of illicit drugs will increase and in turn dissuade people who live in consumer countries (principally the United States) from buying them (Youngers and Rosin 2005b). But after three decades, the supply of drugs reaching the United States is as robust as ever (Mejía 2017). Today consumers in the United States spend some $100 billion dollars every year on illegal substances (Kilmer et al. 2014) and, while cocaine consumption has decreased since 2008,[13] the United States still represents the single largest market for cocaine in the world[14] (UNODC 2016d).

The three largest coca-producing nations are Colombia, Peru, and Bolivia. The most recent UN coca surveys estimate that Colombia has 146,000 hectares of coca (UNODC 2017a), Peru 40,300 hectares (UNODC 2016c), and Bolivia 23,100 hectares (UNODC 2017b). The U.S. drug warriors focus in the Andean region has been the aggressive eradication of coca crops. Eradication is most often done manually: military conscripts, accompanied by heavily armed members of the police, enter small farmsteads to uproot coca plantations (Colombia is the only country in the region to permit the aerial fumigation of coca crops). Coletta Youngers and John Walsh argue that forced eradication is a deeply entrenched aspect of U.S. international drug control policy. They write: "It has the appeal of seeming 'tough' and straightforward—if we wipe out drugs at the 'source,' they won't make it to our shores—and it has attained enormous political and bureaucratic inertia" (Youngers and Walsh 2010: 1). The United States has pressured its southern neighbors to comply with its drug policy goals through an annual process termed certification. This is an evaluation of each country's performance against U.S.-imposed antidrug targets. Countries that do not fulfill U.S. goals are punished by decertification; sanctions include the withholding of development assistance, credit, and trade benefits (Joyce 1999).

Forced eradication puts the burden of the war on drugs onto small farmers who gain the least from the trade and generates multiple harms: eradicating crops destroys local economies, criminalizes some of the poorest and most vulnerable sectors of society, and legitimizes oppressive policing. In the Andean region eradication teams have killed, abused, and seriously wounded scores of coca farmers, torched homesteads, and incarcerated thousands of people. Institutional damage has been further compounded by the impunity that U.S.-backed security forces frequently enjoy (Youngers and Rosin 2005a). Not only is eradication harmful, but also the strategy is grossly inefficient.[15] It generates incentives for poor farmers to replant by forcing up the price of coca while simultaneously denying farmers their only source of income. When crops are eradicated in one area, they simply expand elsewhere, a phenomenon that policy analysts refer to as the "balloon effect" (Dion and Russler 2008; Mansfield 2011).[16]

The enormous cost of the war on drugs, coupled with the fact that it is not actually reducing the flow of drugs northward (see Mejía 2010), has prompted some observers to suggest that U.S. policy on drugs is not a stand-alone issue. It has been argued that the U.S. motivation for escalating its militarized fight against drugs at the end of the Cold War was to justify the build-up of a military presence in the region and thereby secure U.S. corporate interests (Corva 2007; Paley 2014; Tokatlian 2010). Winifred Tate (2015) has studied the implementation of Plan Colombia, the backbone of the U.S. drug war strategy in Colombia[17] (2000 to 2012). Tate argues that the militarization of U.S. drug policy was driven by institutional interests, including the U.S. Southern Command's efforts to enhance its profile, the Clinton administration's concern about being thought of as "soft on drugs," and the expansion of the military-industrial complex into drug enforcement operations.

In the Andean countries, coca cultivation is concentrated in marginal areas, characterized by minimal civilian state presence, limited infrastructure, and high rates of poverty. In this context, the decision to grow drug crops is highly rational, especially in the face of steady demand. Coca is a nonperishable, robust crop, with a high value, and the market for it is relatively stable (see figure I.2). Coca complements subsistence farming and, in the absence of other income-generating activities, is one of the few pursuits that provide farmers with access to cash income, which is essential for survival (Grisaffi and Ledebur 2016: 4). As Peru, Colombia, and Bolivia have their own unique history, culture, and traditions related to coca, each country pursues a different approach to regulation.

Colombia penalizes coca most severely; all aspects of production, consumption, and commercialization are outlawed. The Colombian state has long embraced U.S.-designed and U.S.-funded eradication strategies (although over the past six years Colombia's leaders have begun to question

Figure I.2. Men drying coca. Photo by author.

the sustainability of the U.S. approach; see Collins 2014). Under the auspices of Plan Colombia, the government sprayed an average of 128,000 hectares per year (between 2000 and 2012) with the defoliant glyphosate (also known by its brand name Round-Up). Researchers from Bogota's Universidad de los Andes found that people who live in spray zones suffered from a variety of ailments including skin, respiratory, and gastrointestinal problems, and that exposure to spraying increased the incidence of miscarriages. The herbicides have caused environmental damage (including water contamination and land degradation) and affected food and cash crops, undermining food security (Camacho and Mejía 2015). Spraying pushes peasants off the land, accelerating processes of displacement (Dion and Russler 2008).

Colombia's harsh stance toward coca can be traced to the fact that the country has comparatively limited traditional consumption, and so unlike in Peru and Bolivia there is no widespread support for it (Ramirez 2011: 55). Further, the major guerrilla groups, including the Colombian Revolutionary Armed Forces (Fuerzas Armadas Revolucionarias de Colombia—FARC) and right-wing paramilitaries were known to finance their activities by taxing coca production (Ibáñez and Vélez 2008; Thoumi 2002). Given the illegal status of coca in Colombia, the people who farm it have long been criminalized and subject to repressive measures. In response, the coca growers have mobilized, casting their social movement as a civic action to demand citizenship rights and the inclusion of themselves and the region into the nation-state (Ramirez 2011).

In Peru, coca leaf consumption is common in highland areas, particularly among rural populations, but it is also consumed by middle-class urban professionals and is served as a tea to tourists in Cusco to help them cope with the high altitude.[18] Peru's coca legislation is less rigid than Colombia's, because while the state officially condemns coca chewing and prohibits private coca cultivation, it nevertheless authorizes limited coca production and commercialization for medicinal, scientific, and industrial purposes (Ramirez 2011: 56). All (legal) coca is sold through the state coca company, ENACO (la Empresa Nacional de la Coca), with annual exports valued at approximately $6.5 million dollars (Ledebur 2016). Peru receives significant U.S. counter-drug aid and has ambitious plans to eradicate half the country's coca crop over the coming years (Gootenberg 2014). Coca growers in Peru have mobilized against eradication programs, but unlike their Bolivian counterparts, their political impact has been limited because of internal divisions among growers, distance from the capital city Lima, association with terrorism in the public mind (the Shining Path Maoist guerrilla group continues to operate in coca-producing regions), and a weak identification with indigenous causes (Durand Ochoa 2014).

Long Live Coca, Death to Yankees

Bolivia ranks a distant third in Andean drug production, but given the country's small economy, income from coca and cocaine has always been more significant than in either Peru or Colombia. In 2006 (the year Morales assumed office), the market for dried coca leaf was worth $180 million dollars, representing 2 percent of Bolivia's GDP and 13 percent of the GDP in the agricultural sector (UNODC 2007). By 2016 this figure had increased to $276 million dollars annually, but because of the rise in rents from hydrocarbons and mining,[19] it represented a smaller overall contribution to Bolivia's GDP (UNODC 2017b). Bolivia has two main coca growing regions, the Yungas and the Chapare.

The Yungas, which sits to the north of La Paz, produces approximately 60 percent of Bolivia's coca crop (UNODC 2016b). Here coca is cultivated on steep terraced slopes alongside tropical fruit and coffee. Most of the 30,000 Yungas coca growers claim Aymara descent, but there is also a significant Afro-Bolivian population.[20] The Yungas coca growers are organized into six agrarian federations, which are united into a confederation, the Consejo de Federaciones Campesinas de los Yungas (COFECAY). Coca has been cultivated in the Yungas valleys for centuries, first to supply the Inca kings and later, during the colonial period, the mines of Potosí (Meruvia 2000; Soux 1993). From her research in the Yungas, Alison Spedding (1994) emphasizes the importance of rituals that accompany labor in the fields and the reciprocal modes of labor exchange (known as *ayni*) as a means for the reproduction of social identities. Spedding refers to the coca field as a "total social fact" (Spedding 1997). Yungas coca leaf is highly valued in Bolivia, as the small, green, sweet Yungas leaves are considered to be the best to chew. The Yungas crop is now the country's largest, and a significant proportion is probably destined for the illegal cocaine trade (Farthing and Ledebur 2015: 14).

By contrast, the Cochabamba Tropics, or the Chapare as it is more commonly known, has only been settled since the 1950s. It is a vast region covering more than 24,000 square kilometers (a landmass equivalent to New Hampshire or Wales) stretching over three provinces, Chapare, Tiraque, and Carrasco. The elevation ranges from 200 to 500 meters above sea level,[21] and consists of lowland tropical forests, wide rivers, and floodplains (see figures I.3 and I.4). It is hot and humid; indeed, the name Chapare is derived from *ancha paran*, Quechua for "it's very rainy." True to its name, average rainfall stands at 5,000 mm, with the wettest months being January and February (Eastwood and Pollard 1986). Bolivia's main road (built in the 1970s with U.S. funding) cuts through the region, connecting Santa Cruz and Cochabamba, Bolivia's first and fourth largest urban areas, respectively.

In 2012, the population of the Cochabamba Tropics stood at just under 190,000 people; the majority are migrants from the Cochabamba valleys and mining centers in the highlands, many of whom were previously engaged in militant miners' trade unions (INE 2014). As one farmer explained, "The Chapare, it's a cosmopolitan place, we come from all over the country." According to the 2001 census, over 80 percent of the local population self-identify as Quechua, and most people are bilingual, speaking a mixture of Quechua and Spanish (PNUD 2005: 302).[22] The roughly 45,000 families are dedicated to agriculture: they refer to themselves as *campesinos* (peasant

Figure I.3. A view of the Chapare. Photo by author.

Figure I.4. A typical Chapare house. Photo by author.

farmers), *cocaleros* (coca growers), *Chapareños* (residents of the Chapare), or *colonos* (settlers who came from the Andean region). In this book I use these terms interchangeably in both Spanish and English.

Unlike Peru and Colombia, where coca consumption in restricted, in Bolivia coca use is accepted across most sectors, regions, and ethnicities (Gootenberg 2016: 5). It is best thought of as a national custom, much like drinking tea is for the British. An EU-funded study published in 2013 concluded that about three million Bolivians (30 percent of the population) chew coca on a regular basis, and the majority consume coca as a tea or in the form of other legal coca-based products (Farfán 2013).[23] The most prolific chewers are truckers, peasants, laborers, miners, and small-scale merchants, who value its qualities as a moderate stimulant to suppress hunger and fatigue.[24] The practice of chewing coca has spread to the cities, where some middle-class professionals consume it, and even to the border with Argentina, where it is served on silver plates in elite settings (Rivera 2003). The widespread use of coca in Bolivia has fed into sentiments of what Paul Gootenberg has referred to as "coca nationalism," which, "like most strands of national identity, is a protean or invented tradition" (Gootenberg 2016: 5).

Given the important role coca plays in Andean rituals and society (Carter and Mamani 1986), simply banning the leaf (as UN conventions demand) would have led to massive social upheaval. Thus Bolivia's antidrug Law 1008 (in effect between 1988 and 2017), passed in 1988 under intense pressure from the U.S. government[25] (Albó 2008b: 59), dictates that 12,000 hectares of coca could be grown legally for domestic consumption in the Yungas higher-altitude "traditional zones."[26] Cultivation anywhere outside of the traditional zones (including in the Chapare and frontier lower-elevation Yungas areas) was outlawed and slated for eradication.[27] In this way, legislators turned the Chapare farmers into the "enemy" in the war on drugs (Albó 2002c: 75). As we will see over the coming chapters, the law created tensions between Chapare and Yungas growers, whose respective legal and economic situations have differed significantly.

Beginning in the mid-1980s, the United States launched ferocious coca eradication and interdiction campaigns in the Chapare. Crop eradication provoked a severe economic crisis among growers, who were only eligible for development assistance after losing their main source of income. During escalating cycles of protest and repression (see figure I.5), security forces killed dozens of coca growers and left many more injured (Ledebur 2005).[28] It is argued here that the ongoing military and police repression

Figure I.5. Conflict in the Chapare. Photograph courtesy of Andean Information Network and Dr. Godofredo Reinicke.

turned the Chapare coca growers' union into a powerful force to contest the state's anti-coca policies. One leader explained, "We had to defend ourselves, and so we built this organization to face up to this politics of zero coca, to combat the discrimination of the neoliberal system."

Throughout the 1990s, the Chapare unions, and (after 1996) their political party, the MAS, redefined the parameters of the national coca debate. Pablo Stefanoni (2003: 15–21) explains that while the governments of Bolivia and the United States associated coca leaf with illegality and drug trafficking, the unions emphasized the long history of traditional coca use, arguing that it represents one of the most profound expressions of Andean indigenous culture, not to mention a strategic resource that could be used to promote national development. In this way, the fight to defend coca leaf became synonymous with standing up for national dignity in the face of U.S. intervention, which had taken on increasingly imperial characteristics (Stefanoni 2007; Vargas 2014; Viola 2001). The projection of the coca leaf as a symbol of national sovereignty, captured by the union's call to arms, "Long live coca, death to Yankees," served in part to tie national movements together to bring about the process that put Evo Morales in power (Grisaffi 2010).

And yet, while the Chapare peasants have used the traditional status of the coca leaf to defend their crops against forced eradication, they are nevertheless aware that a percentage of their harvest is used for cocaine production. Moreover, some farmers are directly involved in the artisanal production of coca paste (also known as base paste). There is no way to know exactly how many people are involved in processing drugs, or how much of the coca produced in the Chapare feeds into the illicit trade, but many coca growers assured me that it is the cornerstone of the local economy. While in opposition, Morales and the MAS never had to be explicit on coca's relationship with cocaine: in the face of repressive policing, the promise was simply to end the war on drugs, to demilitarize the region, and to defend traditional coca leaf use. By sidestepping the issue of cocaine, Morales generated unrealistic expectations among rank-and-file union members, and so it was inevitable that, once in office, he would disappoint.

Coca Yes, Cocaine No

As the country's president, Morales must address drug trafficking, not only in response to international pressure but also because the MAS recognizes the negative social and environmental impacts of cocaine production (Kohl and Bresnahan 2010: 16). When Morales assumed the office in 2006, he was, in the words of one union leader, "stuck between a rock and a hard place" (*entre la espada y la pared*). His government could not resume forced eradication; to do so would have alienated the MAS's core support base. But neither could the government allow unlimited coca cultivation, as this would have turned Bolivia into an international pariah. Instead, the government opted to extend a policy originally ratified by the administration of Carlos Mesa (2003–5) in 2004, which allows each registered peasant farmer in the Chapare to grow a limited amount of coca, known as a *cato* (1,600 square meters), and demilitarized the region. The MAS government informally raised the amount of coca that could be grown nationally from 12,000 to 20,000 hectares, which allowed for 7,000 hectares of coca to be grown in the Chapare (the national limit was increased to 22,000 hectares in 2017).[29]

Over the past ten years there has been a gradual softening in international opinion toward coca at a global level: as a result of Bolivian pressure, in 2013 the United Nations accepted the right to traditional coca consumption within Bolivian territory. At the same time, peasant farmers are less resistant to developing alternative livelihoods to coca as a result of government-led integrated development initiatives (Grisaffi 2016; Grisaffi, Farthing, and Ledebur 2017). The Bolivian state, then, can be thought of as a mediator or buffer between these two conflicting poles. The MAS both challenges the absolutism of the international regime (by diversifying coca politics and fighting for the legalization of coca leaf at the level of the United Nations), but also challenges peasants to gradually move away from dependence on coca through its innovative development-first policies and high levels of state investment in the region (including the building of factories and the expansion of basic infrastructure). By 2015 the Bolivian state had successfully brought coca down to its 20,000-hectare national limit, and it had created a new regulatory regime. Significantly, these goals were achieved while simultaneously respecting human rights in coca-growing regions (Farthing and Ledebur 2015). For this reason, Bolivia's new coca policy has been called the world's first "supply-side harm reduction" approach (Farthing and Kohl 2012).

And yet, while these are undoubtedly positive steps, not everyone is sanguine. The cato policy was originally developed with the participation of the coca unions, but it was only supposed to be a temporary arrangement until a study on national coca consumption could be completed, which would form the basis for a new policy. Many rank-and-file members told me that they hoped that Morales would lift the cap on cultivation to allow each member to plant two or three catos (if not several hectares of coca). When this did not occur, some accused the government of selling out, arguing that the cato does not generate enough cash to support a family. More to the point, no modification to the cato agreement would ever have been enough to satisfy expectations, because ultimately the coca growers are dependent on the illegal drug trade (as a market for their crop but also for work), an industry that the Bolivian government cannot and will not support.

The sense of disillusionment with the cato policy, and the coca growers' inability to demand more from Morales, has led some grassroots members to complain of betrayal. Many coca farmers I spoke with said that Morales (and by extension the MAS) no longer looks after them, and that high-level leaders value the maintenance of the party and their own careers over the realization of union goals. This is often narrated in terms of the corruption of grassroots democratic ideals. Rank-and-file members say that leaders do not act as they should; that is, they do not lead by obeying. This contradiction reveals the gap between the aspiration of democracy as a form of self-government and the reality, where external actors (in this case the United States and the United Nations) always impinge on the boundaries of the political community.

The story of the coca growers' struggle from the 1990s to the present day provides an important lens for understanding Bolivia under Evo Morales, the national and international constraints his administration faces, and the MAS's seemingly inexorable trajectory toward top-down, rather than bottom-up, government. But it also makes a broader point about the limits of alternative or vernacular democracies. We saw above that anthropologists of democracy have identified the various forms that democratic practices can take, thus moving away from the liberal ideal that has so often acted as a normative yardstick. But by contrasting the vernacular, the alternative, or the purely local to their received liberal counterparts, this literature also runs the risk of glorifying the former as if they are set in stone. Yet alternative democracies are not statist models, nor can they be isolated from the broader contexts in which they are articulated. As the case of Bolivia's coca growers' struggle shows, Morales's focus on localized models of "leading by obeying" could never have satisfied his bases, whose material livelihoods remain closely entangled in an international drug commodity chain. In short, this book argues that the conditions for the realization of alternative democracies are closely linked to broader political and economic circumstances that both constrain and enable these practices to take hold. As such, its lessons go far beyond the Bolivian case, as these are issues that all social movements have to face.

Structure of the Book

This book is divided into two broad parts: chapters 1, 2, and 3 provide context for the study, while chapters 4 through 7 take different aspects of life in the Chapare and consider how they have been transformed with the MAS in power. The chapters, then, are not in chronological order, but rather tell the story of grassroots mobilization and the limitations and disenchantments that have become apparent over the ten years that I conducted fieldwork (2005–15). I argue that with the MAS in power, rank-and-file union members imagined that a new form of politics would now be possible, one based on the forms of direct democracy found at the grassroots. However, as we see at every step, Morales (and the MAS) has attempted to increase his control over the union, while simultaneously breaking free of the constraints imposed by grassroots organizations.

The first substantive chapter provides the background necessary to understand the rest of the book. It lays out the history of rebellion to illustrate how the insurgency spearheaded by the coca growers has far deeper roots. The chapter introduces the Chapare, including how the coca growers organized into unions to defend their livelihoods. It then examines the trajectory of the MAS party's formation; it stresses how it has developed from its origins as a radical anti-neoliberal party that was driven by extraparliamentary politics, to its contemporary moderate and reformist profile, which prioritizes electoral politics over mass mobilization.

The objective of chapter 2 is to understand the two aspects of coca, its role in traditional rituals and healing practices on the one hand, and the paths by which it enters into illegal circuits on the other. The chapter begins by outlining the traditional uses of coca and the legislation controlling its production and sale. It then traces the history of migration to the Chapare, drawing attention to the way colonization was intimately bound to the growth of the illicit narcotics industry. Finally, it examines coca paste production in the region today. The chapter shows how coca has genuine sacred value, but is also a commodity that is used for cocaine production.

Chapter 3 focuses on processes of governance at the local level. It first identifies some of the central principles of sociality that guide daily life within the base-level union (or *sindicato* as it is known). It analyzes the paradox that, while the sindicato has the ambition to function like a state and exert control over its members (using fines and sanctions to ensure compliance), at the same time there is a drive toward maintaining accountability at the grassroots. It is argued that what makes coercion consensual and socially accepted is the fact that the union's goals are said to reflect those of each and every member, hence collapsing the distinction between executive power and legislative will within the grassroots union. As we will see, it is precisely this link that Morales broke once in power.

Chapter 4 examines how coca growers built an indigenous political identity linked to coca. The fact that coca is outlawed by international treaties meant that they needed a powerful symbolic way of legitimizing their coca production. The discourse of indigeneity allowed coca to become part of a cultural narrative that permitted the farmers to configure a coherent political movement and gave them a moral justification to reach out and form alliances with other social movements from across the country. However, the chapter notes the limits of identity politics, including how, once in power, Morales and the MAS have had to deconstruct this political identity to justify continuing coca eradication missions in national parks and in new colonization zones.

Chapter 5 considers coca control policies in more depth. The chapter explains why the farmers are so reliant on coca for their livelihoods and explores the failure of previous drug war policies to convince farmers to plant alternative legal crops. It then considers how the policies that were pursued once the MAS came to power betrayed expectations regarding coca production. The ethnographic data presented in this chapter expose the weakness at the heart of the MAS project, namely how Morales has been unable to protect the interests of the rank and file, and how this in turn generates feelings of resentment and calls the state's legitimacy into question.

Chapter 6 builds on chapter 3 to consider the union's control of local government. It begins by outlining how the organization of the union is based on Andean self-governing principles mixed with Marxist traditions inherited from the miners who migrated to the Chapare after the closure of highland mines in 1986. With reference to municipal government, the chapter then describes how, at the local level, the party's politics mirror the assembly-style democracy of the peasant unions and how this operates. This experience of local governance shaped expectations of the way the MAS should act in government. The chapter thus highlights the political hopes and aspirations that accompanied Morales's victory in 2005, specifically the idea that, with the MAS in power, members of the union would henceforth exercise direct structural control over the state apparatus through their party.

Chapter 7 considers the mechanics by which the union built a formidable regional presence in the late 1990s and early 2000s. The coca growers' radio station, coupled with the transistor radios that circulate in the Chapare, have provided the communication infrastructure to allow the union to function. It shows how, through satellite networks, the coca unions were able to build common ground with other marginalized groups across the country and form a national movement. However, the case study also shows how the station was hijacked and corrupted by the party, and ultimately replaced by a government-backed media presence. The story of the radio station serves to illustrate a broader point about how the MAS administration has broken its link with the unions and interfered in areas that were previously autonomous.

The conclusion reflects on the hopes and aspirations for a new form of politics that accompanied Morales's victory, but also the disillusionment and despondency that soon set in. It considers what the case study of the Chapare coca growers can tell us about the workings of democracy on the margins more broadly. Theoretically, the book analyzes the contradictions regarding how vernacular conceptions of democracy are enacted and the extent to which the larger institutional framework is able to encompass them. It argues that utopian movements have to find a way of reconciling big ideas with the profane and mundane realities of everyday life and to resolve these contradictions in a way that does not alienate the bases.

1. The Rise of the Coca Unions

Bolivia is a landlocked country located in the geographical center of South America, covering an area roughly twice the size of Spain. The high, rugged mountain ranges and Andean plateau lie to the west, and the jungle and vast lowland plains stretch eastward toward Brazil and Paraguay. The climate varies from humid and tropical in the lowlands to cold and arid at higher altitudes. The country is home to just under eleven million people (Calcopietro et al. 2014: 2), of whom the majority live in the altiplano (Andean plateau), focused in the cities of La Paz and El Alto. Over recent years, economically dynamic Santa Cruz, located in the eastern lowlands, has grown to become Bolivia's largest city. It is estimated that up to 7 percent of the population lives abroad, primarily to work in Argentina, Brazil, Spain, and the United States (Central Intelligence Agency 2016).

Bolivia ranks as the most indigenous country of South America. Most people who self-identify as indigenous are Aymara or Quechua speakers from the altiplano and high valleys, but there is also a large Chiquitano and Guarani population located in the southeastern lowlands. There are a further thirty-two recognized indigenous groups in Bolivia, but they are much smaller, with some numbering no more than two hundred people. Around a quarter of the population self-identify as mestizo. Strictly speaking, this refers to a mixture of indigenous and white European heritage; however, given the fluidity of identity in the Andean region, mestizo is often used to refer to people of indigenous origin who are educated and live in urban areas (Harvey 2002). By far the smallest group (making up around 10 percent of the population) are the white *criollo* elite, who have historically been the most powerful economic and political group in the country (Kohl, Farthing, and Muruchi 2011: xxiii).

Bolivia is one of the poorest nations in the hemisphere (Vargas and Garriga 2015: 5–8). At the start of twenty-first century, GDP per capita was just nine hundred dollars, with 35 percent of the population completely indigent, subsisting on an income of less than a dollar a day (Dunkerley 2007b: 134). While Bolivia's economic status has improved considerably over the past ten years, it still ranks at or near the bottom in many key areas of health and development, including poverty, education, malnutrition, child mortality, and life expectancy, when compared with other Latin American countries (Calcopietro et al. 2014: 2). For most Bolivians, the daily grinding poverty they experience seems to contradict the fact that the country is blessed with an abundance of natural resources including vast reserves of gas, petroleum, zinc, silver, iron, lithium, timber, and immense biodiversity (Kohl and Farthing 2006).

People in Bolivia have repeatedly revolted; and these conflicts have left a deep imprint on Bolivian politics (Albó 1987, 2008a; Hylton and Thomson 2007). The most prominent national heroes are Bartolina Sisa and Tupaj Katari, whose Aymara armies surrounded the city of La Paz and held it under siege for several months in the late eighteenth century in a bid to oust the Spanish colonial occupiers. More recently, audacious forms of neoliberalized "accumulation by dispossession" (Harvey 2004), whereby property, land, and labor are increasingly commoditized and privatized, prepared the ground for widespread social mobilization, making Bolivia the poster child of left-wing rebellion around the globe. Legend says that Katari's last words before being executed by the Spanish were "I alone shall die, but I will return and I will be millions." This phrase became the rallying cry of protestors at the start of the twenty-first century, reflecting the important role that indigenous identity plays in contemporary social movements (Lazar and McNeish 2006).

This chapter traces the long history of rebellion in Bolivia and provides the background for the rest of the book. It discusses how, throughout the 1990s and early 2000s, the Chapare coca unions were in direct confrontation with police and military forces, contesting national-level drug policies. The chapter then considers the context in which the MAS came to power, emphasizing how the MAS has changed from its origins as a radical anti-neoliberal party that was driven by extraparliamentary politics to its more moderate and reformist contemporary profile. The chapter ends with an overview of fieldwork methodology.

The National Revolution

In the late nineteenth century, tin dominated the Bolivian economy, with mining generating 45 percent of Bolivian exports and 95 percent of state revenues (Thomson 2009). For forty years three large mine owners, Patiño, Aramayo, and Hochschild (known collectively as "la Rosca"), largely controlled successive governments. Bolivia's crippling defeat by Paraguay in the Chaco War (1932–35) marked a turning point for the country as it led to a massive loss of life and territory, discrediting the ruling class. The experiences of the rural peasants who served in the army alongside workers and people from urban backgrounds produced a new political awareness and a desire for a more nationalist and equitable development model (Klein 2011: 178–208). The military routing combined with economic decline, and the National Revolutionary Movement's (Movimiento Nacionalista Revolucionario—MNR) 1951 electoral victory, which was not honored, paved the way for revolution. In 1952 miners and peasant militias[1] led by a small middle class, successfully overthrew the mining oligarchs.

The MNR-led government (reluctantly) ceded cabinet positions to the newly formed Bolivian Workers Union (Central Obrera Boliviana—COB),[2] and together they instituted sweeping changes, including the nationalization of the tin mines, agrarian and educational reform, universal suffrage, and reduction in the size of the army. For James Malloy and Richard Thorn (1971: xv), "the Bolivian National Revolution stands alongside the Mexican and Cuban revolutions as one of the most significant events in Latin American history." James Dunkerley (2013: 328–29) explains how the revolution's far-reaching changes affected the population as a whole. Over the following years, the state-owned mining corporation (Corporación Minera de Bolivia—COMIBOL) took direct control of mining interests. The agrarian reform distributed some forty-seven million hectares to over 650,000 beneficiaries over a forty-year period. By abolishing gender and literacy restrictions, the voting base expanded from 200,000 to one million people. Free public education was made available to all.

Sinclair Thomson (2009) points out that the National Revolution was linked to other, less immediately obvious effects. These included increased social mobility as peasants moved to the cities and became more politically and commercially powerful. Meanwhile the unionization of the peasantry allowed for greater state hegemony in the countryside through processes of clientelism (see also Albro 2007: 283). The 1952 revolution was also a turning point for coca. Paul Gootenberg (2016) describes how peasant rebellions dissolved the Yungas hacienda class (see also Leons and Leons 1971). Coca cultivation continued in the Yungas, but production expanded (through the influx of mostly Quechua migrants) to Cochabamba's Chapare region. Migration was accelerated by the opening of access roads and government-backed colonization programs (Fifer 1982).

While the revolution generated a new sense of national identity and gave rise to a qualitatively distinct form of state building (Whitehead 2003: 43), its shortcomings have led some to describe it as incomplete (Malloy 1970). Bolivian sociologist Silvia Rivera writes, "All the liberal promises opened by the Revolution of 1952, that of the full political participation of the Indians and women, of economic sovereignty and self-sufficiency in basic goods, have been shown to be sleights of hand, laying bare the colonial structures that uphold the Bolivian state" (Rivera, cited in Dunkerley 2013: 342). According to Forrest Hylton and Sinclair Thomson (2007: 80), the limitations of the revolution, specifically its inability to resolve the cultural, political, and economic exclusion of the indigenous majority, laid the ground for contemporary indigenous struggle.

The military coup has often been the engine for political change in Bolivia. Since independence in 1825, Bolivia has experienced more than 150 coups or attempted coups. In 1964 the generals left their barracks once more, taking control of the country for the following eighteen years. Throughout this period the COB played an important role in the struggle for democracy against military dictatorship. The miners' unions were the backbone of the COB. Since their formation in 1944, the miners were the most important civil society actors in the country, not only fighting for their own material interests, but also making demands for progressive economic policies, democracy, and human rights. The miners repeatedly brought the government to its knees, through strike actions and protests. The miners paid dearly for their struggle, however. The army crushed dissent, which resulted in various massacres (Nash 1979; Rodriguez Ostria 1991).

In contrast to the miners, the peasants who had only recently reacquired their lands were far more hesitant to rebel, terrified that they could be turned into serfs once more. General Rene Barrientos (president of Bolivia from 1964 to 1969), who was a fluent Quechua speaker, maintained peasant support by promising to uphold the agrarian reform, which granted them land, in return for their loyalty (this arrangement was known as the military–peasant pact). The pact endured for ten years (1964–74) and generated deep divisions between indigenous peasant farmers and the workers' unions.[3] The junta eventually turned against the peasants, however; in 1974 soldiers mowed down peasants with machine guns when they protested over a new tax. This fateful event broke the pact and contributed to the growth of independent peasant unionism in the country (Mallon 1992; Webber 2011: 101).

In 1979, the first (independent) national peasant union, the Unified Confederation of Campesino Unions of Bolivia (Confederación Sindical Única de Trabajadores Campesinos de Bolivia—CSUTCB) was established. It immediately affiliated with the COB to play an active role in the struggle for democracy. A women's organization soon followed, the Bartolina Sisa National Confederation of Peasant, Indigenous, and Native Women of Bolivia (Confederación Nacional de Mujeres Campesinas Indígenas Originarias de Bolivia "Bartolina Sisa"—CNMCIOB-BS). Informally they are known as the Bartolinas, in reference to the eighteenth-century heroine who led the anticolonial revolt with her husband Tupac Katari.

Neoliberal Reforms

Military rule was forced out through concerted struggle led by the COB, and democracy was restored in 1982. A left-leaning government assumed power and found itself facing a severe economic crisis. Inflation soared to an annual rate of 8,171 percent in 1985, and per capita income experienced a downward slide throughout the decade (Hagopian and Mainwaring 2005: 6). On August 29, 1985, Víctor Paz Estenssoro (the historic leader of the 1952 revolution) signed Supreme Decree 21060, which administered a lethal dose of free-market reforms to the National Revolution's import substitution economic model. The shock treatment called for the privatization or closure of state-owned enterprises, froze all public-sector wages, cut welfare expenditure, allowed the currency to float against the U.S. dollar, and abolished import substitution policies and protective tariffs (Dunkerley 1990: 32–9). These cuts deepened throughout the 1990s with the fire sale of the few remaining state-owned enterprises, the rapid expansion of nongovernmental organizations (NGOs), and the decentralization of the state. What happened in Bolivia is part of a more universal process, other faces of which appear in the Global South and East, but also in the advanced economies of Euro-America (Harvey 2005).

The International Monetary Fund–imposed measures did famously succeed in cutting the fiscal deficit and taming inflation, but this came at a high social cost. Jeffery Sachs, the Harvard-trained architect of the reforms, acknowledged that, "although fiscally necessary, the results are stunning, and indeed reflect a social tragedy" (Morales and Sachs 1988: 35). Bolivia experienced a dramatic fall in real wages and an increase in poverty and unemployment as trade liberalization wiped out local businesses (Kohl and Farthing 2006). Local markets were flooded with cheaper imported goods, including staples such as corn and rice, which destroyed peasant liveli- hoods (Urioste 1989). Tens of thousands of state workers, including 27,000 unionized miners, lost their jobs as a result of rationalization, privatiza- tion, and in some instances closure of state-owned companies (Crabtree 1987; Dunkerley and Morales 1986). When the mines were closed down, many of the workers migrated to coca-growing regions, but also to the slums of La Paz and Cochabamba, where they continued their traditions of self-organization and militancy in a new context (Lazar 2008).

Kohl and Farthing (2006) document how the 1990s program of privati- zation led to widespread asset stripping. State industries were vastly under- valued at the time of their sale, and the loss of revenue was not offset by increased tax returns or the gains from foreign investment. Bolivians were faced with higher prices for basic necessities and, given the government's inability to regulate business, cuts in services. The miners saw the railroad that they relied on to export minerals dismantled and carted off to Chile, and the Brazilian company that bought up Bolivia's national airline, Lloyd Aero Boliviano (LAB), stripped the planes for spare parts (Kohl and Far- thing 2006: 109). Meanwhile, the international consortium that took over Cochabamba's water supply in 1999 more than doubled the rates for the urban poor (Laurie, Andolina, and Radcliffe 2002). The hydrocarbon sector sustained the greatest losses of all. Petroleum and gas revenues to the national treasury dropped from an average of US$350 million annually to US$50 mil- lion after 1997 (Hylton and Thomson 2007: 102).

But if the state withdrew from its duties toward its citizens, it strengthened its policing power, a phenomenon Lesley Gill (2000) has characterized as the "armed retreat of the state." The shift to more disciplinary policing (and pu- nitive social attitudes) is a global phenomenon (Koch 2017a; Wacquant 2014). In the Andean region governance has focused on policing drugs. Julian Mercille (2011: 1640) notes how the war on drugs is used as a pre- text to protect free trade agreements, allowing local governments to "contain popular opposition to neoliberal policies." In Bolivia, drug war politics have been used to crush dissent. To give but one example, Law 1008 set disproportionately high sentences for drug-related crimes, locking up thousands of people at the lowest levels of the drug trade pyramid, many of whom were also coca union members (Giacoman Aramayo 2011).

The IMF-imposed neoliberal reforms were not only about addressing macro stability but were also designed to undo the kinds of collective organization and expectations of the state carried over from the 1952 national revolution. This much was made clear by President Victor Paz Estenssoro, who justified the implementation of Decree 21060 as part of a "battle against dual power," an attempt to take power out of the hands of "ultra-leftist" miners who had long exerted influence over government (Stefanoni 2003). In this respect, the policy was successful, according to Jeffery Webber (2005): "the period of neoliberal hegemony, 1985–2000, clearly represented a historic defeat of the left." The old union organizations (most notably the miners' unions) were severely weakened, and prominent figures on the left went to work with nongovernmental organizations or converted squarely to the neoliberal project (García Linera and Ortega Breña 2010: 46). That is not to say that social protest disappeared, however. As we will see, throughout the 1990s the coca growers led massive protests against forced coca eradication.

The 2000–2005 Cycle of Protest

Bolivia entered the twenty-first century burdened by a grotesque "disjunctive democracy" (Caldeira and Holston 1999). Moira Zuazo (2010: 122) writes that the expansion of political rights (following the return to democracy) without economic or social integration meant that by the mid-nineties "popular rural and urban society felt cheated and excluded." This in turn produced a serious crisis in the party system (Mainwaring, Bejarano, and Leongomez 2006; Salman 2006). Starting in 2000, radical left–indigenous movements rose up to contest the government and its market-oriented policies. There never was a coherent plan, but even so, some historians have classified the period 2000 to 2005 as a "revolutionary" epoch (Dunkerley 2007b; Hylton and Thomson 2007; Webber 2010b).

The insurgent cycle of events began with the Cochabamba Water War in 2000, which opposed the privatization of the city's water supply, and peaked in October 2003 when mass mobilizations sought to block the export of natural gas through Chile. In each case, the Bolivian government declared martial law and deployed the military against the population. After the dust had settled, two presidents had been toppled, dozens of people had been killed (with sixty deaths in the 2003 gas war alone), and ex-president Gonzalo Sánchez de Lozada was in self-imposed exile in Miami. An interim government was installed, led by the head of the judiciary, Eduardo Rodríguez Veltzé, and elections were hastily convened for December 2005.

The protestors represented a broad alliance, including the participation of a strong miners' contingent, the federation of the Aymara peasantry, the coca growers' unions of the Chapare, the Regional Workers Central of El Alto, as well as El Alto's neighborhood federations, not to mention a plethora of student organizations, professional associations, unions, and cooperatives. In contrast to the old hierarchical national-level unions, in many cases this new form of collective action was rooted in local issues and concerns and relied on preexisting forms of territorial organization (García Linera 2004; García Linera et al. 2007; Spronk 2007). Sian Lazar argues that the protestors drew on the syndicalist traditions of the displaced miners but also on notions of the *ayllu* (an indigenous form of political organization), and in this way "the working class in Bolivia is reconstituting itself as a political subject, albeit not in its traditional form" (Lazar 2008: 173). Antonio Negri and colleagues (2008) also take up the Bolivian case in support of their theory of multitude.

Significantly, the oppositional movements that mobilized over the period 2000–2005 employed indigenous symbols such as the coca leaf and *Wiphala* (the multicolored flag of the Andean first peoples) to stress a shared history of oppression at the hands of an ethnically different elite group. What makes the embrace of an indigenous heritage interesting is that it is a relatively recent phenomenon for Bolivia's modern social movements, as under the influence of a Marxist left, many activists had previously identified as peasants or workers and mobilized along class-based lines. According to Robert Albro (2005: 449), indigenous politics was an "effective tool for broad based coalition building," as it connected the daily struggles faced by diverse sectors including informal workers, indigenous peasants, and even impoverished mestizos (see also Canessa 2006). Evo Morales was particularly adept at capitalizing on indigenous symbols, prompting political scientist Raul Madrid (2008) to refer to his political style as "ethno-populism."

And yet, while protestors stressed an (inter)ethnic solidarity, they were far from a unitary block. Resistance arose from multiple and diverse popular movements, and action was always contingent on the problems that specific sectors faced at any given moment. Raquel Gutierrez Aguilar writes: "the coca growers joined them [national protests] and added strength to the collective mobilization, . . . although they always kept their own rhythms in mind and focused their attention and effort on resolving their own problems" (Gutierrez Aguilar 2014: 84). Moreover, at times the movements were actively hostile to one another. There was a particularly deep division between the Aymara peasants in the highlands (led by Felipe Quispe) and the predominantly Quechua coca growers' unions. There has been a long-standing rivalry between Aymara and Quechua communities in the highlands (Crabtree and Whitehead 2008: 10). One cleavage was that the coca growers aimed to occupy positions within the state apparatus through their party (the MAS); by contrast, the Aymara communities often sought a more autonomous path (Gutierrez Aguilar 2014: 89).

In spite of these divisions, the popular sectors' demands cohered into a singular narrative. The "October Agenda" (announced in El Alto in 2003 following the "gas war") called for a more socially oriented alternative to the prevailing neoliberal model of economic development, including the nationalization of hydrocarbons, a constituent assembly, and the extradition of President Gonzalo Sanchez de Lozada to face trial for the deaths associated with the gas war (Perreault 2006). The protestors were also involved in a battle over the meaning of citizenship and the forms of doing politics. Movement leaders denounced the actually existing democracy as a sham—nothing more than a closed system operated for the benefit of elite groups. They called instead for a new model of governance, one built on indigenous traditions including authorities who take leadership from below, continuous deliberation, and group rights as opposed to individual rights. From the perspective of the protestors, the goal of the mobilizations was not to destroy democracy (as critics of the popular movements have often claimed), but rather to deepen and to extend it (Albro 2006; García Linera et al. 2007).

The Coca Union's Struggle

When the Chapare was first settled in the 1950s and 1960s, the colonizers who migrated from the highlands formed into self-governing units known as sindicatos (syndicates or agricultural unions). In the first instance, the sindicatos were established as a way to distribute and control land; however, their remit soon extended far beyond that. Given the almost total absence of the state, they became the de facto regional authorities, responsible for many state-like functions (see PNUD 2007), including regulating (often in a coercive way) daily coexistence and interaction between members, establishing private land boundaries, managing and taxing coca leaf markets, and investing in, and building small-scale public works such as roads, schools, health clinics, and river defenses. To this day, the political organization of daily life is left to the unions, but they constantly have to negotiate the terms of their autonomy with an encroaching state. To put it another way, the unions have both an inward-facing role (where they act like a state) and outward-facing duties (when they negotiate with the state).

The coca union has a hierarchical structure (see figure 1.1). The sindicatos form the base of the organization, including anywhere between twenty and two hundred members. Five to eight neighboring sindicatos form a subfederation, known as a *central*, and all the centrals in a municipality (between ten and twenty) are gathered into a federation. There are six federations in the Cochabamba Tropics,[4] organized under the aegis of a centralized committee known as the Confederación de Productores de Coca del Trópico de Cochabamba, or simply the Six Federations. The Six Federations are affiliated to national-level peasant confederations including the CSUTCB.[5] In 1994 grassroots members established a parallel Women's Federation,[6] the Federación de Mujeres Campesinas del Trópico (FECAMTROP), which plays an important role in the Bartolina Sisa Confederation (CNMCIOB-BS).

The first agricultural federation (grouping of sindicatos) emerged in the Chapare in the mid-1960s to represent the interests of the area's peasant farmers before the state, but also within the Bolivian labor movement more broadly. Initially the U.S. embassy in La Paz was slow to pick up on the political significance of this organization. An embassy report from 1982 states: "It is difficult to believe that the coca producers of the Chapare could constitute a political force; these new colonizers, the majority of whom are indigenous, are apparently humble and passive" (Gamarra 1994: 27). The authors were not mistaken in their characterization of the union as apolitical. In the early 1980s, coca prices were high and the peasant farmers were content. Moreover, the union served as a mechanism for governmental control through corporatism (Albó 2008b: 57). The ex-dictator Hugo Banzer was even said to be the godfather to the children of the union's then general secretary. One local coca grower described the

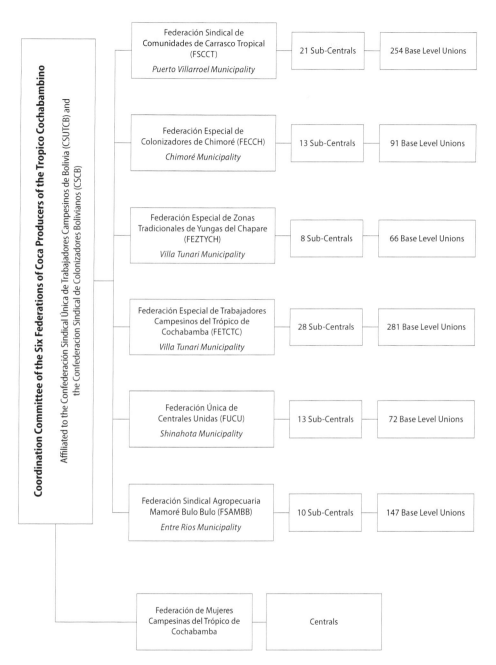

Figure 1.1. Organizational chart of the Six Federations of Coca Producers of the Tropics of Cochabamba.

relationship between the government and unions in these terms: "There were coca unions back then [in the 1970s], but they were tied to the government, managed by the government. The leaders were not chosen by the bases [rank and file], they were chosen by the government." The traditional left, represented by the miners' unions, considered the coca producers to be a petit bourgeois antirevolutionary element (Escobar 2008: 194).

The political apathy of the Chapare unions reversed when tens of thousands of miners migrated to the region in the mid-1980s after structural adjustment and the collapse of the international tin market left them jobless. The miners brought their traditions of class solidarity, organizational skill, and revolutionary consciousness with them. As one ex-miner said: "I was a miner, I didn't have fear, I knew how to light dynamite. I knew the union life." He went on to say that because of people like him "more leaders were formed here in the tropics, we strengthened the unions." The arrival of the miners coincided with a time of growing discontent in the Chapare; coca prices were falling, and impending antinarcotics legislation (Law 1008) threatened to outlaw coca cultivation in the region altogether. What is more, the state, pressured and financed by the United States, had started to show its teeth.

On June 27, 1988, the union organized a large-scale protest against Law 1008's imminent passage. The state response was fierce; the security forces (the Rural Mobile Patrol Unit—UMOPAR) killed twelve coca growers during a violent confrontation on a bridge over the Chapare River, an event that is remembered as "the Massacre of Villa Tunari." One of my coca grower friends who was present that day recalled how he had to jump into the river to escape the bullets. He was lucky, he knew how to swim; others did not and they drowned. From that point on, the Chapare farmers had a class enemy against which their own solidarity came into sharp focus. The defense of coca gave the farmers a common cause with fellow colonizers; enemies were easy to define, including anybody who tried to prevent them from making a living with coca, be it the government, the military, or the U.S. embassy. Coca was not just a crop that the peasants grew, but a way of life that reflected the moral worth of the cultivator.

Evo Morales, who was born to an Aymara-speaking highland family of peasant farmers, first migrated to the Cochabamba Tropics in 1980 at the age of twenty-one (following his parents, who migrated there after a severe drought in the highlands wiped out their crops). His passion lay with football, and he became the secretary for sports of his sindicato in 1982. The murder of a local peasant farmer at the hands of the military (who burned the man alive) stirred his outrage and led to his interest in politics. Morales's charisma, intelligence, and organizational skills ensured that he rose quickly through the union's ranks. In 1988, shortly after the Massacre of Villa Tunari, Morales and a group of associates, who called themselves the "Anti-Imperial Front" (Frente Amplio de Masas Anti-Imperialistas—FAMAI), were elected to the leadership of the Federation of Peasant Workers of the Tropic of Cochabamba (Federación Especial de Trabajadores Campesinos del Trópico de Cochabamba—FETCTC), more commonly known as "Federación Trópico," the largest of the Chapare's six agricultural federations (Morales would become leader of all six Chapare Federations in 1994). Mobilizing under the slogan "Long live coca, death to Yankees," the federations broke with the previous corporatist traditions to demand the right to land, the demilitarization of the Chapare, an end to coca eradication, and the modification of antidrug laws.[7]

In the wake of the power vacuum created by the decline of the COB (which had pushed social and economic justice since the 1952 revolution) caused by neoliberal policies, the coca growers emerged to become one of the most powerful labor movements in the country, taking a leading role in the CSUTCB in 1991 (Van Cott 2005: 57). Do Alto and Stefanoni (2010: 306) write that with the expansion of the U.S.-financed drug war, like the miners before them, "the coca growers came to think of themselves as the vanguard of the popular movement." The coca unions developed sophisticated organizational forms and increasingly were able to mount formidable opposition to the state. Their repertoire of protest included setting up camps in city plazas; blocking Bolivia's main road, which runs through the Chapare; laying siege to military camps; and undertaking long marches to the capital city La Paz, events that vaulted Evo Morales onto the national stage (Laserna 1999). Coca growers also undertook spectacular acts to draw public attention to their plight, including hunger strikes, self-crucifixion, and sewing their mouths closed.

The women took a leading role in protests and marches (see figure 1.2). Leader Juana Quispe explains: "We, the cocaleras [female coca growers], we had to defend our territory with our lives, and we were prepared to do it. We didn't have fear of bullets or death." Women would go at the head of the march because the military was reluctant to hurt them; Juana confirmed, "they would hit us, but only calmly [gently], leave us a bit blue and

Figure 1.2. Women leaders marching at the launch of a congress in 2006. Photo by author.

yellow [bruised] . . . but nothing too bad, not like how they would give it to the men." Zabalaga (2004) records how the women would provoke the soldiers by protesting wearing only a bra with a target drawn on their bodies, daring them to shoot. In December 1995 during Sanchez de Lozada's first administration (1993–97), the female coca growers marched to La Paz, some 600 km, mostly uphill, to speak "woman to woman" with the first lady of the nation about the abuses carried out by eradication forces in the Chapare (Agreda, Rodriguez, and Conteras 1996; Camacho Balderrama 1999).

Drawing on their experience as military conscripts, male coca growers established self-defense committees with the aim of preventing the security forces from eradicating coca plantations. These groups were armed with bolt-action rifles (Mausers) dating back to the 1930s Chaco War against Paraguay, and homemade land mines known as *cazabobos* (fool hunters). Union leader and local mayor Feliciano Mamani explained: "There was never any justice for us, that's why we organized the self-defense committees. If they fought against us with arms, then we responded with arms." It is important to note, however, that fire fights with troops were never more than isolated incidents, and the coca growers were never considered to constitute a guerrilla force (Ledebur 2002).

The coca growers built alliances through domestic and international support networks of NGOs and activist organizations, or what Deborah Yashar (2005: 71–74) calls "trans-community networks." The Bolivian-based Andean Information Network played a pivotal role in facilitating union leaders' participation in international forums. There was also a growing peasant-to-peasant movement throughout the Andes with the mission to defend coca, which the growers considered sacred. The first Andean Council for the Producers of the Coca Leaf (Consejo Andino de Productores de Hoja de Coca— CAPHC), which included Peruvian, Colombian, and Bolivian growers, was held in La Paz in 1991. At its second council meeting (held in Cusco in 1993), the assembly elected Evo Morales as its president (Yashar 2005: 185). Besides holding regular work meetings, the CAPHC arranged for its representatives to attend meetings and conferences in Europe, the United States, and other countries in Latin America and the Caribbean (Cabieses 1997: 80–82).

Throughout the nineties, the astronomic political ascent of the coca growers' union and the national presence they developed plagued one Bolivian government after another, which were facing considerable pressure from the United States. During the Banzer administration (1997–2002), the government effectively outlawed the union by arguing that, as coca is illegal, here was really no need for a union representing coca growers' interests (Orduna and Guzman 2001). The Chapare was declared a "red zone" subject to special policing measures, thereby instituting a permanent "state of exception" (Ramirez 2010: 84–85).[8] Farmers were denied their civil rights; union leaders were forced to live on the run; and base-level unions often held their meetings in secret locations, away from the main road and hidden from the helicopters that circled above (see figure 1.3). Union leader Don Franco Pacheco recounts: "I remember once . . . we were having our meeting and just then the UMOPAR [militarized antidrug police] turned up. They fired tear gas at us to disrupt our meeting, even though we hadn't done anything. We hadn't even insulted them, nothing!" Meanwhile, Don Angel Mamani, an ex-leader in his forties, explained: "Back then politics was illegal in the Chapare. The leaders, well, we couldn't even walk around with a notebook, it was a crime." I was told that the security forces would enter the region at night with the aim of arresting leaders. To safeguard against this, the leaders would often sleep in the jungle or in freshly dug graves. Don Franco joked, "In those days the cemetery was my bedroom."

Figure 1.3. Military police search Chapare residents. Photograph courtesy of Andean Information Network and Dr. Godofred Reinicke.

The state made efforts to bribe and co-opt leaders; if this was unsuccessful, they were arrested and charged with terrorism. Take the case of Doña Marcela Herrera, a union leader who was arrested and charged in 2002 for "armed uprising." Doña Marcela explained that the police framed her by planting dynamite and weapons at her house; she was then taken to the military camp, where she says she was imprisoned and tortured. Many leaders had similar stories; it was said that the public prosecutor kept an Uzi machine gun in his office, which he would force coca growers to pose with for incriminating photographs. Some leaders were quite simply victims of extrajudicial killing. In 2001 Casimiro Huanca, the leader of one of the six federations, was shot dead at point-blank range by a member of the Expeditionary Task Force, a paramilitary unit set up and run by the U.S. embassy. The officer responsible faced no punishment for the crime (Gill 2004: 187–88).

Government forces made repeated efforts to silence Radio Aurora, the coca union's radio station. Over the period 2000–2001, the public prosecutor sent dozens of letters to the station demanding that it cease and desist broadcasting messages designed to "incite the cocaleros to block roads, disturb the peace, and prepare them for confrontation with the armed forces," as stated in one such letter. The local union organized a permanent guard around the station to defend against attack, but they were no match for the militarized antidrug police. One night in February 2002, over twenty heavily armed members of the Mobile Rural Patrol Unit (UMOPAR) broke into the station, impounded the FM transmitter, and arrested the union members who attempted to stop them. After several months of protests and roadblocks, the transmitter was eventually returned to the union, though I was told that it was badly damaged and had to be replaced.

The coca growers have a coherent narrative pertaining to the U.S.-backed war on drugs. Any cocalero or cocalera will explain that U.S.-led efforts had absolutely nothing to do with tackling the illicit drug trade, but rather were about obliterating organized peasant resistance to the neoliberal development model. In a 2006 interview, Doña Apolonia Bustamante, a leader in her mid-forties, put it this way: "The United States, they want to snuff out oppositional movements that don't fit with their vision. They saw that we were unionized. They were scared about a powerful social movement here in the Tropics. And so they thought about it, and they decided to do away with the organizations, and that is why they attacked us repeatedly." She went on to explain how the focus had previously been the fight against communism, "but today it's the war on drugs." Local mayor and coca union leader Don Feliciano Mamani told me: "Behind the war on drugs there are other interests. Interests in natural resources, and in dismantling the unions of the Chapare." He went on to explain that the aim was to move peasant farmers off the land so that transnational companies could take control and employ them as a cheap labor force.

The Birth of the MAS

In November 2013 I interviewed Don Marcelo Moreno, the leader of the United Centrals Federation of coca growers. We sat in the federation's tatty offices surrounded by peasant leaders vying for his attention. The walls were plastered from floor to ceiling with campaign posters. Marcelo spoke about the formation of the MAS; he explained how in the early nineties, "We marched, and we thought that politics could be changed with protests, but they didn't have any impact." He went on to describe how the unions would sign agreements with the government, but they would never be honoured: "The neoliberal state had all the power. . . . They [the elites] were playing on the football field, and we didn't even have one player, we just watched from the sidelines. That's when we decided we needed our own political party."

Moira Zuazo (2010: 121–22) writes that the MAS emerged from two contradictory tendencies. On the one hand, it is the product of the crisis of democracy provoked by the government's adherence to neoliberal orthodoxy (and militarized coca eradication), but on the other it also emerged in direct response to the new political spaces opened up via the decentralization of the state. Throughout the 1990s, governments throughout Latin America, under the guidance of the World Bank, decentralized administrative authority. In 1994 the first Gonzalo Sanchez de Lozada administration (1993–97) passed the Popular Participation Law (Ley de Participación Popular—LPP), widely recognized as one of the most ambitious efforts to reform the state in the entire region. The LPP created over three hundred municipalities nationwide, legally acknowledged more than 15,000 local grassroots organizations, and decentralized 20 percent of national revenues to these municipal governments. It also called for elections to be held for mayoral and council member positions throughout the country, and mandated participatory budgeting and oversight by local organizations.[9]

Restructuring was justified on the grounds of increasing public participation and good governance. However, some academics have been critical of such initiatives, which they maintain are simply the most recent element of a neoliberal governing agenda. The aim, it is said, is to further break up the state and to consolidate new modes of regulatory relations (Peck and Tickell 2002; Veltmeyer 1997). Critics of the LPP in Bolivia maintained that one of its principal motivations was to shift the locus of political struggle in the country from the national level to the more controllable local level, thereby neutralizing opposition movements. However, it has since become clear that the reverse was true. Instead of localizing politics, decentralization actually contributed to the emergence of indigenous peasant-based political parties that subsequently became the most important counterweights to neoliberal hegemony (Kohl 2002; Postero 2007; Van Cott 2005).

The LPP meant that for the first time town halls were actually worth fighting over, as they became the principal vehicle for implementing public works.[10] In direct response to the spaces opened out under the LPP, confederated peasant unions (led by the coca growers) were driven to set up their own electoral vehicle. At a 1995 congress held in Santa Cruz titled "Land, Territory, and the Political Instrument," the unions[11] jointly established the Assembly for the Sovereignty of the People (Asamblea por la Soberanía de los Pueblos—ASP), which ran in local elections as the United Left

(Izquierda Unida—IU). The same year the ASP-IU contested elections in the newly formed municipalities, and won ten Cochabamba town halls, including all five in the Chapare. Municipal government proved to be a good training ground for the nascent party, which quickly developed a national profile. The United Left won four seats in Congress in the 1997 national elections, with Evo Morales winning a seat in Congress with the country's highest majority (Morales achieved 70 percent of the vote in the Chapare electoral district) (Assies and Salman 2003: 37). Pablo Stefanoni (2010: 147) argues that these early electoral victories diminished the possibility of armed struggle (particularly in the Chapare).

The ASP was short-lived, however. A leadership struggle between ASP leader Alejo Veliz (an indigenous peasant leader from Cochabamba) and Evo Morales led to a split in the party. In 1998 Morales and the coca unions formed their own party, the Political Instrument for the Sovereignty of the People (Instrumento Político por la Soberanía de los Pueblos—IPSP), which later ran in elections as the Movement Towards Socialism (MAS), the name by which they are known today (Madrid 2011). In 2002 Morales and the MAS came within a whisker of winning the presidency, and gained eight senate seats and twenty-six in the lower house (do Alto and Stefanoni 2010: 308). Don Marcelo Moreno (introduced above) summed up: "At first it was just a union fight but later it changed. Then we had two arms, union struggle and political struggle. That's when we entered the field; now whoever plays best wins."

As the MAS grew in stature, the party came under siege. Morales was arrested, beaten, and tortured on numerous occasions, and he was expelled from Congress in 2002 for the part he allegedly played in inciting protests that led to the death of two policemen. During the 2002 electoral campaign, U.S. Ambassador Manuel Rocha threatened voters that the U.S. government would cut all funding to Bolivia if the electorate voted for Morales (*Los Tiempos* 2002). Contrary to his intention, such attacks only bolstered Morales's popularity by confirming that he was a true outsider fighting against the tyranny of the neoliberal system. This chimed well with the electorate at a time when the rest of the country was convulsed in mass social protest against the prevailing neoliberal model (Assies and Salman 2003; Van Cott 2003). When the results came in and the MAS did far better than expected, Morales quipped that Rocha was his best campaign manager to date.

Don Angel Mamani, an ex-miner turned coca grower who was present at the founding meeting of the ASP in Santa Cruz, explained the motivation for establishing the party: "The previous political system was not participatory; only senators or members of congress had the right to propose a law, and they were just agents of the World Bank, the IMF, you know? Particular interests. A union leader couldn't make a law! That's why we set up the political instrument [political party], so that we could all participate." The aim of the political instrument (as the MAS is more often known in the Chapare), then, was to take social movement demands to the national arena, but also to get its movement leaders elected so they could enter into positions of state power.

At the beginning, party affiliation was premised on membership in a social organization (Zuazo 2010: 122). Grassroots movements worked together to form a "network of alliances" and thereby expand the party at a national level. Base-level organizations were responsible for choosing their own candidates to run on the MAS ticket and setting their own priorities. In return they had to commit to support the presidency of Morales and back the MAS's core agenda. Grassroots organizations also had to provide resources and labor in support of the MAS (including sewing flags, painting banners, but also paying for transport, food, and entertainment for MAS leaders). In this way, the MAS was able to mount a national campaign in spite of its limited resources—see figures 1.4 and 1.5 (Gutierrez Aguilar 2014: 90). In a 2003 interview, Evo Morales described the functioning of the MAS in the following way:

> [The MAS] is a political movement that expresses the aspirations of social organizations in their struggle for national demands, and those of the popular sectors. The organic base is precisely in the organizations, before which political leaders and their public representatives (councilors in the municipalities, deputies, and senators) are accountable for their actions and receive the main directives for their action. . . . As a movement linked to social organizations, the bases participate both in controlling the actions of their representatives and in the selection of candidates for public office. (Morales 2003)

In the early days the MAS had no party bureaucracy to speak of, and most of its candidates were social movement leaders rather than career politicians (including Evo Morales). In essence, the party was run by and for its social movement base (Madrid 2012: 163; Regalsky 2010). The MAS then had a "dual character," linking the world of socially rooted movements on the one hand with formal politics on the other (Harten 2011). Drawing attention to

Figure 1.4. Coca growers at a rally in support of the MAS party. Photo by author.

Figure 1.5. A pro-MAS rally in Cochabamba. The banner reads "Coordinator of the Six Federations of Cochabamba. Long Live Coca, Death to Yankees." Photo by author.

this unique feature of the MAS, Evo Morales has stated, "where trade union organizations function well, there is no need for a parallel party structure" (do Alto and Stefanoni 2010: 311).

The Transformation of the MAS

In 2013, I asked union leader Marcelo Moreno about the functioning of the national MAS party. He confirmed that it continues to operate as an extension of the union organization. He told me: "Look, this [the MAS] is not a party. It's a social and syndicalist movement. The social organizations and the political instrument are like husband and wife, they work together . . . the organizations are sat above the ministers, it is a matrix institution. We [the unions] control the government." To make his point, Don Marcelo impressed upon me how the unions could convene an assembly and demand the participation of any member of Congress, senator, or even the president, and that they would have to come. "Our job is to guide the members of Parliament," he told me. "They come here [to the Chapare], and we put them right." But does Evo listen? I asked. Marcelo replied, "Really, Evo didn't propose that he would be president. NO! We [the unions] told him 'you are going to be president,' and so he listens to us, he has to."

The MAS undoubtedly challenges taken-for-granted ideas about what democracy is and how it can be practiced. However, as a governing party the MAS could never function in the same way as it did when it stood only for the coca growers. Where social movements have made the transition to governing elsewhere in Latin America and beyond, the literature indicates that they invariably take on a more bureaucratic and hierarchical structure and disconnect from the grassroots organizations from which they emerged (Deschouwer 2008). This was certainly the case for Pachacutik in Ecuador (Collins 2004) and the Workers Party (PT) in Brazil (Hunter 2010).[12] In this respect, the MAS appears to be no different. Analysts have argued that since 2002, when the MAS became Bolivia's main opposition party, it lost its revolutionary potential. They say it has transformed into a more traditional political party dedicated to winning elections, and that it is increasingly characterized by vertical decision making and centralist tendencies (Anria and Cyr 2017; Harten 2011; Zegada, Torrez, and Camara 2008).

The step up from being a local movement rooted in the Chapare to a national party with both urban and rural bases presented a number of challenges. In order to gain votes, MAS party leaders have had to make alliances with diverse popular and middle-class movements, tone down their radical message, and make compromises, even with those who were once deemed to be enemies (Zuazo 2010). Given the lack of expertise in the social movement ranks, today most people who hold key positions in Evo's cabinet are not indigenous social movement leaders at all, but rather have urban middle-class backgrounds and only joined MAS during the campaign[13] (Anria 2016a: 470; Stefanoni 2007: 32). Finally, the MAS functions within the preexisting liberal political system, and this has inevitably imposed restraints on how and when popular sovereignty can be exercised (Rockefeller 2007: 177–78). Moira Zuazo (2010: 120) writes that as a result, "the role of social movements has diminished . . . their role driving the process of change is increasingly irrelevant."

Nancy Postero (2017: 17) argues that the MAS's decision to condense power into the central state has generated "vehement dissent" at the grassroots. This much was evident in the Chapare, where the predominant rank-and-file visions of the MAS did not align with Marcelo's account of radical bottom-up control. Union members repeatedly expressed to me that they were aggrieved about the integration of outsiders into the party structure. Don Enrique Huanca, an ex-miner turned coca grower, put it this way: "We don't have people who are well prepared for government and so we have to have outsiders. Most of the government ministers are ex-ADN-istas, MNR-istas, NFR-istas [members of different political parties]; more than anything they are *oportunistas* [opportunists]. Meanwhile, those of us who have been with the MAS for the longest, those who fought the hardest, well we are not recognized . . . we are back working in our fields." Enrique went on to voice concern that the union had lost power to a group of unaccountable representatives in La Paz, people who could not be trusted. He told me: "These rich ones, these city-folk, they say they are MAS-istas [members of the MAS], but they don't know anything. They haven't suffered or fought the way we have. Some of us were talking, if one of them betrays the MAS, then we were thinking we should bring them here to the tropics, to let the bases decide what to do with them. To enact community justice, just like we would do to any union leader." Enrique believes that the bases should have more control over leaders, including the right to physically punish anyone who betrays the movement. He was by no means alone in his concerns regarding the way the party is led; base-level members frequently echoed these sentiments to me.[14]

The tension between the unions and the parliamentary block is evident at meetings as well. Sentiments such as "the bases are not exercising satisfactory control over the ministers," "the authorities do not come down to inform the bases sufficiently," and "when the federation convenes a meeting then the ministers should be present" can often be heard (Stefanoni 2003). At one union meeting I attended, an angry union member shouted at the leaders on the presidium, "We are not just supporters of this government, we are the government so they [the elected officials] have to respect our wishes." In this context, statements such as "we are the government" can be read as an effort to hold leaders accountable rather than a statement of fact.

In Government

Bolivia has been sucked dry by 500 years of rampant extractionism (which has destroyed ecosystems and dislocated indigenous communities); it has rarely had any political stability; and, until the MAS entered office, it had patchy infrastructure at best. The challenges Morales and the MAS faced when they came to power, then, were formidable. The MAS called its "process of change" a "decolonization" of the state.[15] On entering office, Morales focused on three key areas. First, he promised to make the state participatory by institutionalizing features of direct democracy found in Bolivia's social movements. Second, he proposed ending the neoliberal development model that had caused so much damage. Finally, Morales claimed he would reassert national sovereignty, including allowing indigenous peasants the right to grow coca and taking back control of natural resources (see Postero 2017: 33).

Over its eleven years in government, the MAS has had many notable triumphs: the middle class has expanded to include 10 percent of the population, economic growth (thanks to rises in commodity prices until 2011 and Bolivia's successful negotiation with multinationals for a greater share of the profits) is higher than it has been for decades (in 2013 Bolivia's GDP grew at a rate of 6.8 percent; see the *Economist* 2017); and there have been major advances in terms of civil and social rights. Conditional cash transfers,[16] a new minimum wage, and investment in health, basic infrastructure, and education have improved the lives of the poorest and most vulnerable sectors of society[17] (Farthing and Kohl 2014). The figures speak for themselves: extreme poverty has fallen from 38 percent in 2005 to 17 percent in 2014, and the gap between the richest 10 percent and the poorest 10 percent has shrunk from 128 to thirty-nine times (BIF 2016).[18] Along with bringing the Dakar rally to Bolivia, one of Morales's most popular and instantly recognizable projects has been the installation of the longest urban cable car system in the world, which links the cities of La Paz and El Alto.

There have been significant advances in expanding the participation of women and indigenous peoples in government (Albó 2007). After the 2014 election, 53.1 percent of the seats in the national parliament were held by women (World Bank 2016b). During its first administration, the MAS convened a popularly elected assembly to rewrite the constitution; delegates included people who were left out of previous rounds of institution building such as women, workers, and indigenous peoples (Rousseau 2011). The text was put to a national referendum in January 2009, and it was ratified into law with a 61 percent "yes" vote.

MAS's efforts to reinvent the state and the economy have not gone uncontested, however. The agro-industrial oligarchs in Bolivia's eastern lowlands (known as the half-moon) have posed the most serious threat to the MAS administration. These landowning elites have mounted obstacles to even the most modest social and economic reforms proposed by the MAS government. In 2008 an alliance of pro-autonomy capitalist elites (with implicit U.S. backing) and their foot soldiers the Cruceño Youth Movement (a group of young, fascist thugs) unleashed a wave of violence including[19] attacks on police officers and the massacre of at least eleven indigenous peasants in the state of Pando (Fabricant 2009). As a result of the pressure exerted by the right wing, Morales's ambitious land reform program had to be scaled back (Webber 2017).

The desire for rapid economic growth, along with foreign interest in key industries, has increased pressure on the Bolivian government to search for new forms of resource extraction (particularly natural gas and mining) and large-scale development projects. The associated reliance on foreign capital has hampered Morales's ability to redesign the economy along more egalitarian and sustainable lines. Rather than expropriating foreign and privately owned firms, all Morales's nationalization of the hydrocarbons sector (a key campaign promise) really meant was a renegotiation of the contracts. The terms now in force have boosted state revenues dramatically, but there have been no substantive changes in the current structure of capital accumulation.[20] Moreover, the social and environmental impacts of the extractive industries remain the same (see Bebbington and Bury 2013; Gudynas 2011; Hindery 2013). Critical scholars on the left have argued that in spite of government rhetoric, the state continues to be fundamentally liberal, and the country has not only continued, but rather has expanded its reliance on market capitalism (Hindery 2013; Molina 2010; Webber 2010a; Zibechi 2015). Such claims have been contested by MAS supporters, however (Fuentes 2011).

In February 2016, Morales faced his first electoral setback since 2002, when he lost a referendum to amend the constitution so that he might stand for a fourth consecutive term[21] (his third under the 2009 constitution). The referendum vote cannot simply be read as a rejection of the MAS party or its political project, however.[22] As Arkonada (2016) argues, it was a vote against Morales standing for yet another term, rather than a vote in favor of a return to neoliberal orthodoxy. Still, the MAS faces significant challenges going forward. Bolivia is suffering from a severe drought, the effects of which are made worse by poor water management (Farthing 2016). Economic growth, which sustained Morales's popularity for most of his eleven years in office, has lost momentum as a result of falling commodity prices since 2011.[23] Finally, scandals, strikes, and clashes between protesters and police have turned some supporters against the government (Achtenberg 2016; Anria and Cyr 2017; Perreault 2015; Ravindran 2016; Regalsky 2010; Webber 2012).

Academics have debated the continuations and ruptures between the MAS agenda and the 1952 revolution (Dunkerley 2007a, 2013; Thomson 2009). For most commentators, 2006 is a poor imitation. Forrest Hylton (2011: 245) writes: "Whether the issue is natural resources, education and literacy, infrastructural development, or agrarian reform, the MNR reforms at mid-century were more radical and far reaching than anything MAS has accomplished in the twenty-first." Meanwhile, Jeff Webber (2016) refers to the MAS's process of change as a "passive revolution." This book adds to the debate over the MAS in power by telling the story from the perspective of its core support base, the coca growers' unions of the Chapare.

Methodology

The first time I visited the Chapare in January 2003 I was a tourist. The bus ride took ten hours, as opposed to the normal six, as heavy rains had made the uneven road difficult to transit. When I got off the bus I noticed two

Figure 1.6. A view of a village in the Chapare. Photo by author.

things immediately: the overpowering heat and the massive military presence. Troops were being moved from place to place in large trucks (known
locally as caimans, on account of the fact they are long and green), and
helicopters ran continuous laps in the sky above. On that visit I became
interested in the political organization of the coca union. I returned to the
Chapare two years later, this time to carry out ethnographic fieldwork for
a PhD. This was followed by subsequent trips for postdoctoral research. In
total, I spent over thirty months carrying out ethnographic research in the
Chapare. The longest stints of fieldwork were carried out on two separate
trips, from 2005 to 2007 and 2013 to 2014, with further shorter trips in 2008,
2011, and 2015.

From the very beginning, I lived in Aurora, a quiet village with a population of approximately four hundred people distributed across roughly
eighty households. The village has a small hospital, a market, a high school,
and a Catholic church (see figure 1.6). Before starting fieldwork, I first had
to seek permission from the general secretary of the federation and the
local base-level union (the sindicato) where I hoped to live. Once I had
received their support I moved into a pension located in the village. At first
I was treated with a great deal of suspicion. My arrival coincided with the
winding down of the drug war, and people feared that I was an agent from
the U.S. embassy come to spy on them.

In order to confirm that I was indeed a student writing a thesis, I immediately set about interviewing high-level union leaders and municipal councilors. This was a successful strategy insofar as I got to know who was who, and the leaders became aware of my presence. The interviews did not yield interesting data, however. Interlocutors generally repeated the union's official line, a heroic story focused on the struggle to put Morales into power and the traditional uses of coca leaf. Ultimately, these interviews revealed nothing more than what I could have gleaned from reading a newspaper. The only way to get reliable data on coca growers' perspectives on the union, the MAS, and the coca–cocaine economy, then, was to build relationships of trust. But I faced a problem: most people were busy all day working in their fields, and so I was left with very little to do and nobody to speak with.

I soon realized that I needed to be more proactive about meeting people, and so I visited Radio Aurora, the coca union–owned and -operated radio station. The station, which was located in the village, occupied a shabby one-story building next to the coca market (it has since expanded into a two-story building). When I first visited in 2005, the director was a forty-year-old man called Epifanio Condori. Epifanio had already heard about the foreigner living in the village, and he agreed to collaborate with me. He introduced me to reporters Sergio Cayo, Grover Munachi, and Leyla Mamani, all of whom were from coca grower families, owned land in the region, and as such were intimately tied to the union's struggles. From that point on I spent most days with them.

The radio station turned out to be a strategic site from which I could witness the dynamic flows that constitute social and political phenomena in the Chapare. Members of the audience, including peasant farmers, union leaders, municipal officials, and national-level politicians (including Evo Morales), would regularly turn up at the station to drop off a message, ask for advice, or speak on the radio. Sitting on the station's porch, then, was a great way to meet people and keep abreast of local comings and goings. In addition, most days the reporters would travel to the town hall, federation headquarters, or distant communities to collect stories for their evening news programs, and I would accompany them. My affiliation with the radio gave me access to closed-door meetings but also allowed me to travel all over the region and to be treated as an ally rather than an outsider.

Municipal government was another important locus of union activity. Leaders would regularly go the town hall to petition the councilors and the

Figure 1.7. Fishing on the Isiboro River. Photo by author.

mayor (who themselves were members of the coca union) for public works for their community. During fieldwork I visited the town hall on average three times a week, where I attended meetings, interviewed leaders, and accompanied the councilors and mayor on their frequent field trips to examine the progress of public works. I also built relationships with functionaries including technicians, security guards, and drivers (most of whom were from coca grower families).

My research was not only focused on the dramatic events of union politics, however. Over the months, I developed relationships with local families. I spent many days hanging out at people's homes, cooking together, going to markets, celebrating birthdays, attending weddings and funerals, helping people to farm, and tagging along on fishing and hunting trips (see figure 1.7). In this way I entered the more intimate spaces of Chapare life, and I became privy to the insider perspectives on the unions and the MAS. Many Chapare campesinos own second homes in the outskirts of the city of Cochabamba, and they constantly move between the two places, and so I carried out research there as well.

Everyday sociality is gendered. As a young man I was privy to my male informants visiting bars where they would drink heavily (sometimes for several days at a time). I had less access to those spaces that seemed to be exclusively inhabited by women. Moreover, the coca union leadership is male-dominated, and hence a lot of the voices in this book are those of men, and it is skewed toward their perspective. I did, however, make efforts to seek out female leaders and base-level members; their voices come through, but not as forcefully.

In this book I focus on landowning families who represent the bulk of the population. However, we should not lose sight of the large number of landless workers resident in the area. They are normally men who do not have the money or connections to buy land and join a sindicato. They work for established farmers on a day rate, doing things like chopping down trees, planting rice, harvesting coca, or burning scrub.[24] Some combine agricultural work with coca paste processing. Many of these workers are temporary migrants who return to their places of origin in the highlands during the rainy season when there is less work available. Some landless laborers have settled permanently in the Chapare and run farms for others on a sharecropping basis (they are known as *partidarias*). Itinerant workers are not members of the union (only the landowner is); they are, however, subject to its authority and often participate in union activities (including meetings and protests) if the landowner is unable to attend.

Mindful of the debates surrounding the issue of emotionally driven ethnography (D'Andrade 1995; Gledhill 2004; Scheper-Hughes 1995), I made efforts to seek out and talk with non-coca growers including military commanders, police officers, teachers, policy makers, national politicians, and right-wing leaders of the opposition. I carried out over sixty formal interviews; most were in the Chapare, but I also traveled to the cities of Cochabamba, La Paz, and Santa Cruz to interview people. A final point on anonymity: all names in this book have been changed[25] apart from those of public figures such as Evo Morales. The names of the villages mentioned in this book are also made up, as is the name of the coca growers' radio station. I have not changed the names of larger towns and municipalities. I conducted most of my research in one of the six federations; thus, when I talk about "the federation" I am referring to Federación Trópico, the largest federation in the region.

I began my first period of fieldwork in September 2005, only three months before the election that would bring Morales to power. Throughout this book the reader will have the impression of a before and after, around the pivot of the MAS victory. On occasion, coca growers retrospectively romanticize elements of union life, stressing the grassroots control they used to exercise over leaders and that the union has somehow been corrupted. There is no way of telling whether these narratives are actually true. In any case, I am interested in narratives of the past as critical commentaries on the present, rather than as narratives in their own right. In addition, there is a tension between the voices of leaders, who (mostly) articulate the official position of the union, and the grassroots members who make critical commentaries about the union. As we will see, the two readings do not always align.

2. The Lowest Rung of the Cocaine Trade

I read your study on the coca growers of the Chapare and the conclusion that they are humble farmers who are not involved in drug trafficking made me laugh out loud. It's the same as saying that a shepherd in the United Kingdom doesn't know that they use wool to make sweaters. If there was no drug trafficking then they wouldn't have anywhere to sell their coca leaves, it's that simple. The rest of your article is quite believable, but it lacks depth. Saludos, Adolfo.

This was an email I received in October 2014 from Adolfo Chavez, a Bolivian from La Paz. Adolfo was drawing attention to a bias he had noticed in my research, namely that I prioritize the coca growers' political platform at the expense of paying attention to the reality of drug trafficking. Adolfo was correct; I had indeed shied away from exposing anything that might potentially be damaging to the union. In previous blog posts and academic articles I had simply avoided the issue of drug production entirely or else reiterated the coca growers' mantra that "coca is not cocaine" (see, for example, Grisaffi 2010).

But as Philippe Bourgois (1995: 12) has argued, we have to tell the ugly reality as it is, not as we want it to be, if we are to understand injustice. To not expose this reality would mean to become complicit in the causes of structural violence. It is important, then, to recognize that Bolivia is caught at the very lowest rungs of the international drug trade, and produces significant quantities of low-value coca paste, the first step toward refining pure cocaine. In a 2006 interview, the commander of the regional antidrug police force told me that there were hundreds of drug processing workshops operating all over the Chapare[1] (most were located either close to or in the Isiboro National Park). Coca paste production is not restricted to the Chapare, however; it takes place throughout the country, in both rural and urban areas.

A 2011 UN Office on Drugs and Crime (UNODC) report indicated that the Cochabamba Tropics produces almost 28,000 metric tons of dried coca annually, of which only 1,800 tons pass through the legal market in Cochabamba (located in the district of Sacaba). To put it another way, only about 7 percent finds its way into legal channels (*La Razón* 2011). This is not to say that the rest goes to drug trafficking, however. César Guedes, former UNODC director in Bolivia, noted that consumers and merchants often purchase coca leaf directly from the Chapare for sale in the mining centers and in the Santa Cruz department, which is the country's largest market for legal coca leaf (Farthing and Ledebur 2015: 46). But while a great deal of Chapare coca leaf undoubtedly is used for traditional purposes (far more than the official figures might suggest), it would be blinkered to ignore the reality of drug production, particularly because my friends in the Chapare stressed that a lot of coca paste was produced there, and some claimed it is the foundation of the local economy.

Estimates for the country's annual cocaine production differ by a large margin. Some Bolivian academics suggest about twenty metric tons[2] (Burgos Gallardo 2017), but U.S. assessments are ten times that figure (Schultze-Kraft 2016). According to political economist Jose Carlos Campero, in 2010 the coca–cocaine circuit was the third largest source of revenue for Bolivia, after hydrocarbons and mining (Schipani 2010). The truth is, nobody actually knows how much cocaine is produced, and estimates are often politically motivated (Robinson and Scherlen 2007). Even so, it is important to recognize that the Chapare is a node in a broader illicit network, and the region cannot be understood without attention to how it connects to this network.

The objective of this chapter, then, is to understand the two faces of coca: its role in traditional rituals and healing practices on the one hand, and the paths by which it enters into illegal circuits on the other. The chapter begins with an overview of coca, outlining its traditional uses and the legislation controlling its production and sale. It then traces the history of migration to the Chapare, drawing attention to the way colonization was intimately bound to the growth of the illicit drug industry. The final part examines coca paste production in the region today, including who is involved, how it is made, and what workers can realistically expect to earn. This chapter illustrates that the coca leaf produced in the Chapare has healing powers and ritual efficacy, but it is also a commodity that historically has been the main source of income for farmers.

The Importance of Coca

"I chew coca like a horse!" laughed Don Alfredo Higuera, as he stuffed hand-fuls of coca into his cheek, stalks and all. "I could chew banana leaves, but I don't, because they don't have what coca has. Coca has vitamins, calories, and nutrients. Without coca I am lazy." Every day before starting work in his fields Don Alfredo, a coca farmer in his mid-fifties, put a wad of coca leaves into the side of his mouth and nibbled on some *lejía*[3] (a soft, dark, tarry substance), which acts as a catalyst to help release the leaf's active properties (chewers might also use bicarbonate of soda). Over the following hours Alfredo would slowly suck the juice out of the leaves, spitting excess green saliva on the floor. Alfredo would chew coca for most of the day, refilling his *pijchu* (mouthful of coca) once every couple of hours or so. He explained: "We chew coca to help us work, and it does us no harm. Every day we chew coca, it gives us strength and bravery, don't you see? It gets rid of our tiredness, our hunger." Chewing coca in this way was referred to locally as *bolear* or *pijchar* (see figure 2.1).

Coca (*Erythroxylum coca*) grows in semitropical areas at elevations of be-tween 200 and 1,500 meters. As Alfredo explains, coca is used as a physical and mental stimulant, and to suppress feelings of hunger and fatigue. Stud-ies have established that this form of coca consumption increases tolerance for physical labor and helps the lungs absorb more oxygen, along with a host of other life-enhancing factors (Bolton 1976; Burchard 1992; Plow-man 1986). The coca leaf is a source of vitamins, as well as calcium, iron, fiber, protein, and calories (Duke, Aulik, and Plowman 1975; Penny et al. 2009). A 1995 study by the World Health Organization (WHO) stressed its positive therapeutic uses. The report stated that its legalization would benefit humanity. However, as a result of U.S. pressure, the WHO never of-ficially published the report (Metaal et al. 2006: 7–8).

Archaeologists have found ceramics depicting coca chewers with bulg-ing cheeks along the Peruvian coast (and even some preserved leaves), indicating that coca use might date as far back as 1,800 BC (Plowman 1986: 24–27). Historically, coca use was not as widespread as it is today, how-ever. At the time of the Incas, coca leaves were considered to be precious and were usually reserved for the nobility and religious ceremonies. Garcilaso de la Vega, one of the earliest chroniclers of the conquest of Peru, writes: "It [coca] was not so common as it is now"; he goes on to explain that "only the Inca and his relatives and some chiefs, who the king favored and had mercy upon" had access to coca (de la Vega 1943: 177). John Murra (1986: 49–50)

Figure 2.1. A bag of coca leaves for chewing. Note the bag of bicarbonate of soda next to it. This is mixed with the leaves to extract the alkaloid. Photo by author.

stresses that coca use was restricted mainly because it was not readily available, as it came from lower altitudes along with hot peppers and maize.

It was only with Spanish colonization that coca use expanded. The Spaniards disapproved of coca because of the role it played in native ritual and its concomitant association with the devil (O'Phelan 1995: 141). Even so, they could also see that it offered certain advantages. Under colonial rule, indigenous peoples were forced to provide tribute to the crown in the form of labor (known as *mita*); in this way, millions of indigenous Andeans ended up working (and dying) in the silver mines of Potosí. The Spanish soon realized the miners could work longer and harder when allowed to consume coca.[4] Coca then was used a form of compensation, and the use of coca rapidly became more prevalent throughout the indigenous communities (Gagliano 1994; Klein 1986). The Spanish Crown understood that it could profit from the lucrative coca trade, and in 1573 Viceroy Toledo gave up trying to suppress coca and taxed it instead (Flores and Blanes 1984: 156).

Acullico, or coca chewing, is a cornerstone of basic sociality. Peasants and workers share the leaves. An invitation to chew coca, then, is not simply an offer to consume, but rather to engage in a social relationship. This point is vividly demonstrated by Catherine Allen (1988), who explains the elaborate rituals that accompany the act of sharing coca leaf, including selecting the best leaves, the way they are offered, and the invocation of earth beings. Even in contexts where everyone has their own supply of coca (as is the case in the Chapare), people still invite one another to chew. The ensuing conversations often focus on the quality of the leaf, with farmers competing over whose coca is better. The leaf they share is homegrown; most Chapare farmers cultivate a small plot of organic coca for their personal consumption, which is carefully tended and of higher quality than the coca they sell in the market.

June Nash (1979) observed the link between sharing coca and building solidarity and class consciousness in Bolivia's tin mines. At the bottom of every mineshaft the workers have built a statue of a devil, who they refer to as the *Supay* or *Tio*. The devil is considered to be the owner of the mine and can bring good and bad luck. As such, he is the central focus of many ritual events, ranging from elaborate llama sacrifices to daily offerings of cigarettes, coca leaves, and alcohol, known as the *Ch'alla*. Nash argues that the observance of such preconquest rites allows workers to come together and share their problems, thereby contributing to building class consciousness and collective identity. In this way, Nash questions the idea of a universal proletarian class; she shows how the miners have a sense of collective identity that transcends the structural situation they find themselves in.

Coca serves important social and cultural functions; it is a central element of rituals in indigenous peasant communities, and it is considered to be sacred (Carter 1996; Carter and Mamani 1986; Henman 1992). In the Chapare, people use coca in monthly burnt offerings to the *Pachamama* (an Andean earth deity). The offering, known as a *Q'owa*, is a piece of newspaper stacked high with streamers, herbs and coca leaves, sugar tokens fashioned into objects of desire (such as education, travel, work, and housing), and on special occasions a llama fetus (see figure 2.2). To make the offering, the Q'owa is placed on top of burning charcoal; it should not flame up but should gently smolder. The tokens that melt are those desires that have been acknowledged by Pachamama. As the Q'owa burns, generous libations of alcohol are poured in a counterclockwise direction around the offering (see figure 2.3). During the process participants drink beer, chew coca, and smoke cigarettes (alcohol holds an important position similar to coca in Andean society; see Harvey 1994).

Figure 2.2. A Q'owa; note the coca leaves and llama fetus. Photo by author.

Figure 2.3. A woman celebrates the Q'owa. Photo by author.

Coca is also used for divination, and to cure a range of ailments from headaches to bad stomachs. Don Alfredo told me, "Coca is good for healing. When I have a stomachache I drink some coca tea, and it gets better; others mix it with alcohol. But not me! This old man knows how to cure himself with tea and nothing more!" When I asked peasant farmers why coca is so special, I was told about how humans first became aware of it. In one narrative it was the Virgin Mary who first discovered its calming effects while watching Jesus on the cross. Other origin myths attribute coca use to *Inti*, the sun god of the Incas. One older female coca grower told me, "It's for the Pachamama but for the Virgin also—that's why coca is important."

The power of coca was vividly demonstrated to me when my landlady, Doña Mercedes Aguayo, fell ill. One day she began to suffer from a constant hiccups, uncontrollable vomiting, and blurred vision. She was referred to a hospital in the city of Cochabamba, where the doctors diagnosed that she was suffering from complications arising from diabetes. After two weeks Doña Mercedes was showing no signs of improvement. She became impatient with the cost and ineffectiveness of the medical treatment and discharged herself. I urged Doña Mercedes to return to the hospital, and I offered to pay the bills for her, but she would hear none of it. Instead, she spent the following three weeks at home in bed. Sebastián (Mercedes's son) lived in the city and had been visiting his mother regularly while she was in hospital. Concerned by the turn of events, he traveled to the Chapare to see if he could convince Doña Mercedes to return to the clinic, but she refused. Given her resistance, Sebastián offered to contract a local Yatiri (traditional healer) to conduct a divination and healing ceremony, to which Doña Mercedes agreed.

The Yatiri was a middle-aged woman who had lived in the Chapare for over twenty years, but was originally from the high valleys. She instructed Sebastián to place a bag of coca leaves on his mother's head and leave it there for one night. The following morning he removed the leaves and took them to the Yatiri's house. She cast the leaves onto the ground and read them. She informed Sebastián that the earth was angry because, ever since Doña Mercedes had joined an evangelical group four years previously, she had stopped making monthly burnt offerings to the earth (evangelical pastors disapprove of such rituals, which they link to the devil). During this period the land had continued to give her good harvests every year without fail. The result of this oversight was that the earth now wanted its payback and had taken Doña Mercedes's *anima* (soul/spirit). The Yatiri told us that the only way Doña Mercedes would get better was if a ritual cleansing (*limpieza*) was performed and offerings were made to the earth. That night an elaborate Q'owa was done at the site where Mercedes's soul was said to have been lost.

Following the completion of the relevant rituals, coca leaves were again placed on Doña Mercedes's head, and were again read by the Yatiri, who was able to confirm that the rites had been successful. Remarkably, two days later Doña Mercedes got out of bed and walked around the house for the first time in more than a month. After one week, she was putting on weight and soon returned to work in her fields. Doña Mercedes considered that she was cured because of the actions taken by the Yatiri and the power of coca. Despite her belief in the efficacy of the Yatiri, it is worth bearing in mind that during the entire episode she continued to take the medication that the doctors at the hospital had given to her. Notwithstanding Doña Mercedes's syncretic approach to health care, when people say that coca has special powers, that it heals, or that the Pachamama has to be fed, then as anthropologists we have to take such claims at face value, regardless of whatever else might happen to the leaf (see de la Cadena 2010).

Coca Legislation

The reason Andeans have long held coca in such high esteem is precisely because it contains cocaine alkaloid; this is what makes coca powerful, but also dangerous in the eyes of lawmakers. A German pharmacologist first isolated the active property of the coca plant in 1859, and cocaine soon became a popular legal stimulant in the United States and Europe. One of the most famous early users of the drug was Sigmund Freud, who between 1884 and 1887 penned five essays extolling its virtues as a way to cure depression, treat alcoholism, and increase libido, among other things (Freud 1984). In the late 1800s coca leaf also became popular in northern countries. It was used to produce myriad tonics that were available over the counter, the most famous of which was Coca-Cola. Paul Gootenberg (2008: 25–26) argues that the popularization of cocaine and coca-based products abroad changed the way it was viewed back home in Peru. Coca went from being something associated with lower-class indigenous culture that was derided and looked down on, to something modern, that elites living in the capital city of Lima could be proud of. But toleration of coca and cocaine was short-lived. Evidence of addiction led to the outlawing of cocaine in the early 1900s and set in motion events that would eventually lead to the criminalization of coca leaf as well (Gootenberg 2008: 105–42).

In 1949 a UN commission visited Peru and Bolivia with the mandate to "investigate the effects of chewing the coca leaf and the possibilities of limiting its production and controlling its distribution." The subsequent report vilified coca chewing as a disgusting habit that contributed to the "racial degradation" of the indigenous population (AIN 2004). The report stated that "It induces in the individual undesirable changes of an intellectual and moral character hindering the chewer's chances of obtaining a higher social standard" (Metaal et al. 2006: 5). The study has since been discredited as inaccurate, poorly researched, and racist. Even so, on the basis of this report the UN officially took the position that coca chewing was a form of drug addiction and should be outlawed (Metaal et al. 2006: 6).

In 1961 the UN listed the coca leaf as a Schedule One drug alongside the most dangerous and restricted substances, including heroin and cocaine, on the UN Single Convention on Narcotics, the most important international legal framework for drug control. The UN convention calls on signatory governments to eradicate all coca bushes, even those that grow wild, and to abolish the traditional practice of coca leaf chewing within 25 years of ratification (Bolivia's military government ratified the convention in 1976). Subsequent conventions have upheld these hardline anti-coca positions (Metaal 2014). The 1961 convention thus provided the justification and legal framework for subsequent U.S.-backed militarized crop eradication campaigns in the Andean region.

The 1961 UN convention contains an important caveat—the so-called Coca-Cola clause, which allows the export and use of de-cocainized coca leaf as a flavoring agent.[5] Every year Peru's state-run coca company (ENACO) exports tens of tons of coca to the Stepan Company, based in New Jersey, which is the only firm in the United States with permission to import coca leaves and process coca extract (the cocaine that is taken from the leaves is sold for medical purposes). The Stepan Company sells its coca extract exclusively to the Coca-Cola company (Gootenberg 2004: 247). The Coca-Cola Company, then, is legally permitted to sell a coca-based product across the globe. Andean farmers, however, are not. Under the 1961 convention, raw coca leaf and manufactured coca products such as teas, soaps, liquor, cakes, and candies are outlawed. This includes Bolivia's own take on the famous soft drink, launched in 2010, which is called Coca-Colla. In Bolivia *Colla* is used to refer to highland peoples of Quechua or Aymara descent and derives from Collasuyu (also spelled Qullasuyu), a region of the Inca empire.

Bolivia has challenged the legal status of coca leaf. In the early 1990s Bolivian President Jamie Paz Zamora (1989–93) followed a course of "coca diplomacy," which drew upon the coca growers' own distinction between coca and cocaine. The president visited Europe to promote the export of coca leaves in the form of herbal tea, toothpaste, and wine. He also formed a commission at the WHO to ensure the protection of the domestic legal market for traditional uses (Painter 1994: 89–90). However, Paz Zamora's efforts were undermined when, in April 1994, he was linked to key players involved in the cocaine trade (Menzel 1996: 89–91). It was not until Evo Morales came to power that a Bolivian president would once more dare to argue that coca in its natural state is not a drug and that it could benefit humanity.

Bolivia's 2009 constitution gives coca leaf legal protection for the first time, declaring that it is part of the nation's cultural heritage, its biodiversity, and a factor for social cohesion (Vazualdo 2014). Accordingly, Morales has led the fight to decriminalize the leaf at the international level. In 2012 Morales stood before the UN Commission on Narcotic Drugs in Vienna, holding a coca leaf aloft, and declared: "We are not drug addicts when we consume the coca leaf. The coca leaf is not cocaine. We have to get rid of this misconception . . . this is a millennia-old tradition in Bolivia, and we would hope that you will understand that coca leaf producers are not drug dealers" (UNDP 2016: 10). The UN Single Convention's outlawing of coca contradicts the UN's own 2007 Declaration on Indigenous Rights, which promises to uphold and protect indigenous cultural practices.

In 2011, Bolivia made efforts to amend the 1961 UN Single Convention on Narcotic Drugs to legalize the practice of coca leaf chewing, with the full support of the UN Permanent Forum on Indigenous Issues. However, the United States and the International Narcotics Control Board (a quasi-juridical organ responsible for the convention's implementation) condemned Bolivia for undermining the international drug control regime and lobbied to get the G-8, several European countries, and Mexico behind them. When Bolivia failed to secure its proposed amendment, the Bolivian Congress voted to withdraw from the Single Convention and sought permission to rejoin with a formal reservation for traditional uses of coca leaf. Fifteen countries blocked the move,[6] but ultimately Bolivia was successful. The legalization of coca chewing in 2013 was a major international victory for Bolivians; however, the reservation only applies to its national territory, and the international export of coca or coca-based products remains proscribed (Jelsma 2016).

Bolivia overturned Law 1008 in March 2017 and replaced it with two new laws, one for coca and one for controlled substances (Bolivia is also drafting a new penal system code). The first of these laws, the General Law on Coca, permits 22,000 hectares of coca production nationally (14,300 hectares in the Yungas and 7,700 in the Chapare).[7] Morales launched the new law at a massive event in the Chapare, where he told thousands of supporters, "We won the battle. The coca leaf represents our region, the Andean region, Bolivia, and the social movements. . . . Coca won, now by law it's guaranteed for life" (*Los Tiempos* 2017c). The second law, on controlled substances, will strengthen state mechanisms to combat higher-level drug trafficking organizations (Medrano 2017). The penal reform will address the minimum mandatory sentencing in Law 1008, under which low-level traffickers can end up with a sentence far longer than someone convicted for murder (Giacoman Aramayo 2011).

Colonization

In the city of Cochabamba, buses for the Chapare depart from a dusty street close to Lago Alalay, a shallow lake covered in thick green algae. The sides of the buses are covered with murals depicting an idealized tropical landscape of palm trees, flowers, and rivers. The company offices sport Day-Glo banners that announce "express service direct to the hot Tropics"; inside, bows and arrows crafted by indigenous Yuqui artisans (native to the Chapare region) hang on the walls. The combination conjures an image of an exciting and exotic place. No matter if it is a peasant farmer or an urban professional, the Chapare is always spoken about as a frontier replete with extreme weather, wild animals, and abundant land.

Ever since the period of Spanish colonization, the Chapare has been viewed as a promising resource base from which to develop the regional economy of Cochabamba. However, due to the difficulty of access and limited investment, early attempts to set up camps and open roads into the tropics all ended in failure (Flores and Blanes 1984: 76; Larson 1988: 253–58). The turning point was heralded by the 1952 revolution. With U.S. backing the National Revolutionary Movement (MNR) government built a road to connect the eastern city of Santa Cruz and promoted the directed colonization of the eastern lowlands. This was done as a way to avoid dealing with the social inequalities such as landlessness and growing poverty that remained after the revolution (Gill 1987: 38; Sanabria 1993: 43). The government believed that if they populated the east they could ensure that neighboring countries would not encroach onto Bolivia's territory. This was a paramount concern given that Bolivia had lost a significant chunk of land to Paraguay in the Chaco War only twenty years previously (De Franco and Godoy 1992: 382).

Prior to colonization, the Chapare was not a pristine or untouched land, however. Small groups of hunter-gatherer and fishing peoples, including the Yuracarés, Yuquis, and Trinitario-Mojenos, have occupied the Chapare for centuries (long before government-backed programs bought Quechua migrants to the area). The Yuracaré population encompasses around 3,000 people; historically, they were highly mobile, but have now made permanent settlements along the banks of the Chapare River. The Yuracaré continue to hunt, fish, and gather forest products for subsistence, but they also cultivate a range of crops (including coca), and extract timber to earn cash (Becker and Leon 2000; León et al. 2012). The Yuqui, who were first contacted as late as the 1950s, number fewer than two hundred people, and many are not proficient in Spanish. Today some Yuqui people intermittently live on the streets of the town of Chimore (located in the Cochabamba Tropics), where they beg and hawk crafts, such as the bows and arrows mentioned above (Jabin 2014; Stearman 1996).

The first wave of migrants to the tropics consisted of mostly Quechua-speaking peasants from the Cochabamba valleys who traveled to the Chapare under the auspices of the National Colonization Institute, which promised them land, tools, and credit (Bruzzone and Clavijo 1989: 207–18). Don Julian Cruz came to the Chapare as part of the directed colonization in 1964; his motivation was simple: "Back then in the highlands, there was nothing for us, but at least down here there were lands to work." Initially he was nervous about the move; "people said that there were snakes and tigers here, and wild Indians with bows and arrows!" (Don Julian is referring to the lowland Yuracarés and Yuquis.) But the promise of a new life made the risks worthwhile. Don Julian remembers how government agents selected and transported him to the Chapare on a truck, a journey that took more than a week. On arriving in the tropics, government agents provided the so-called pioneers with a plot of land measuring five hectares, basic tools (a machete and a hoe), seeds, and a lamp. Julian told me: "They [government agents] were in charge; if you got bad land, then that was it, you could not choose better."

It takes a while for a farm to become productive; land has to be cleared and plants have to mature. Thus, Julian and his friends survived the first couple of years eating handouts from the World Food Program and working for the few established peasant farmers in the region, who paid them with bananas and yucca. They also fished and hunted the abundant game, including tapir, wild turkeys, and boar. Colonists like Julian faced a range of challenges, including learning new tropical farming techniques, getting on with settlers from different cultural backgrounds, and overcoming feelings of discouragement bought on by the immense heat, heavy rain, mosquitoes, and isolation. "They were some of the hardest years of my life," Julian told me (for accounts of the early colonization of the Chapare, see Bruzzone and Clavijo 1989; Fifer 1967; Rodríguez 1996).

Most settlers were unhappy about the limited freedom implied by directed colonization programs, such as technicians deciding what crops should be grown (they did not permit coca, as it was listed as a controlled substance under UN treaties) and dictating the places where people could live. Consequently, the majority of new arrivals to the Chapare avoided getting involved with government programs, but they did take advantage of the penetration roads and other planned infrastructure, and spontaneously settled the land (Eastwood and Pollard 1986; Wennergren and Whitaker 1976).

Knowledge about the availability of land traveled via word of mouth, so that new migrants invariably ended up in a place where they already knew somebody. Thus, many settlements are composed of people who were previously neighbors in the highlands and were named after established villages and towns in the highlands. The settlers established small family-run farms on plots measuring between five and twenty hectares, where they grew a range of crops including rice, yucca, bananas, and oranges, and raised a few chickens and pigs for subsistence. From the early days of colonization, coca was a crop that the farmers (who were not associated with government programs) grew primarily to sell on the market, and it accounted for the bulk of their cash income (Laserna 2000).

The Coca Boom

At the beginning, the pace of migration to the Chapare remained low, there were high rates of abandonment, and temporary rather than permanent migration was the norm (Wiel 1983). But this all changed in the late 1970s when increasing demand for cocaine in the United States (and to a lesser extent Europe) made coca paste (an intermediate stage of the cocaine production process) the nation's most profitable export commodity. By the late 1980s the illegal coca–cocaine trade in Bolivia generated over one billion dollars annually, an amount greater than the income gained from all legal exports and foreign loans combined (De Franco and Godoy 1992: 387). This in turn pushed up the price of coca. Farmers recall that in the early 1980s a pound of coca cost over nine dollars (by contrast, in 2013 a pound of coca cost only four dollars). In response to the elevated prices, coca cultivation in the Chapare expanded dramatically, from 13,000 hectares in 1978 to 55,000 hectares only a decade later (Painter 1994: 15).

The roots of Bolivia's cocaine trade can be traced back to the 1950s, when small amounts of coca paste were produced in Bolivia and smuggled to Chile, Argentina, and Brazil, where *pitillos* (cigarettes laced with coca paste) were becoming popular (Henkel 1986: 71). When cocaine production really took off in the late 1970s, the trade was largely driven by Colombian traffickers who were searching for cheap coca paste to transport to Colombia, where it was refined into pure cocaine and from there exported to the United States (Gootenberg 2012: 164–66). Local cattle ranchers (mainly in the departments of Beni and Santa Cruz) worked with the Colombians to organize the refining and transportation of the drug outside of the country. These wealthy farmers were ideally placed for the business as they owned planes, airstrips, and large expanses of land in remote areas of the country; but most importantly they were well connected with political and military elites[8] (Dunkerley 1984: 318–19; Painter 1998).

The cash flow generated by cocaine corrupted bankrupt governments. By the late 1970s Bolivia won global infamy as the hemisphere's first narco-regime, where drug oligarchs like the lowland clan of Roberto Suárez "captured the state and economy" (Gootenberg 2008: 275–286). Between 1980 and 1981, the dictator General Luis García Meza used the military to run the illicit trade (Mesa, Gisbert, and Mesa 2003: 728–30). One local shopkeeper told me how he used to observe conscripts processing coca paste next to the village and then transporting the drug to the military base for export. The timing of the so called "coca boom" (1979–85) was opportune: it occurred just as the rest of the country was passing through a moment of acute economic crisis, including hyperinflation, mass unemployment, and a prolonged drought in the highlands (during the 1982–83 growing season). The cocaine economy is credited with directly supporting jobs for between 10 and 20 percent of the Bolivian population in the mid-1980s

(Painter 1994: 50). It has been argued that the cocaine trade dampened the effects of neoliberal restructuring by providing employment and much-needed foreign revenue (Blanes 1989; Estellano and Nava-Ragazzi 1994; Toranzo 1997).

Throughout the 1980s highland peasants were forced from their land by the combined processes of *minifundio* (smallholdings), where agricultural families lack sufficient land to even minimally support themselves,[9] a severe drought, and later structural adjustment policies that led to floods of agricultural imports, against which they could not compete. Tens of thousands of people descended on the Chapare region to seek livelihoods in the burgeoning coca–cocaine economy. The impoverished peasants and miners who migrated to the region had no idea what cocaine was or about its negative impact. In the words of union leader Doña Maria González, "as coca farmers we didn't know about this drug. What type of drug? We don't know, because as farmers we chew coca to help us work, and it does us no harm whatsoever."

While miners in the highlands fought collectively and created one of the most militant unions in the Americas, some of them had developed an individual survival strategy as well. Years of progressive pauperization, military interventions, and cuts in the subsidized food stores, led many miners to migrate to the lowlands, where they could make money growing coca and processing coca paste. Don Emeterio Lujan, an ex-miner turned coca grower, told me: "The miners . . . we always thought that this was going to happen. Governments, like García Meza . . . there was nothing for the people. Instead of being there, suffering in the mine, and working without getting paid, there was opportunity here . . . at least in coca." At the same time that they were protesting mine closures, many had already begun laying claim to land in the Chapare. Emeterio explained that a group of miners would take turns once every three months to travel from the mines to the Chapare to hold a meeting on the land. He said this process of colonization began ten years before Decree 21060 (the presidential decree that closed down mines) had even been issued.

The Chapare's population ballooned from 24,000 in 1967 to an estimated 350,000 in 1989 (Perez 1992: 28). For the new migrants, there was plenty of waged work in the labor-intensive process of coca-leaf planting, harvesting, and drying (see figures 2.4 and 2.5). There were also opportunities to work as laborers processing coca paste in the artisanal workshops located close to the coca fields. At that time wages for unskilled workers

Figure 2.4. A man works with a machete. Photo by author.

Figure 2.5. Drying coca leaf by the side of the road
in a Chapare town. Photo by author.

in coca paste production were higher than wages earned in urban areas (Healy 1986; Rivera 1991). As people flocked to the region, severe labor shortages arose in highland villages, which had a negative impact on agricultural production (Sanabria 1993).

Don Alfredo Higuera liked to recount the boom days when money was easy to come by and the Chapare was the place to go. He recalled how back then there was very little control of the drug trade: "The workers used to stomp [process] the coca by the village. They made good money, those *pichicateros* [small-scale coca paste producers]!" Alfredo explained how luxury cars traversed the muddy tracks around the village: Colombian drug traffickers bought kilos of cocaine in the street "as if it were flour"; prostitutes were flown in from Brazil on small planes, and the drugs were taken out. He said, "the peasants used to wipe their ass with dollar bills, they thought that the money would never stop!" He went on to describe how peasants from the high valleys would turn up, messy, hungry, and lost, but within a month they would have ditched their *abarcas* (rubber sandals) and *chulos* (traditional Andean hats) and be wearing a suit and "three gold watches . . . even if they couldn't tell the time."

With a regular cash flow generated by coca, the "colonists" were able to improve the situation of their families, as well as their own status (Blanes 1983). Income earned from coca (and coca paste) production allowed migrants to send remittances to their families in their places of origin, ensuring the survival of highland communities (Sanabria 1993). The cocaleros were able to invest in small businesses (such as a hardware store, truck, or car to run as a taxi) and houses on the periphery of the city of Cochabamba (Shakow 2014: 69–71). Thanks to the coca (and coca paste) trade, today the coca growers represent an emergent middle class whose disposable income sets them apart historically from other impoverished peasants in highland Bolivia (see also Pellegrini 2016). And yet internationally they remain on the lowest rungs of the international cocaine trade, classed as criminals and outlaws. This brings us to the present day.

The White Factory

The optimal time to plant coca is during the rainy season when the ground is wet and soft. Milton Acero walked ahead of me, poking holes with a stick (about the size of a broom handle), and I followed behind dropping a coca sapling into each hole and closing the earth around it. During one of our many breaks we sat chewing coca leaf in the shade of a tree. Milton joked about the T-shirt I was wearing, which in large letters across the back read "coca no es cocaína" (coca is not cocaine) (I had bought it in a tourist market three weeks before). Milton said, "Well, sometimes it is . . . actually normally coca is cocaine." Until that point I had only ever heard people say the opposite. Wary not to offend him, I insisted that coca is a natural stimulant; it's sacred and has nothing at all to do with the illegal drug. To which he replied, "Come on, Tomás, where do you think all the coca really goes? You think people can chew all this coca? If there was no cocaine then there would be no coca trade. It all goes to the 'white factory' [cocaine trade]."

This encounter with Milton came after I had already been visiting the tropics for eight years, but still his frankness surprised me. Over that time I had witnessed flashes of the illegal drug trade, including car chases, suspicious movements of coca leaf, and barrels of chemicals late at night, but for a long time nobody would talk to me about it. Most people either avoided my questions or flat-out denied it went on. I had tried in every possible way to make clear to people that I was not judgmental; going out in the heat to plant coca and chewing the leaf to stress solidarity was one way to do this. During an extended field trip in 2013, Milton and others rewarded me for my perseverance and opened up about this controversial issue. One local trafficker, whom I will call Don Jose Cortez, took great pride in recounting his tales of smuggling coca paste, his friendships with renowned Colombian traffickers, and the time he spent in prison in both Peru and Brazil in the 1990s. It was through these contacts that I built up an understanding of the local cocaine trade.

Each peasant central has a union-owned and -operated coca market; this is normally a large barn (known as a *galpon*) located in the center of the village. Only coca is traded in this space, but these barns often double as meeting places for the unions. There is a class of accredited coca merchants, who are mostly women and members of established coca grower families. They are known as *coca chakas* after the leaf-cutting ant that is common in the region. It is a (relatively) lucrative activity; the merchants jealously guard their position and exclude any outsider who wants to enter the trade (in the village where I lived the trade was dominated by five sisters, their cousins, and female in-laws). Coca is sold soon after it is harvested and dried. Every day growers would turn up at the market in the late afternoon or early evening with four or five sacks of coca weighing 50 pounds each. The coca is weighed and the price per pound is debated.

This is not a free market, however; most merchants have established relationships with growers whom they always buy from, and they often extend them lines of credit (sometimes buying half the crop before it has even been harvested).

The law dictates that all coca should be sold through these primary coca markets,[10] and that it should then be taken to the coca market in Sacaba, on the outskirts of the city of Cochabamba, so that it can enter the legal circuits for traditional uses including chewing, processing tea, celebrating the Q'owa, and so on. However, according to my informants, the system is very "leaky," with most coca traded in the Chapare feeding into the local cocaine trade. Coca merchants say that they divert coca leaf to the illegal trade because it is the only way they can make any money. They claim that when they sell coca through the legal channels the prices are so low that they end up losing money. According to one source, in 2013 the drug workers paid up to two bolivianos per pound (about twenty-five cents) over the legal price.[11] Given that it takes up to 300 pounds to process one kilo of coca paste, the difference soon adds up.

Coca merchants sell the coca they have bought to intermediaries, who arrange for the coca to be delivered to the *monte* (jungle), where the coca paste production sites function. For example, one night in July 2007 I hitched a lift on a beat-up truck through a remote region of the municipality where I was living. At two in the morning, the driver stopped at an official coca market, bought up more than thirty bags of coca from the accredited merchants, and then continued through the jungle, dropping off coca sacks every few miles with young men who were waiting by the roadside. The men heaved the bags onto their backs and then disappeared into the dense foliage. The laborers were carting off the coca for use in the artisanal coca paste factories (known locally as *fabricas*).

The first step in cocaine processing is relatively simple. The drug workers macerate shredded coca leaves in a mixture of gasoline, sodium bicarbonate (baking soda), and sulfuric acid, to extract the cocaine alkaloid. These days most drug workers use leaf shredders and adapted cement mixers to turn over the mulch. But these are recent developments. When I began fieldwork in 2005, everything was done by hand. Most workshops relied on young men (known as *pisa-cocas*) to stomp on the coca for several hours to mix up the solution. Production sites employ three to four people and, when working at full capacity, can process up to of three kilos of coca paste per 'entrada' (session—normally one night).

The owner of the production site sells the finished product to a local buyer, called a *rescatista* (who is normally a local businessperson). The rescatistas buy up coca paste from several different sites, and once they have amassed several kilos, they arrange for it to be transported out of the region, generally by teenagers or members of the large itinerant population who are always on the lookout for work. Whether by foot, road, or river, the transporters have innovative strategies to hide the drug so that they can pass through or avoid the police checkpoints. Coca paste is concealed in car door panels, under truckloads of oranges, packed into powdered milk tins, or taped to children's stomachs. Some carry the paste by foot to the city of Cochabamba, a five-day trek with the risk of robbery. People also go on canoe trips along the winding rivers all the way to the department of Beni, and further toward the frontier with Brazil. Local coca farmers mentioned that there are a handful of Peruvian and Colombian businesspeople operating in the Chapare who buy up locally produced coca paste and fly it out of the region on small planes.

The coca paste still needs to be refined into pure crystallized cocaine (cocaine hydrochloride), but this is a complex process, requiring more skill, equipment, and expensive, difficult-to-obtain chemicals. Much of Bolivia's coca paste is refined outside of the country (along the border with Brazil), although laboratories have also been discovered within Bolivian territory, including in the Chapare's Isiboro Secure National Park (Sanchez 2011). The location of laboratories shifts continually, however. Police raids have revealed that some of these laboratories have a workforce of up to twenty people. They are very different operations from the rudimentary Chapare coca paste production units.

Can You Get Rich?

To process one kilo of coca paste, the drug workers (pichicateros) require 100 liters (about twenty-six gallons) of gasoline (which can be reused up to three times). However, the Morales administration has put tight controls on the movement of precursor chemicals. For instance, Chapare gas stations allow people to buy only one tank per day, and they add pink dye to it, which makes it less attractive for coca paste production. Consequently, some taxi drivers (known as *cisterñeros*) smuggle fuel from the cities, doubling the sale price in the Chapare. Other precursors, including chalk and caustic soda, also come at a premium because of tight government controls.

When the pichicateros cannot get hold of the correct chemicals, they improvise, for example, using cement instead of chalk to process paste.

Coca leaf represents the most costly element in the production chain. Between 2008 and 2014, the price of coca doubled to twenty-eight Bolivianos per pound (four dollars), most likely as a result of government controls restricting the production and commercialization of coca leaf. On average, it takes 300 pounds of coca leaf to process one kilogram of coca paste, which means that at 2013 prices the pichicateros spent over $1,200 on coca leaf alone. It costs approximately $1,500 to produce one kilo of coca paste; this includes overhead costs to pay off loans for the initial equipment (mixers, tanks, leaf shredders), coca leaf, precursor chemicals, labor, and transport. In the Chapare, one kilo sold for between US$1,650 to $1,700 dollars in 2013, meaning that net profits for coca paste producers were as low as $150 dollars per kilo (Grisaffi 2014).

It is also important to note that production is not constant. Pichicateros tend to spend far more time idle than working. This is because they lack sufficient capital to cover the costs of the inputs until they have sold their previous batch of paste, but also because it is often difficult to obtain the necessary chemicals, which slows or even stalls production. In addition, the pichicateros take frequent breaks from processing in order to avoid drawing attention to their illicit activities and risking arrest; as one man put it, "we often have to let things cool down." Along with irregular production, there is also a high margin of waste—if they mulch coca carelessly, it spoils, and the entire batch has to be thrown away. As a result of these factors, most production sites make fewer than ten kilos of coca paste per month.

Pichicateros earn good money, but they do not get rich from manufacturing coca paste; all it allows them to do is to save up to buy their own plot of farmland, small business, car, or even a house. These are modest ambitions, enough to buy a beat-up Toyota station wagon, not a Mercedes-Benz or Land Rover. These cars are generally not for personal use but rather are operated as taxis. Many claim that once they have amassed the requisite capital to invest in a productive activity, then they will abandon their illegal activities. Older farmers confirmed that they had done just that; after acquiring their own plots of land where no credit was available, they had decided the risks far outweighed the benefits and had subsequently dedicated themselves to farming instead. One man said, "When you work in *pichicata* [processing drugs], you spend the whole time looking over your shoulder, you can never relax, it's just too stressful." The drug trade, then, is something that people pass in and out of; farmers might engage intermittently in illicit activities to make some extra cash, but it is never a full-time occupation.

According to both Milton and Jose, a large portion of the Chapare population has, at one time or another, been directly involved in the illegal industry, perhaps working as a lookout, pisa-coca (coca stomper), or smuggler (of drugs or precursor chemicals). In Milton's own words, "everyone's involved somehow." Just as in any other industry, illegal coca paste production is stratified, with owners of the means of production and others who sell their labor. The three key roles in coca paste production include the *peon* (day laborer, also known as a *maton*), the *químico* (chemist), and the owner of the production site.

The laborers represent the majority of the workers in the local coca paste industry. They undertake manual tasks such as carrying the heavy bags of coca and precursor chemicals to the production site, shredding coca leaves, processing the coca, and acting as lookouts. The majority are either recent migrants to the region (who combine processing cocaine with work as farmhands) or local teenagers who want to earn extra spending money. The owners of the production site are very careful to hire only people who are "*de confianza*," that is to say, people who are known and can be trusted. Most laborers earn about thirty dollars a day (agricultural labor pays less than half that) for work that is tiring, irregular, and harmful to their health (as a result of the chemicals used). It is also very risky: if caught, they face eight years in prison. In a 2006 interview a fourteen-year-old coca stomper described wading around in a toxic mulch of coca, gasoline, and acid for several hours a day. The fumes gave him a terrible headache, and his flimsy rubber boots let in gasoline that turned his toenails green. He told me, "It's the hardest work there is, you have to carry barrels of chemicals, sacks of coca, sleep in the jungle . . . it's terrible. You sweat more than you have sweated in your life!"

The next rung on the ladder is the químico, or chemist. These are mid-level technicians familiar with the basics of processing coca paste, including the quantities of chemicals that are needed and when they should be added. These semiskilled laborers are normally people who have previously worked as coca stompers. Over time they have learned how to cook the drugs and have built trust with the owner of the fabrica (factory). The chemist earns 200 bolivianos (around thirty dollars) for every kilo of coca paste produced, which means that on a good day they can earn up to ninety dollars, but that would be exceptional—average earnings are more like sixty. The químico can complement this wage by skimming off any extra production and selling it privately.

At the top of the local production ladder are the owners of the production sites. Not just anyone can set up their own factory; they need the capital, land, and contacts to make it work. Given that precursor chemicals are in short supply, the smugglers will only sell them to their established contacts (just like the coca leaf trade, then, this is not a free market). As a result, the owners of production sites tend to be local coca growers from large families who have been established in the region for years. If caught, the owner faces fifteen years in prison, and consequently they rarely work directly in coca paste production. The owner makes the most money from the operation; a generous estimate would be US$2,000 a month, less than is earned by an assistant manager at McDonald's in the United States (Grisaffi 2014).

People who enter the drug industry have the opportunity to build contacts that can lead to additional work opportunities. For instance, a person who makes a name for himself as a proficient químico might be asked to work processing coca paste elsewhere in the country. Meanwhile, someone who builds a reputation for being trustworthy and competent might secure a contract driving cars packed with drugs to the city of Santa Cruz. Some people have even been involved in international trafficking. To give but one example, Milton was invited by a contact of his uncle's to smuggle drugs across the border to the port of Iquique in Chile. This required him to hike for four days across a high-altitude desert (altiplano) with twenty kilograms of cocaine on his back. The hardship this involved should not be underestimated—the temperature plunges to 15 degrees Celsius below zero at night, and there is very little fresh water available. For this he was paid just $2,000. Milton did this on three separate occasions. He decided that it was far too risky when, on his third (and final) mission, he was almost captured by a Bolivian antidrug police unit.

Grassroots Perspectives on the Drug Trade

As far as most farmers are concerned, participation in the drug trade is not a moral question; coca paste manufacturing and smuggling are simply ways to make a living. We could go further and say that the opposite is true: from the perspective of most farmers, the U.S. government is immoral for criminalizing their livelihoods, while simultaneously generating demand for the product. Don Jose told me, "They attack us for growing coca, but it is the *Yanquis* who want this stuff [cocaine], they go crazy for it." Still, there is a certain irony. While the coca growers promote a leftist political agenda and profess a hatred of the United States, the illegal drug trade is quintessentially a free market, and entrepreneurial in spirit. Moreover, the farmers are reliant on consumers in the United States and Europe to generate a demand for their product.

People who are directly involved in the so-called white factory (*la fabrica blanca*) are deemed to be respectable members of their community; everyone knows who they are, and they are looked up to. The cocaine trade, then, creates status distinctions in community life between those who occupy the higher rungs of the local trade (the rescatistas and factory owners) and those whom they employ (the coca stompers, smugglers, and lookouts). Owners of the workshops, rescatistas, and coca merchants (who divert coca to the illicit trade) tend to have more disposable income than those who are not involved in these activities. As a result, they are "invited" (that is, they are asked, but there is strong social pressure to accept this commitment) to sponsor community activities such as paying for a school graduation trip, bankrolling the local football team, or providing the sound system for a fiesta. This type of relationship is common in highland and valley indigenous communities (Abercrombie 1998). The practice of selecting sponsors for communal activities redistributes resources and can be understood as a leveling mechanism. To give but one example, Milton was selected by members of his community to sponsor a dance troupe in honor of the local saint. Everyone knew that he was a pichicatero, but this did not preclude him from taking on such an important (not to mention religious) role.

Coca growers will (on occasion) denounce the illicit activities of their neighbors to the police. This is not driven by a desire to see the local trade wiped out, nor to attack a competitor, however. Rather, the involvement of the police is generally a way to "get back" at someone for a personal grievance, which might have nothing to do with the drug industry per se: a denunciation might be motivated by an outstanding debt, a perceived lack of respect, or marital infidelity, among other issues. A man I will call Hernan was pulled over while transporting five kilos of coca paste. He was arrested, charged, and spent the following six years in prison. Hernan suspected that his neighbor had tipped off the police as a way to get revenge over a long-standing dispute over the boundaries between their respective farms. Drawing inspiration from Insa Koch (2017a), I argue that in these instances the police are used as an ally to pursue personal vendettas, rather than to seek an abstract idea of justice.

One of the reasons the illicit trade is tolerated in the region is that, while drugs are widely available (coca paste can be smoked in a hand-rolled cigarette known as a pitillo), local consumption is virtually unheard of. Drug use is very much seen as a *gringo* (foreigner) problem. Moreover, coca paste manufacturing does not generate the kind of chaos and disorder found at higher levels of the chain. This can be put down to the fact that there is a stable market for coca paste, and the product is of relatively low value. Thus, if the militarized police find a production site, the workers simply run away rather than risk a confrontation. Disputes between people who work in the drug industry mean disputes between neighbors, and they tend to be resolved in a pragmatic rather than a violent manner. For example, when I asked Milton about the most serious confrontation he had witnessed during his time as a drug worker, he told me a story about when he was still a teenager and worked as a coca stomper. On this occasion, Milton had mulched the leaves carelessly and the entire batch had spoiled. His uncle (who owned the fabrica) held Milton's parents responsible for the lost earnings and demanded they pay him $1,000 dollars to cover the costs. After a verbal argument, they split the difference and paid five hundred dollars. Compared with other countries in the region, Bolivia has very low levels of violence. According to the United Nations' 2014 Human Development report, Bolivia had the fourth lowest homicide rate in Latin America (AIN 2014). As a result of the strong unions and the role they play in policing behavior, the Chapare is a very peaceful place. We will return to this issue in the next chapter.

Conclusion

To outsiders, coca farmers routinely deny knowledge of the cocaine trade, principally because the stakes are high, and the threat of having their livelihood destroyed or even going to prison looms large. It is disingenuous of the growers to say they are ignorant of what happens to the coca leaf they produce. A large number of people benefit directly or indirectly from the illegal industry: it generates a market for coca leaf, provides employment opportunities (in production and smuggling of drugs, coca, and precursor chemicals), and has multiplier effects throughout the informal sector. Local shops, bars, builders, transport firms, and other small businesses all depend on the industry to keep them afloat.

But even though the cocaine trade forms the cornerstone of the local economy, neither the farmers nor the pichicateros are the major beneficiaries of this industry. It is estimated that less than 1 percent of the final retail price of cocaine makes its way back to the coca growers and drug workers in the Andes (Painter 1994: 145). The majority of drug workers, including coca stompers, lookouts, laborers, and chemists, receive relatively low wages for dangerous and demanding work. These people can therefore be thought of as the proletariat of the cocaine trade, as opposed to "drug barons" (Aguilo 1986; Leons and Sanabria 1997).

As far as the coca growers are concerned, the fact that coca leaf is used in drug production does not detract from its sacred status. The leaf is sacred precisely because it contains the cocaine alkaloid. The same people who sell coca to the pichicateros, process coca leaf into drugs, or grow it with full knowledge of where it will end up also use it to heal themselves, to make offerings to earth deities, and in divination ceremonies. They do not see this as a contradiction. When the coca growers say "coca is not cocaine," they are stating a heartfelt truth; sure, it can be cocaine, but that's not its essence.

3. Self-Governing in the Chapare

In June 2007, there was a rally in the town of Ivirgazama, 70 kilometers from Aurora. The committee of the Six Federations had called for 100 percent of the rank and file to be present, so there must have been at least forty thousand coca growers packed onto the sports field. The event was held to celebrate the successful completion of the government's mass literacy program, which involved the deployment of Cuban educators all over the country. Farmers stood with other members of their base-level union under hand-painted banners that bore the name and affiliation of their sindicato, followed by the word *Present*. After several hours of waiting in the powerful tropical sun, President Morales finally arrived. The music from the political campaign was played over the speakers. The announcer animated the masses, yelling, "Wave your flags! Show me your banners." People bore placards that read: "Thanks to Evo I wrote this!" and "Now I can write, thank you." Unfortunately, many were marred with poor spelling and grammar.

Morales began his speech by calling out the names of various sindicatos and centrals: "Can I see my old central . . . San Francisco?" He peered out over the crowd; a shout of "Present!" erupted from the right-hand side of the stage. "How about central Eterezama?" Again, there was applause and cheering. Morales made reference to the huge numbers of people who had spontaneously come to show their loyalty and support for his government and the process of change. "The opposition say that we pay you to be here! That's why so many of you turn out! But we don't pay anybody, you are here because you are conscientious," he said.

Later, Don Tito Paracas, a farmer in his late thirties who had also been at the rally, laughed at Morales's speech. "They don't pay us to be there, but they fine us if we don't go!" He smirked while rubbing his thumb and forefinger together to indicate money. With this he was alluding to the union's system of sanctions, which means that anyone who does not participate actively in union activities is fined. He said, "we have to be organic." Being organic, or *vida organica*, refers to the union as a living organism that requires constant maintenance (Lazar 2013: 85). Thus, "to do organic life" means to participate fully in union activities, which might include attending rallies like the one described above, joining in collective work parties, participating in regular meetings, or going to a demonstration.

Classical theories of liberalism developed in Western Europe argue that individual rights should triumph over group rights. This narrative has been incredibly powerful, driving the democratization agenda in the postcolonial world (Hickel 2015: 5–8). One of the implications of this trend is that collective forms of political organization that do not appear to safeguard individual rights (such as the right to vote and the secret ballot) are seen as autocratic or a form of "dictatorship." The Chapare coca unions have been repeatedly denounced in the national and international press as an example of *dictadura sindical* or union dictatorship (ANF 2001a; Choque 2010; *Clarin* 2008; *Los Tiempos* 2015a). Commentators in the media and opposition politicians characterize union leaders as overlords who run the union for their own benefit; they say that in the Chapare "you have to do what you are told," "there are fines," and "they punish dissent." One article described Evo Morales as the "King of the Chapare" and wrote that "an autocratic-union system" operates there (ANF 2001b). This view is clearly articulated in a documentary available on YouTube,[1] with the title "The Union Dictatorship of Evo Morales," which was widely commented on in the Bolivian media in 2011 (*La Patria* 2011).

Development workers from the United States shared this view of the unions. Take, for example, this USAID report from 2003, which states:

> In the Chapare . . . both social capital and the institutional base are very weak. People live mainly in isolated, very small settlements with little or no social infrastructure to bring them together, which exacerbates the breakdown of social cohesion (common social patterns and relations), caused by the fact that the population has migrated to the region from various parts of Bolivia. This dispersion and lack of cohesion is aggravated by the lack of a viable state presence in the region. State institutions, particularly in the justice and social service

sectors, tend to be weak or absent, or available only in the largest towns. This social and institutional vacuum has facilitated the ability of the well-organized unions and their federations to be dominated by coca interests, to impose their agenda and interests on the majority population. (Jackson et al. 2003: 6)

The authors of this report characterize the coca growers as isolated, confused, and subject to an oppressive union that imposes its will from above. The authors fail to acknowledge that the coca growers themselves built the union and participate actively in managing their own affairs.

As we saw in the introduction to this book, anthropologists have long argued that if we simply look at the procedural elements of democracy (voting, elections, and so on), we fail to understand the cultural specificity of democratic practices (Cook, Long, and Moore 2016; Paley 2008). They have also argued for a more relational understanding of citizenship (Koch 2015; Lazar 2008). Drawing on the aforementioned literature, what this chapter shows is that the dictatorship that is so feared by those grounded in liberal theory is located in particular understandings of sociality that prioritize ideas of reciprocity, mutual dependence, and equivalence over individual self-fulfillment. As we will see, these ways of relating to one another are not unique to the coca growers, but rather are anchored in a deeper Andean culture, which can be traced to the ayllu, an indigenous form of community organization. Coca growers do not see democracy and antiliberal attitudes as mutually exclusive, but rather as interlinked projects. This can be exemplified by analyzing the way in which politics is organized at the most basic level in my field site, namely the sindicato.

In what follows, I describe how the sindicato has the ambition to be like a state and to control its members, but at the same time there is a drive toward maintaining its connection to the grassroots by promoting equivalence and participation. In other words, there is a mixture of both (spontaneous) participation by those who call themselves members, but also coercion leveled at anyone who is considered to transgress communal values. It is this mixture of equivalence and the threat of coercion that gives the sindicatos their potentially autocratic character. I do not try to reconcile this contradiction, but rather explore dictatorship as an element of self-governance that repeats itself throughout the entire union structure. The chapter ends by examining how the union takes responsibility not only for governance of coca grower communities but also for the region at large.

Ayllus and Sindicatos

In 2014, at the inauguration of a new high school in the Chapare, Evo Morales[2] gave a lengthy speech in which he recounted his first experience of syndicalism in the Cochabamba Tropics, and contrasted it with the indigenous system of self-governing found in his community of origin in the Aymara highlands: "When I arrived in March 1980 at Sindicato San Francisco—Kilómetro 21, I still did not know the union structure of the Tropics of Cochabamba. In the land where I was born, the indigenous authorities were in charge, the *malla t'allas* and the *mallkus*. There was no sindicato [agricultural union]. I was surprised by the syndicalism in the Cochabamba Tropics."

The form of community organization in the Bolivian highlands during the pre-Conquest era (and still operational today, particularly in the southern altiplano, including where Morales grew up) was known as the ayllu, an elaborate, kinship-based economic and political system that covered a large territory spanning different altitudes, or what are known as ecological steps (Murra 1995). This system allowed the community to produce a diverse range of agricultural products, raise livestock, and trade extensively between these different zones. Within the ayllu there is no private property or market relations; rather, the inhabitants rely on *ayni*, which refers to "a symmetrical exchange of delayed reciprocity between equals, usually manifest in labor exchanges," or simply put, mutual aid (Allen 1981: 165). In addition, ayllu members practice *faena* (also referred to as *minka*); these are public workdays when all the members of the community are expected to work together to maintain communal goods such as the roads or irrigation systems (Isbell 1978: 167). Economic anthropologist Enrique Mayer (2001) has shown how resilient these forms of reciprocity and exchange are, even in the face of the capitalist system.

Within the ayllu, leadership positions are rotated based on age and prior experience, and involve both men and women (Harris 2000a; Rivera 1990: 100–101). The leaders' duties are to ensure the economic well-being of the community, to distribute resources (including land), and manage relationships between community members. Thomas Abercrombie describes how the leaders have to shoulder a heavy economic burden by paying for saint's day celebrations, which can be read as a form of redistribution, or leveling device, among community members (Abercrombie 1998: 81–89). Silvia Rivera (1990: 101) has described these community offices (or *cargos* as they are known in Spanish) as the ayllu's "own electoral mechanisms."

The origins of the sindicato (or union), can be traced to the 1930s when, following the Chaco War, labor organizers connected to Marxist political parties began to organize in the Cochabamba valleys to demand rural schools and agrarian reform (Gordillo 2000; Weismantel 2006: 94). Following the National Revolution, the MNR government sought to supplant the traditional ayllu community structures with trade union organizations, as part of its modernizing project to turn "Indians" into peasants. The MNR designated the peasant union as the primary organization for carrying out land redistribution (under the 1953 agrarian reform bill) and for governing local affairs. Agricultural unions subsequently spread throughout the Bolivian countryside and became the principal vehicle for community-based organizing (Conzelman 2007: 106). The spread of the union form generated tensions with the traditional ayllus in some areas of Bolivia (Platt 1983; Rivera 1990).

There is a large and growing body of literature that traces out the continuity and ruptures between the ayllu form of organization and contemporary social movement practice (Bjork-James 2013; Conzelman 2007; Gutierrez Aguilar 2014; Zibechi 2010). For example, Sian Lazar (2008) has considered how the neighborhood federations and informal street traders' associations she studied in El Alto are based on Andean self-governing principles such as reciprocity, consensus building, and high levels of community participation, mixed with Marxist traditions inherited from the displaced miners (who settled in the slums following the closure of the mines in the 1980s), such as electing authorities formally rather than rotating them by age and prior experience.

Andean forms of organization have also traveled east to the newer colonization zones in the state of Santa Cruz. Nicole Fabricant (2012) explains how landless movement (Movimiento sin Tierra—MST) activists have embraced the concept of the ayllu in order to shape new ways of governing and producing, and to forge new collective identities. That said, Fabricant is careful not to romanticize these emerging indigenous practices; she notes that MST activists replicate some of the same hierarchies found in the dominant society (particularly in relation to gender). She argues that grassroots agendas are by no means pure, but rather are better imagined as hybrid, informed by indigenous conceptions but also by mainstream ideals such as economic success, liberalized markets, and individualism.

The point is, we cannot draw out hard and fast distinctions between the ayllu and the union forms of organization, as the two bleed into one another, blurring the boundary between "Indian" and peasant (Albó 2000). The Chapare unions build on the heritage of the ayllus, the strong tradition of peasant unionism from the Cochabamba valleys, but also on the Marxist traditions bought to the Chapare by the displaced miners.

The Agricultural Unions

In the previous chapter we saw that moving to the Chapare was a promising life change; some migrants went out of choice, others because they were forced (as a result of mine and factory shutdowns or drought in the highlands). But those who spontaneously settled the land (that is to say, those who did not get involved with the state-backed colonization programs) did not make that move on their own: when they arrived, there was already a well-established structure of local governance in place, one dominated by the sindicatos, which decided what would be done with the new arrivals, where they would be given land, and what their obligations would be to the local community in turn. This helped the new migrants find a foothold in this unstable region where there was almost no state presence (PNUD 2007).

While the role the unions play in self-governance might appear exotic at first glance, it is worth noting that scholars have described how informal systems of governance continue to exist alongside formal institutions and state processes elsewhere in Latin America, but also in the United States and Europe. In each case, processes of self-governance exist because the state is either absent or else purposely excluded (Arias 2017; Karandinos et al. 2014; Koch 2017a). The gangs that operate in prisons in the United States provide a vivid example of just this phenomenon (Skarbek 2014).

Joining a sindicato is not really a choice; anybody who wants agricultural land in the Chapare has to become a member. However, each sindicato puts strict conditions on who can join. Normally, they only allow people to affiliate who are already known to the community, and only then once they have proven their commitment to the organization by participating in communal work parties and meetings. For example, I knew one man who was allowed to join the sindicato where I lived because his brother was already a member (so the local community knew him), but more importantly he was an excellent football player and they wanted him for their team. The upshot of this exclusive selection procedure is that sindicatos are cross-cut by kinship relations, old friendships, and alliances between families, which are often expressed as godparenthood.[3] Members would describe the sindicato as being a bit like an extended family; in many cases this was not an analogy but was in fact true as sindicatos are composed of large kin groups who intermarry.

Membership in a sindicato comes with a clearly determined set of rights and duties, which are outlined in the unions' statutes. A condensed version of this is kept by all members on a blue A5 membership card, which people diligently keep in a plastic pouch to protect against the constant damp. The card has a grid where attendance at monthly meetings, civic parades, and other important events is logged, and on the flip side the card lists the rights and duties of each affiliate. It reads:

Rights of affiliates:

- To a voice and vote at all meetings and to have their opinions heard.
- To choose and be chosen for leadership positions
- To be informed about union matters, above all economic management
- To benefit from the projects carried out by the sindicato
- To have a just hearing if denounced
- To receive full assistance in the case of emergency or need

The second section goes on:

The obligations of the affiliates include:

- To comply with the rules outlined in this statute
- To abide by the decisions of the assembly
- To hold positions in the union
- To fulfill all manner of contributions, be it labor or cash for the benefit of the organization, or to execute any project that might be of benefit to the community
- To assist when the leader convenes an activity

The sindicato has the power and authority to ensure that people stick to these rules. Don Alfredo Higuera (whom we first met in chapter 2) told me, "When we say something, we make people respect it. We are very strict, but very united." Any member who does not honor his or her commitments to the group faces a range of sanctions, including fines, the loss of the right to grow coca, or community work (such as litter picking, cutting the grass, or painting buildings), and this is backed up by the threat of expulsion from the community and the confiscation of land. As a result, there is strong pressure to conform to communally determined goals.

In the Chapare, land ultimately belongs to the union, and the sindicato can take it back from any member if they do not comply with their obligations. For instance, land is supposed to fulfill a productive function; if a plot is left uncultivated, the union will declare it fallow and assign it to someone else. Or, if someone fails to attend the regular meetings or pay their *quotas* (subscription fee), they risk losing their land (when I began fieldwork in 2005, anyone who missed three meetings in a row without good reason would have their land taken from them). When a plot is repossessed, it is referred to as being *caducado*, the literal translation being "expired" or "lapsed," indicating that ownership is only ever temporary. The idea that ultimately land should belong to and benefit the community reflects deeper Andean ideas regarding land and its connection to livelihood, security, food production, social welfare, and the maintenance of cultural identity (Abercrombie 1998; Harris 2000b; Isbell 1978; Spedding 1994).

Today, *caducaciones* (repossessions of land) occur rarely; nevertheless, the threat of it remains real and present in people's minds. The union's control over land is the key to the organization's strength. The union's use of sanctions is by no means unique; social movements across Latin America punish members if they do not abide by communal laws (Derpic and Weinreb 2014; Starn 1992). For instance, in Chiapas (southern Mexico), indigenous peoples who opposed the "communal consensus" defined at village assemblies were deprived of rights and expelled from their community (Gledhill 1997: 94). To fully comprehend the power the sindicato exerts over its members, it is instructive to consider the role it plays in administering justice and arbitrating disagreements.

No Man's Land

The rains had come late and the temperature was hitting 40 degrees Celsius. I accompanied Grover (a reporter from the coca growers' radio station) to the closest large town to cover a story about an attempted theft of a motorbike. At the police station, Sergeant Rojas sat behind a wooden desk surrounded by cardboard files and stacks of paper. He knew Grover well and immediately agreed to be interviewed for the news program. The sergeant gave a dry, factual account of the crime. A seventeen-year-old boy had been caught attempting to steal a motorbike in the center of the town. The local residents had caught him in the act and brought him to the police station. The sergeant contrasted the behavior of the townsfolk with the rural coca growers. He said, "The problem is, sometimes, the sindicatos like to deal with things internally, their own way." He urged the listeners that if they catch a criminal, they should bring them to the police station because "the police are the state, and the state is the MAS, and so the people should trust us."

Once Grover had turned the voice recorder off, the sergeant spoke more candidly about the problems faced by his officers. He explained that there are many parts of the region where the regular police simply cannot go. In order to enter some of the sindicatos, they first must ask permission from union leaders, but it is often not granted. He spoke about several cases where the sovereignty of the state was severely undermined, including the sindicatos taking police officers hostage, police being beaten by sindicato members, and one case when a peasant union demanded the police hand over a criminal already in their custody so that they might enact their own punishment. It was, he said, "*la tierra de nadie*" (a no-man's land).

High-level union leaders expressed similar concerns. In November 2013 the Six Federations, along with the association of municipalities of the tropics (known as the *mancomunidad*), called an emergency meeting to discuss citizen security. Don David Arce, a high-level union leader, explained that there had been a spate of violent lynchings, which had been covered by the press. This was making the Chapare (and by extension the Morales administration) look bad, and had to be stopped. He acknowledged that in the past the peasant farmers had had their differences with the police, but "now we are in government and so we have to work with them." Don David then urged the rank and file to honor the official legal procedure. "If you catch a criminal you have to take him to the police, compañeros! You can't always burn people." With this he was referring to how some communities have been known to set criminals on fire as a punishment. He summed up: "We are the state, but that means we have to respect the state." David's words captured the key problem the union is facing: while union members harbor ambitions to control the state, they do not want to be controlled by it.

The Chapare, then, is a region where the state does not penetrate effectively. This is not to say that there is no law in the Chapare—there is; it's just not the state that enforces order, but rather it is the union. In rural areas, most crimes are not reported to the police or pursued through official legal procedures; rather, they are dealt with internally—a phenomenon that has been observed throughout Bolivia and Peru (Goldstein 2003; Starn 1999). "First you go the sindicato," I was told, "because it is like your family." Others said, "when you live in an organization you are subject to the organization," "here we do things organically," and "around here the federation is the law." Dealing with problems internally is said to be preferable because it is faster, simpler, and cheaper than engaging with the mainstream legal system.[4] What is more, people simply do not trust the police or legal professionals, whom they describe as "more criminal than the criminals."

Each sindicato elects a secretary of justice (also known as a sheriff or *corregidor*) from its ranks;[5] he (I only ever met male sheriffs) is responsible for maintaining order and administering justice in the locality (when I first arrived in Aurora, I had to seek permission from the sheriff as to whether or not I would be allowed to stay in the village). The sheriff holds regular consultations and organizes *rondas* (night watch) on weekend evenings between 11 PM and 2 AM. The sheriff, accompanied by members of the community (including men and women), patrols the village to ensure that no untoward activity is taking place. The rondas regularly escort amorous teenagers home to their parents, close down local bars that sell alcohol to minors, and incarcerate violent drunks in the *calabozo* (a small cell) until they sober up. Some sheriffs are more proactive; for example, Don Carlos Ribera, who was the sheriff of Aurora when I conducted my first period of fieldwork, tackled youth gangs by demanding that the parents bring their children to a meeting where they were forced to confess to their crimes, and some were subject to a public whipping.

More complex and long-standing problems such as disputes over property, land, honor, and debt are bought to the sindicato's monthly meeting, where the issue is debated and resolved with the participation of all union members present (see figure 3.1). The sindicato's power extends right into the home; for instance, an aggrieved spouse can bring a case against their partner for infidelity or battery. The sindicato has a range of sanctions at its disposal, including fines, enforced community work, incarceration, or even the expulsion of a member from the community. Because the sindicato is unencumbered by bureaucratic inertia, weight of evidence, and due process, it can solve problems quickly and easily.[6] When I asked about how the collective could judge someone guilty, I was told, "You can just tell if

Figure 3.1. A monthly sindicato meeting held in a barn, where issues of justice are decided by all present. Photo by author.

they are guilty, they can't hide it . . . they are scared when they are stood up there in front of everybody."

During fieldwork, I attended many meetings where disputes were successfully worked through. Take, for example, the case of Doña Blanca Ledezma and Doña Dominga Mercado, whose agricultural fields abutted one another. The previous year Doña Dominga had spent several weeks clearing and planting orange trees over a large area. However, as the boundaries between the fields are poorly defined, she had mistakenly done all of this on her neighbor's land. Given the amount of time and money she had invested in this endeavor, Doña Dominga felt that it was only right that she should be allowed to claim it for herself; after all, prior to her efforts the land had been left uncultivated. Doña Blanca disagreed, saying that it was her land and so the plants belonged to her. A tit-for-tat conflict ensued. Doña Dominga chopped down trees on Doña Blanca's land to spite her, and in retaliation Doña Blanca entered Doña Dominga's house and smashed her television set. The conflict threatened to escalate as both had extended family in the sindicato whom they had mobilized to support them.

This issue was bought before the sindicato meeting. Both parties were given the opportunity to tell their side of the story, and the problem was then opened out to the floor. People yelled at one another, there was crying and screaming. Some made threats that the sindicato should split into two separate communities because "we really cannot live together." Eventually, after two hours of deliberation, a solution was agreed. Doña Blanca would have to pay Dominga $300 for the workdays she had put into clearing and planting. But Blanca would get to keep all of the land's production going forward. It was also agreed that if Doña Blanca did not pay the fee, then all sindicato members would go together to harvest her coca and the proceeds would go to Doña Dominga to clear the debt. The aggrieved parties were then encouraged to shake hands. Initially, they refused but after more shouts they reluctantly clasped each other's hands for a fraction of a second and immediately withdrew. The aim of sindicato justice, then, is to find a solution that reconciles the demands of both parties. This is important because it reduces the possibility of a conflict spiraling out of control, risking a breakdown in community cohesion. This form of restorative justice is common in rural indigenous communities throughout the Americas (Hammond 2011; Sieder 2002; Van Cott 2007). For instance, the Rondas Campesinas, studied by Orin Starn (1999), imparted justice in a way that involved the participation of large numbers of people and an appeal to community sentiment.

In theory, the sindicato should only deal with low-level misdemeanors, while criminal matters should be taken to the police, but in practice this rarely happens. For serious crimes (murder, rape, and theft of expensive items), the sindicato's retribution is severe. Punishment includes stripping the suspect naked and then tying him or her to the *palo santo* (a tree that is home to thousands of poisonous biting ants), tying up the culprit and dousing them in petrol, hanging by the neck, or burying them in sand with only their head sticking out. If the members of the community know the accused, then, with adequate contrition, he or she will generally escape serious harm. Outsiders are less lucky, however; over a five-year period (2008–13), nineteen people were killed by lynching in the Chapare (Vásquez 2013).

During a lynching everyone is expected to participate. An older female shopkeeper told me about a time when a thief was caught at the market where she owned a stall. The suspected criminal was made to stand on a chair with a noose around his neck; like every other store owner, the woman was given a stick and was instructed to hit the culprit at least once. The logic is that by involving everyone, all are made complicit and a wall of silence is guaranteed to surround the event. While this behavior might sound brutal, most coca growers support the idea of violent punishment. People say that violent acts send a strong message that will deter people from committing crime in their area. I was told, "the criminals are afraid to come here" and "they don't dare commit crime here." Lynching is by no means unique to the Chapare, but can be witnessed right across Bolivia (Derpic and Ayala 2016; Goldstein 2004). Some have read lynching as a logical response, a way to ensure security when the neoliberal state is failing to fulfill even its most basic duties (Goldstein 2003, 2005). But the case of the coca growers reveals a different story. The coca growers have no truck with liberal ideas regarding the inherent worth of the individual; rather, according to their vernacular logic, anyone who transgresses communally held values loses all rights, even the right to life.

The organization of the sindicato and its use of force may justify the dominant view that it is authoritarian. As the examples offered here illustrate, there is little space for negotiation, and transgression of basic communal norms is heavily sanctioned. However, such a top-down perspective tells only half of the story. What it cannot reveal is the extent to which members voluntarily comply with the rules imposed, and even show active support for the sindicato's punitive reach. Building on the foundations laid by political anthropologists, I suggest that we cannot understand how people engage with politics on the margins unless we first comprehend how it is rooted in deeper social processes of care and commitment to people and place (see Ferguson 2013; Koch 2016, 2017c; Lazar 2017; Spencer 2007)— or, to put it in the terms of my informants, the factors that make someone a "real member."

Reciprocity

I bumped into Don Carlos Ledezma walking along the street late one afternoon. Carlos is a local farmer and fisherman. He is short, fat, and has a head of thick, curly black hair. I hadn't seen him for over a year, and we greeted each other with enthusiasm. He asked how I was getting on and why I was visiting the Chapare yet again. Carlos was surprised to hear that I was still working on the book. "What, it's not finished yet?" he inquired. "So this book—are you going to tell the truth?" "What do you mean—the truth?" I asked. "Are you going to write about the syndical dictatorship that exists?" Don Carlos launched into a withering critique of the bullying he claimed to have experienced at the hands of other sindicato members. He complained that the leaders are abusive and take unnecessary fines. He said, "and what do they need it for? For their own pocket! The leaders live like kings with our money!" He went on to say that the leaders grant special rights to their kin group (including the right to grow additional plots of coca) while the rest suffer. "Why doesn't anyone say anything?" I asked. "The same people are afraid so they don't say anything, they don't want to get on the wrong side of the sindicato," he said.

What Carlos was talking about sounds a lot like the sindicato dictatorship described at the beginning of this chapter. Moreover, Carlos was by no means the only one to voice these concerns. Coca growers often grumbled that because of the fines, they were forced to toe the line. But when I asked the same people if others should be punished if they do not fulfill their community-oriented duties, most agreed that they should. Thus, coca grower commitment to vida organica (organic life) cannot simply be reduced to the effective use of sanctions. Gilmar Condori, a young union leader, put it this way: "Do you think that the people only participate because we threaten to whip them or fine them? No! People participate because they are conscientious!" He went on: "Of course some people do not like to go [to meetings and rallies], they just look after their own personal interests. So what else can we do with them?" In this reading, sanctions are not fundamental, but they are useful as they address the "free-rider problem," ensuring that all coca growers pursue collective rather than individual goals (Edelman 2001: 287–89).

People do not simply belong to a predetermined community; rather, they have to actively build their community through various forms of participation. For example, Sian Lazar (2008: 118–43) explains how the collective sense of self in the neighborhood associations and (in)formal trade unions she studied in El Alto was generated through active participation in cultural events such as fiestas, religious festivals, dance fraternities, and popular assemblies (see also Lazar 2015). Anthropologists have argued that some of the most important everyday "group making work" that indigenous Andeans are engaged in are the rituals that accompany their labor in the fields, communal work parties, fiesta sponsorship, fertility rituals, and a rotating system of community offices, all of which are grounded in the fundamental notion of reciprocity (Abercrombie 1998; Harris 2000b). Krista

Van Vleet (2008), who worked in the Bolivian highlands, goes further than most to argue that ayni (exchange) is the basis of all social relationships, even kinship.[7] Reciprocity then is a core organizing principle of Andean indigenous communities, and it is through engaging in these networks that people come to be considered *jaqui*, or a "real person" (Albó 2002b: 10).

The profound sense of solidarity engendered between sindicato members cannot simply be put down to shared abstract characteristics (such as class, or speaking Quechua), owning land in the same area, residence, or for that matter kinship. Rather, taking the lead from the aforementioned scholars, I argue that it is constantly reaffirmed through daily Maussian exchanges[8] that express care and commitment to one another and tie people into dense relationships of debt and dependency (see also Piot 1999: 52–75). In the Chapare, low-level daily exchanges include gifts of food, drinks, or invitations to sit and chew coca together. To give but one example, during fieldwork I found it very difficult to walk around the village without being invited into my neighbors' homes to eat. As there was no way to turn down these invitations, I regularly ate up to four lunches in a row. As far as I could tell, this hospitality was extended to others. People commonly greeted me in the following manner: "Where did you get lost?" and then proceeded to berate me for not calling on them to receive their hospitality. There was a demand, then, to engage with and to rely on people, but in turn to be relied on. I was also asked for loans, favors, and to act as a godparent to several children.

Work was another area where people demonstrated their commitment to one another. For example, some tasks, such as clearing land (for slash and burn agriculture) or harvesting certain crops, require more than one worker. In these instances, the landowner might hire someone to help them, but often they practice ayni, that is, they work for one another for free (on the understanding that this work will be returned in the future). Ayni is seen as a positive way of working because people work together as equals, but it's also described as "fun." People enjoy working alongside their friends, as they can chat and eat together. Ayni, or sharing, can be enacted in other ways too; for example, farmers frequently borrow farming tools from one another, even high-value ones such as a chainsaw or outboard motor for a boat. I also heard of instances of people lending unused portions of land to friends, relatives, and *compadres* (people they are tied to through godparent relationships) so that they might farm it, and this was done at no cost.[9]

Figure 3.2. On the way home from a football tournament with trophies for the winning team. Photo by author.

Apart from these personalized exchanges, people are also expected to contribute to the broader community by participating actively in the union, attending meetings, paying their quotas, and participating in communal work parties for the benefit of the community; that is, they have to *do* organic life. It is also expected that union members should be present at parties, drink together, and even play sports on a local team (there are both male and female football teams and leagues for older and younger people—see figure 3.2). When it comes to important life cycle events such as weddings and funerals, the entire community shows up. At the funeral of a close friend, almost two hundred people descended on the widow's house and stayed there for many hours to pay their respects. Some even spent the following night at the cemetery, where they kept the corpse company, drinking huge quantities of beer and praying. This was spoken of as a form of exchange. One man told me, "it's a day on loan"; the expectation was that, when the time comes, community members would come to one's own funeral to say the appropriate prayers to hasten the soul's journey to its end destination.

For coca growers, then, a good person is not a self-reliant individual, but rather someone who demonstrates loyalty and care toward people and place, and who in turn is dependent on others. People who honor this commitment are described as being *bien cumplido*, that is, someone who is conscientious and who has fulfilled their duties. These ideas become central to boundary-drawing processes between insiders and outsiders. Only those who live up to moral expectations are considered to be true members of the sindicato deserving of its protection. In a similar fashion, Sian Lazar (2008: 186) notes that El Alto's neighborhood associations demand full participation in "organic life" (including attending meetings, demonstration marches, and civic parades called by the association), and those who comply "have a greater call on the protection provided by that association."

While stressing the importance of reciprocity and participation, I do not want to suggest that there is an inner circle of family and community with self-evident solidarity and trust vis-à-vis outsiders. Peter Geschiere (2013) argues that we too easily forget that in Marcel Mauss's original formulation, the obligation to return a gift is always fraught with an element of fear and danger. He comes to the worrying conclusion that intimacy is always intrinsically dangerous, and that the most threatening aggression comes from within families and among neighbors.

Equivalence

My neighbors in Aurora seemed to be forever at each other's throats, bickering, fighting, and trying to get one over on each other. To give an example, high levels of mistrust characterize the process of buying and selling coca. The farmers accuse the merchants (who are often their neighbors) of using scales that are rigged; meanwhile, the merchants insist on unpacking and repacking large sacks of coca to check that the farmer has not hidden any stones in the bag to unfairly increase its weight.[10] In the Chapare, a common idiom for talking about rivalry was in terms of *celos* (jealousy) and *envidia* (envy); indeed, I was often told to be careful because "there is a lot of envidia here." This talk reflects the idea that nobody wants their neighbor to get ahead of them, particularly because another's gain is often considered to come at one's own expense. Foster (1965) referred to this as the "limited good" and considered it to be universal in peasant communities. While this idea has been thoroughly criticized (Gregory et al. 1975), it provides elements that help to explain what is going on in the Chapare.

To mitigate self-interested behavior, the coca growers strictly enforce an ethic of equivalence; everyone had to be the same. This much was evident in everyday, mundane interactions. For instance, whenever I went to a restaurant for lunch with coca grower friends, everyone would order exactly the same dish, even if there were several different plates on offer for a similar price. Or when it came to drinking beer, people would always share the same bottle, all present would drink at exactly the same pace, and nobody would leave until it was decided that everyone would leave together. Leveling mechanisms are found throughout the Andes—for example, the fiesta cargo complex common in the highland ayllus (Abercrombie 1998)—but also in peasant communities more broadly. The aim is to minimize class differences within the community and check individual power (Wolf 2001: 201).

Within the community where I conducted fieldwork, there were explicit mechanisms in place to level economic disparities. For example, anyone who "got on" was "invited" to be a sponsor for community activities, including paying for the school graduation, sound systems for a fiesta, or the dance troupe for a religious celebration. As a relatively wealthy outsider, I was selected to be the sponsor (known as a *padrino* or godfather) for a great many community events, including paying for the annual fireworks display to celebrate the radio station's anniversary, which I did for three consecutive years at a cost of around $300 per year. I was also asked to help out on an individual basis to cover health costs, wedding preparations, and even a loan to buy a farm. In return, I was feted as a generous and kind person who was allowed to walk freely around the village and was welcome into people's homes. I thought I was doing great, building relationships and settling in (even if I was blowing most of my research grant on gifts); my landlady was less sure. She berated me for being a fool, claiming that the neighbors were "abusing me."

Anyone who does not participate appropriately in community-oriented activities loses rights within the sindicato. One base-level member explained: "Anyone who is not cumplido [fulfilling their duties], well, they lose the right to a voice. They are ignored. For them it's difficult to defend themselves against the accusations of the other compañeros [comrades]." This much was vividly illustrated in the case of Don Nelson Quispe. Nelson really had no interest in participating in vida organica: he skipped meetings, reluctantly turned up for fiestas, and rejected calls to sponsor community events. As a result, he was marginalized within the community. People said that he was arrogant and thought of himself as better than others. Worse still, people spread rumors about him, including one suggesting he was an informant for the U.S. embassy. One day local union members invaded Nelson's land, pulled up his coca, and denied him the right to replant it. Stating that he had not fulfilled his duties. Nelson's cato (legal coca plot) was then reassigned to another member who was said to be "bien cumplido." To an outsider, this looked like an abuse of sindicato authority, but to the people involved it made perfect sense. Nelson had failed to complete his community obligations, and therefore was not considered part of the community.

There is a large and growing literature on the individualizing tendencies of capitalism in general, and neoliberalism in particular (Beck and Beck-Gernsheim 2002; Brown 2015). It is tempting to interpret the self-interested behavior described above (exhibited by Nelson Quispe) as something new, a result of these very processes. But this would not be correct. The ethnographic literature indicates that Andean rural communities have always been characterized by a tendency toward individualism and factionalism, alongside a strong communitarian ethic (Albó 1985, 2002b: 9–32; Vincent 2017), something Xavier Albó (1977) has described as the "Aymara paradox." Moreover, we have seen that when people act in self-interested ways, other members of the community look at them negatively and sanction this behavior. Individualism, then, is considered to be rule breaking, as opposed to something that is condoned or aspired to. Sanctions thus become a moment where collective ideals are reasserted.

In sum, the communal structure overcomes individual desires through a mixture of spontaneous participation, peer expectation, but also bullying and coercion. By now we can begin to understand how some of the elements of sharing, reciprocity, and exchange coexist alongside the potential for coercion and punitive control that we considered at the beginning of the chapter. In the following pages, I consider how the principles found at the level of the sindicato are scaled up to inform the practice of the union as a whole.

Scaling Up

Just like the sindicato, the Six Federations cannot be treated as a given community characterized by some sort of elemental solidarity. It is a massive organization, with over 45,000 members, and is in a constant dynamic tension of unity and division. The rivalry between sindicatos is vividly demonstrated at football tournaments. Individual sindicatos take the annual federation league very seriously. In theory, teams composed of sindicato members slug it out over the season to compete for the big prize, which is normally a cow (to be barbecued) and US$2,000 in cash. The prize itself does not motivate the teams; rather, participants take great pride in their sindicato, and they play for glory. The passion the game elicits is intense: the winning team of the 2013 competition only included four members from the sindicato it claimed to represent; the rest of the side was composed of professionals drafted from the city, who were paid a flat rate of US$200 per game. The leader of the sindicato in question estimated that over the course of the tournament his community had spent over US$6,000 on players.

Inter-sindicato rivalry can take a more sinister aspect, however. Take, for example, the constant internecine conflicts over territory and river management. The tropical rivers in the Chapare have massive erosive power. Consequently, when people attempt to improve defenses on their side of the river, the residents on the opposite bank complain (fearing the water will be deflected and cut further into their own territory). Often negotiations break down, and strike parties to destroy river defenses are a common occurrence. During fieldwork, I heard of sand being put into the petrol tanks of heavy machinery (used to build the defenses), dynamite used to blow up infrastructure, and violent fights breaking out between people living on either side of the river. Such acts inevitably provoked retaliatory attacks and even roadblocks to inconvenience members of rival sindicatos (one roadblock I observed lasted for three months).

However, while different parts of the union, including sindicatos, centrals, and federations, might pursue their own self-interested course of action, there is also a drive to achieve collective goals. In the Chapare, the same people who fight each other one day (be it on the football field or in a dispute over territory) will put their conflicts to one side and unite against an external threat. In localized disputes (within the sindicato), people mobilize kinship relations against their neighbors, but these same people will stand together to fight a rival sindicato. Centrals fight other centrals, federations fight with federations, and together they fight outsiders, including the state if need be.[11]

The way alliances are scaled up is clearly illustrated if we examine coca grower actions to prevent the military and police forces from eradicating coca in the 1990s and early 2000s. When the troops entered a locality, the farmers would use fireworks (known as *petados*) to alert one another to their presence. Villagers armed with sticks, slings, and machetes would convene in an attempt to stop the eradication. Doña Justina Rodriguez, a leader in her forties, recalls, "The sindicatos would help one another, like ayni. Let's say the soldiers came here, to our sindicato; the seven sindicatos that make up our central would come to help to get rid of the soldiers. The neighboring central would help out too. As soon as we heard the signal, it didn't matter if we were eating lunch, breakfast, in bed, at night; we had to rush to help. We had to get there before they eradicated the coca."

The coca growers take great pride in their sindicato, and just like an individual union member, people describe specific sindicatos as being bien cumplido. This is used to signify that a sindicato has fulfilled its duties toward the broader union structure. For example, when the federation calls large-scale public events, each base-level sindicato will try to outdo one another in terms of how many people they can mobilize for it. This much can be seen if we refer to the initial example of the rally in Ivirgazama (at the start of this chapter). Morales called out the name of each base-level union, and the members expressed their pride that they were attending in large numbers by shouting "Present" and cheering.

However, while there might be spontaneous participation, the federation can also coerce sindicatos to comply with federation mandates. The federation has a range of sanctions at its disposal to ensure that sindicatos stay in line. For example, sindicatos that do not turn up for union meetings or mass rallies in sufficient numbers are fined. They might also be denounced on the coca union's radio station; this ritual of public naming is thought to bring shame on the sindicato in question and is a powerful tool to ensure compliance. For this reason, coca growers often referred to the radio as a "judge." Union leaders also explained that the town hall (which has been run by the unions since 1995) could cut public works funding to wayward sindicatos. In an area where many people do not count on basic amenities, this is a serious threat. One union leader explained in relation to coca control: "If you go to the town hall and your sindicato has not respected the cato [the limit on coca cultivation], it's like having a criminal record. No one will attend to you."

In the Chapare, higher levels of the union are responsible for arbitrating disputes between subordinate levels. For example, if two sindicatos come into conflict, then the duty to solve the problem falls to the central, and so on up the hierarchy. In 2013, I attended a meeting that was convened to solve a conflict between two rival centrals over the boundaries of their respective territories. The meeting was presided over by Don Oscar Comacho (the general secretary of the federation), who asked all present: "How are we going to fight between brothers and sisters? This is not right. We are like a family; if the husband and wife cannot solve a problem, then they take it to their godparent who then solves it for them." In this instance, Don Oscar, as the general secretary of the federation, cast himself as the godparent, positioned in a hierarchical relationship to the centrals. Oscar went on to say, "there is no higher authority that the federation, you have to respect our decision!" Thus, just as in unions elsewhere in Bolivia, "conflict resolution processes highlight the importance of scales of hierarchy" (Lazar 2008: 186).

The notions of equivalence and envy can also be observed at the level of the federation. When driving through the Chapare, the casual observer will be surprised to note the huge number of sports stadiums. There is no apparent justification for the quantity of these expensive and underused facilities, other than the fact that if one sindicato has a stadium, then the neighboring sindicato wants one too. Such public works are thought to be a source of prestige and, in the eyes of coca growers, are an indicator of "development."[12] In the words of one long-serving public functionary at the town hall, "each sindicato wants everything [infrastructure], and they want to have the same, if not bigger and better than the next village."

We have seen how the dynamic processes including the sense of duty, equivalence, and coercion which govern the lives of individual members also apply to the union structure as a whole. In the final section, I zoom out further, to consider how the coca union not only self-governs, but actually assumes the role of the state, so that others who live in the region and have no formal connection to the union are also subject to its authority.

We Are the State

The rain was heavy; it hadn't stopped for the best part of two weeks. I was traveling in the federation's white Chinese-built pickup truck with Don Oscar, the general secretary of Federación Trópico. We arrived at the UMOPAR antinarcotics checkpoint. Here the militarized police search cars for coca paste and chemicals used to process drugs. Don Oscar wound down the window and with a flick of his hand dismissed the police officer who wanted to review the vehicle, with the words *We are the state*. Then a man wearing a blue anorak and holding a clipboard came to the window to collect the road tax. Oscar told him, "We don't pay." With this he accelerated onto the main road and toward town. Oscar commented on the events at the checkpoint: "They know the car, . . . it's very distinctive [on account of the fact it has large stickers promoting the MAS on the side], so they should know that *we are the state*." The subtext here is that the police and tax collector should therefore know not to interfere with him. But of course, Oscar is not the state; he is a union leader and holds no officially recognized public office.

Oscar's claim that "we are the state" makes sense because in many instances, the union actually is. Examples are numerous: local transport firms are required to send a representative to the federations' monthly meeting to provide a report. The union has the power to set fares and routes and to arbitrate disagreements between different firms. The federations exert similar powers over other small businesses operating in the region. For instance, the union would come down hard on shops that sold products that were defective or expensive, and the union frequently closed down bars if they were thought to be disreputable (for example, if they sold alcohol to minors, or if there were fights).

Since the MAS came to power, the union has also been able to exert control over state-owned institutions, including schools (in 2008, the federation fired leaders of the teachers' unions who mobilized against the MAS for a pay rise), hospitals (the federation demands hospital directors provide reports at their meetings), and the state coca monitoring institution (the director is a coca grower who answers to the union); but most surprising of all was the way the union could now command the military. Once thought to be an enemy, the security forces are now at the beck and call of the union. More than once I witnessed Don Oscar call on the local military commanders to send him a squadron of soldiers to undertake heavy manual labor on behalf of the union (for example, moving equipment, construction work, digging holes, and so on). Such work was unpaid and was referred to as "community service." The military would also provide logistical support (such as the loan of trucks), as and when the union required these services.

The union also exercised direct control over state-owned enterprises including the honey, juice, paper, and coca processing plants located in the Chapare (all of these enterprises were built during the MAS administration). In October 2013, I participated in a union commission to provide oversight of the fruit juice processing plant, which had been performing poorly. The commission (consisting of seven union leaders and one municipal councilor), which was headed by Don Oscar, met with the factory's three managers, all of whom were university graduates from the city. Oscar opened the proceedings by stating the reason for the visit. He explained, "We are in government; that means it is our task to monitor you. We have to teach you how to run this place better." A smartly dressed manager, who was male and in his late thirties, acknowledged the shortcomings, but blamed them on technical as opposed to human error. He added, "We have a professional auditor who checks on how we are doing, and he says that we are performing well." This comment irked Oscar, who saw it as a refutation of union authority. In response, Oscar said, "We are going to educate you. You are going to learn to work as we work. When a union leader does not fulfill his role, then his deputy takes over. This is how you are going to work also." With that he fired all three managers on the spot. The point to take from this is that the coca unions are not simply responsible for self-governance; they have increasingly taken on state-like responsibilities in the region at large. We will return to this issue when we consider municipal government in chapter 6.

Conclusion

In this chapter, we have seen how the unions work to address common problems, from administrating land and dealing with transport to managing relationships between members. The unions are also responsible for governing sectors of the economy and state institutions that formally have nothing to do with the union. The Chapare unions, then, represent the region's primary civil authority, practicing a de facto autonomy (Gutierrez Aguilar 2014: 80).

Critics of the unions draw on examples such as the repressive forms of community justice and the sanctions and fines leveled by the unions to describe them as autocratic, coercive, and corrupt. My initial response was to reject such interpretations as simply the racist ideas of the urban elite. I wanted to believe that coca grower militancy was down to individual commitment to an ideal. It's not just that I was naïve; the idea of individual commitment also forms part of the official discourse embodied in the idea that people are "conscientious" (something Morales alluded to in his speech at the rally described at the beginning of this chapter). Over the course of fieldwork, it became increasingly difficult to sustain this view, however. The unions did indeed appear to be hierarchical and authoritarian: indeed, being a member of a sindicato entails submitting oneself to the organization entirely.

There is tension between the idea that within the sindicato everyone is equal, while at the same time the union has the ambition to be like a state, and everyone is kept in check through coercive practices. From the inside, however, this does not look like the dictatorship so feared by external commentators. Through ethnographic examples, we have seen that "dictatorship" is not simply a top-down process but rather an integral part of self-governance. What makes coercion consensual and socially accepted is the fact that the union's goals are said to reflect those of each and every member, thus collapsing the distinction between the power of leaders and the will of the rank and file. However, as we will see in the chapters that follow, it is precisely this link that Morales broke once in power. This, in turn, has led some coca growers to say that today the union really is characterized by "union dictatorship."

This chapter reinforces the need to understand democracy within its own specific cultural context. The "sindicato dictatorship" thesis is informed by an underlying assumption that there is a normative model of democracy, and any deviation from it represents a departure from, rather than a step toward, democracy. The danger in holding a normative view of democracy—and measuring all political practice against this ideal—is that vernacular conceptions are not recognized as legitimate forms of political expression. This chapter alerts us to the fact that there are multiple understandings of what makes a political system moral; thus, the same democratic system could be understood as working properly or in crisis, depending on the observer's perspective. Claims of "dictatorship," then, tell us less about the quality of democracy and more about the mismatch between prevailing political ethics and the normative ideal.

Finally, the case of the Chapare sindicatos disrupts how we think about unions in the West. If a union was composed of extended kinship groups who patrolled the streets at night, intervened in martial disputes, sanctioned its members, and was responsible for local governance, most people in the Global North would label it as nepotistic, vigilante, or corrupt. But these are exactly the characteristics of the coca union. From the coca growers' perspective, anything less holistic just wouldn't be considered a union. The coca union, then, encourages us to think of radical politics anew, transcending the role of a union as a mere vehicle for workers' demands to something much deeper and ingrained in daily life (see also Lazar 2017).

4. From Class to Ethnicity

It was 2007, and Radio Aurora was celebrating its tenth anniversary. The festivities, which extended over three days, included a bicycle race, a marathon, a fireworks display, and live music. The most eagerly anticipated event, however, was a beauty pageant to select the "Sovereign Cholita." In Bolivia, *cholita* is used to describe young single women who wear traditional Andean clothing.[1] In the weeks preceding the contest, Radio Aurora ran an advertisement that stipulated that only *cholitas originarias*—that is, women who habitually wore such clothes and were therefore considered to be "authentic"—would be allowed to compete. The aim was to select the woman who demonstrated the most autochthonous characteristics.[2]

The event took place in the disused market close to the radio station. The audience of more than 500 people was packed tight, and many more stood on chairs and low walls outside the venue. The eight judges were all high-ranking union leaders or municipal officials (both men and women), and each wore a garland of coca (which had been awarded to them by the staff at the radio station in recognition of their status). They sat facing the stage behind a table, which was covered in the colorful flag of the Andean first nations, known as the Wiphala. Grover and Leyla (the reporters) acted as hosts for the night. Both were dressed in green to represent coca leaves. Leyla raised a cheer for the contestants and welcomed them onto the stage. The six young women took turns demonstrating their "traditional" outfit. Each had her hair plaited into two thick braids, and wore a *pollera* (a layered, gathered skirt traditionally worn in highland Quechua- and Aymara-speaking communities), an embroidered blouse, a shawl, and gold earrings. Some of the contestants held a Wiphala and adorned their outfits with coca plants (see figure 4.1). One woman had a handwritten

Figure 4.1. Contestants in the Sovereign Cholita beauty pageant. Photo by author.

note pinned to her blouse, which in Quechua read, "Our traditional cultures should not be forgotten."

Leyla asked each contender a number of questions about her favorite foods, music, and national politics, including naming members of Congress and the Senate. Leyla then asked them to make a short speech about why they should be selected. Most of the women were not confident public speakers and mumbled into the microphone. The person who eventually won the contest, however, gave a rousing speech in which she recounted the story of the battle to defend coca, including a reference to the massacre of Villa Tunari. She ended with one fist in the air and shouted, "Long Live Coca!" The audience responded with rapturous applause. The winner was awarded a set of nine cooking pans along with a sash, tiara, and scepter, which she was informed she could wear at civic events over the following year. All six contestants were honored with garlands of coca and a dusting of confetti in their hair.

While at first sight beauty pageants might appear to be frivolous (and sexist) events, anthropologists have shown how they have been used as platforms to advance political agendas (Besnier 2002; Gustafson 2006). In this case, the aim of the pageant was quite clearly to link coca leaf to an idealized indigenous heritage; coca leaf was worn by the contestants, people were awarded garlands of coca, the emcees wore green to represent coca, and in the speeches, coca leaf was said to be sacred. The beauty contest surprised me because, having lived among the coca growers for some time by then, I knew that identity politics were of little interest to many. Sure, most people were involved in coca production, and coca leaf had genuine sacred value, but the kind of overidentification with the leaf, externalized here in the selection of the authentic Sovereign Cholita, did not resonate with everyday life. On the contrary, if people held onto any identity, it was the tradition that they had inherited from the valley peasants and miners, namely a class-based one.

While the coca growers' unions are indigenous, in that they are composed of Quechua speakers, it is not an indigenous movement per se. Indigeneity is not a salient aspect of people's identity; indeed, most coca growers do not consider themselves to be indigenous, a label they associate with a set of negative characteristics. Class is still important in how politics is organized internally, and the sindicato looks quite different from the traditional ayllu form of community organization, which was described in the previous chapter. Moreover, the unions have never made specifically ethnic demands; rather, they have always revolved around addressing material concerns, principally the right to land and the legalization of coca leaf production. In this chapter I try to make sense of this seeming contradiction. I ask: How and why has indigenous politics taken center stage? And what are the consequences of this shift?

In what follows I argue that it was by no means inevitable that the coca growers would mobilize around indigenous cultural difference in order to justify their oppositional politics. In the face of militarized coca eradication campaigns, the coca growers mobilized to defend their right to grow coca. However, the criminalized nature of coca meant that the arguments inherited from the miners regarding class and the right to dignified work were no longer valid. The farmers needed a new discourse, one that would legitimate why they should be given the right to grow coca that extended beyond their immediate economic requirements: indigeneity was one way this could be achieved. This shift in discourse reflected a broader turn toward indigenous rights that occurred throughout the Americas in the early 1990s. As we will see, this strategy opened political space and enabled the farmers to articulate their demands, but it has also silenced others, an issue that we will return to in the conclusion.

We Aren't Indigenous

Pablo Montero stood on a stage in the sports coliseum at Lauca Eñe, the headquarters for the Six Federations. Two hundred delegates rested on the banked seating, chewing coca and sweating in the midday heat. The meeting had been called in preparation for the inauguration of the assembly to rewrite the constitution in August 2006. Aware that presidents from all over Latin America, not to mention the world's media, would be present in Sucre for the inaugural "First Nations Parade," the union leaders had decided to go well prepared, including dedicating one day to practice marching in an orderly fashion.

Pablo's voice crackled over the microphone. "All of Bolivia's thirty-six ethnic groups will be there, wearing their traditional costumes, the Yuquis, the Yuracarés, Mojeños, Tsimanes, Trinitarios, the Guaranis. . . . They are all going to be there with their feathers and face paint, their typical costumes. Us, the Six Federations, we are not going to be outdone. We also have to march in the typical dress of the Cochabamba Tropics." I was surprised by this announcement, because as far as I was aware the farmers had no traditional costume to speak of. Pablo went on: "And so it has been decided that the men shall wear black shoes, dark blue trousers with a pale blue shirt, and women will wear a blue pollera [the layered skirt mentioned above], a light blue blouse, and a white hat." Some women rebelled, shouting, "I'm not wearing a pollera!" and "I don't even own one!"[3] After battling for half an hour over what constituted appropriate "traditional dress," it was decided that at the very least it should be predominantly blue. Pablo returned to the stage to sum up: "So then, we are the blue soldiers, just like the Venezuelans are the red soldiers . . . this is our uniform, and with the flags as well . . . we are going to make an impact!"

On the way home after the event, I traveled with Don Hugo Zurita in his old Toyota Corolla, which vibrated ferociously as we bounced along the cobbled road. Shouting over the din, Don Hugo asked if there were indigenous people in my home country (the United Kingdom). The four passengers crammed into the back seat leaned forward to catch my answer. I explained that the UK was populated by waves of immigration going back millennia and that nobody could really claim to be a native. To this Hugo exclaimed, "Ah, so everyone is from elsewhere? You are people who have no culture or traditions then, not like us, we are Originarios [first peoples]." Hugo's self-assured declaration that he and his passengers were "first peoples," proud descendants of the Quechua nation,[4] hides a more complex story, however. Many Bolivians have indigenous roots, but, as Andrew Canessa argues, "no longer identify closely with the life-ways and cultural values of their communities of origin" (Canessa 2014: 20). The coca farmers have an ambivalent relationship to their status as an indigenous people: they self-consciously debate their "typical dress" (which is nothing more than "predominantly blue"), and, as is evident from Pablo's comments, they see themselves as quite different from (if not superior to) those who paint their faces and wear feathers in their hair.

Alison Brysk (2000: 6) describes how there is an enormous diversity among those who self-identify as indigenous in South and Central America. For her, the most fundamental distinction is that between highland and lowland peoples. Brysk notes how highland indigenous peoples are mountain peasants, heirs of the Inca and Aztec empires. Most speak Spanish (as a second or even their only language), live in urban areas, and often work in the informal economy. Lowland indigenous peoples, meanwhile, inhabit jungle and savannah areas, and some rely on hunting, fishing, and gathering for their subsistence. These dispersed, egalitarian, clan-based societies are much smaller in number and have been in contact with outsiders for only a few generations. In Bolivia lowland peoples refer to themselves as *pueblos indígenas* (indigenous people), and highland peoples have adopted the term *pueblos originarios* (first peoples).

Highland Quechua and Aymara speakers have been settled agriculturalists for thousands of years and involved with states and markets for at least five hundred (Larson and Harris 1995). These highland peasants do not consider themselves to be indigenous: for them the real "indigenas" are the lowland peoples, whom they have on occasion classed as savages and see as very different from themselves (see Canessa 2012b). The majority of coca growers hail from either the Cochabamba valleys or the mining centers, both areas where people traditionally did not self-identify as indigenous. Brooke Larson (1988) points out how many Cochabamba Indians escaped the hacienda system, and managed to migrate to become miners, smallhold farmers, or workers in textile production. Thus, ideas about class and *mestizaje* (race mixture) took hold early on in the Cochabamba valleys (see also Rivera 1987: 150). For their part, the miners embraced modernity in the form of Marxism and considered themselves to be proletarians, and despite being of indigenous peasant origin, they saw the indigenous groups surrounding the mining centers as backward (Harris and Albó 1976; Platt 1983).[5]

To this day, coca growers, be they of valley peasant or miner origin, continue to resist being labeled as indigenous. For example, when I asked my neighbor Don Waldo Delgado if he was indigenous, he looked offended, saying, "Hell no, we are not indigenous!" He insisted that his parents had been miners, lived in the city, and were therefore modern. When I spoke to my friend Sergio Cayo, whose parents came from the Cochabamba valleys, he insisted that he was a mestizo, even if he spoke Quechua. To make sense of these comments, it is instructive to take a closer look at the coca growers' relationship with lowland indigenous peoples, including the Yuracarés, Yuquis, and Trinitario-Mojenos who live among them, and who the coca growers identify as being the *real indigenas* or *los tribus* (the tribes).

The Indigenous Territory and National Park Isiboró-Securé (more often known by its Spanish acronym, TIPNIS), located in the Tropics of Cochabamba, is home to forty-seven Amazonian indigenous communities totaling over 4,500 people (Yashar 2005: 206). A red line demarcates the agricultural colonization area of the Chapare from TIPNIS. In theory, the coca growers are not allowed to cross the imaginary line; however, in practice this rule is seldom respected. Farmers regularly enter indigenous lands to plant coca, fish, hunt, and engage in illegal logging. Land invasions have on occasion provoked violent conflicts. I was told stories of farmers being attacked by "wild savages" with bows and arrows, and counterattacks on the part of farmers armed with bolt-action riffles.

Any narrative of colonization is one that needs to justify its acts of violence: commonly done through terra nullius, the idea of the untouched land, or of the land being underused or empty. This includes not only the physical environment; it is also a statement about the people who may live in it (Stocks 2005: 87). In the Chapare, the rhetoric is no different; during fieldwork I constantly came across acts of *othering* as the coca growers (read: colonizers) made conceptual boundaries between themselves and their lowland indigenous others (read: colonized). One farmer told me: "Most of them [Yuracarés] ran away into the jungle, but some of them have become civilized already. They didn't want to give up their lands . . . but we conquered them with alcohol, cigarettes, and salt."

Don Raymundo Rodríguez, a coca grower and local deputy mayor, and hence a person of significant local importance, described the predominant understanding of the lowland indigenous minority in the following terms, "A lot of people [coca farmers] do not respect their rights. They look at them as if. . . . How can I say? They look down on them, as if they are inferior, of a lower rank, just like that."[6] Coca farmers were particularly aggrieved about lowland indigenous mobilization, which had halted the construction of a new road in the Chapare in 2011.[7]

Coca growers do not consider themselves to be "indigenous," a label they associate with being backward, dirty, and uncivilized. And yet at the same time they present themselves to outsiders as overtly indigenous, and hold elaborate events like the beauty pageant described at the start of this chapter to celebrate this identity. To understand this seeming paradox, we need to understand how throughout the 1980s and 1990s indigeneity came to be a recognized language within the landscape of Bolivian politics, and why the coca farmers have latched onto this concept as a powerful political trope.

Indigenous Politics

Over the past thirty years, as class-based movements have lost their central role (as exemplified by the declining influence of the COB in Bolivia), peasants and workers have embraced an international language of indigenous rights to articulate their demands, fitting into what Tania Murray Li (2000) has referred to as the "tribal" or "indigenous peoples slot." The San of Botswana (Solway 2009), Adivasis in India (Shah 2010; Steur 2009), dispossessed peasants in southern Mexico (Harvey 1998; Nash 1995), and Afro-descendent movements in Colombia and Central America (Anderson 2007; Ng'weno 2007) are all arguing for rights to land, citizenship, and resources based on the fact that they are indigenous. Thus, indigenous culture now plays an essential role in the construction of collective identities and in making claims against the state in Latin America and beyond (Jackson and Warren 2005; Lucero 2008).

There are a number of reasons why indigenous movements became so important in the 1990s. Peter Wade (2007: 112–50) explains that, on the one hand, neoliberal reforms, with their promotion of free markets and the withdrawal of the state, hit indigenous peoples particularly hard (see Hall and Patrinos 2005). But, on the other hand, they also advanced a progressive pro-democracy, multicultural agenda. For example, in Bolivia the first Sanchez de Lozada administration (1993–97) signed the International Labor Organization's Convention 169 on indigenous rights and pushed through amendments to the constitution that recognized Bolivia as a multicultural and pluri-ethnic nation.[8] While some academics have been highly critical of multicultural reforms, seeing them as a way to contain indigenous mobilization (Hale 2002), others have noted that these concessions opened spaces for new forms of political expression and participation of various kinds (Gustafson 2009; Postero 2007; Yashar 2005). Second, over the past twenty years, multilateral organizations as well as transnational NGOs have increasingly come to promote the development and protection of the rights of indigenous people and have provided vital support networks (Andolina, Laurie, and Radcliffe 2009; Brysk 2000; Rappaport 2005). In this context, being a "hyper-real Indian" (Ramos 1998: 267–83), offers marginalized groups certain advantages.

But while indigeneity has empowered some marginal groups, there have also been voices of warning. Adam Kuper (2003) has cautioned about the ways in which new forms of racism are likely to emerge with the resurrection of essentialist notions of identity. Peter Geschiere (2009) has examined just this issue, showing how in Cameroon the question of who belongs is pertinent in political struggles between tribes, but how the same vocabulary emerges in debates over the integration of immigrants in Holland. Others have noted how those who are less able to present themselves as indigenous are excluded from access to special rights, despite being equally poor and marginalized (Hooker 2005; Stocks 2005). Anna Tsing (2007: 52) argues that "frames for indigeneity are also spaces for disagreement. Not everyone can fit into these frames."

To understand Bolivia's contemporary "indigenous awakening" (Albó 2008a), we need to go back to the 1952 National Revolution. At that time the MNR government attempted to assimilate the indigenous population through the homogenizing and modernizing discourse of mestizaje, or race mixture. Under the new regime the pejorative term *Indians* was abandoned in favor of the term *campesinos* (peasants). The government encouraged indigenous groups to establish peasant unions to replace traditional Andean forms of community organization (the ayllu). Silvia Rivera Cusicanqui writes that the liberal reforms instituted after 1952 relied on a "cultural package of behavioral prescriptions designed to turn the unruly but 'passive' Indian into an active mestizo 'citizen': property-owning, integrated into the capitalist market, and 'castilianized' (speaking Spanish)" (Rivera Cusicanqui 2010, cited in Postero 2017: 9).

From 1952 onward, mestizaje became the dominant model for citizenship in Bolivia; everyone was considered to be equal, and the only difference was supposed to be one of class. The official disavowal of race did not mean that racism disappeared, however. From her work in highland Peru (where similar policies were rolled out), Marisol de la Cadena (1998) explains how racism became silent through the historical transformation of concepts of race into concepts of culture. Dress, education, residence, work, musical tastes, concepts of hygiene, and food preferences became crucial markers of whiteness or nonwhiteness, irrespective of the color of a person's skin (see also Colloredo-Mansfeld 1998; de la Cadena 1999; Orlove 1998). Peter Wade (1993) also challenges the idea that "race mixture" is liberating, showing how in Colombia mestizaje is not actually about mixture, but rather is a process of social and cultural whitening.

Mestizaje only succeeded in burying ethnic politics for a short period of time in Bolivia. In the early 1970s, a small group of highland Aymaras, inspired by the pro-Indian intellectual Fausto Reinaga, began to organize as a union, blending class and ethnic discourses. Known as Katarismo, the movement took its name from Tupaj Katari, the eighteenth-century anticolonial rebel. Activists argued that the discrimination and oppression indigenous peasants experienced was a result of their subaltern class position but also had cultural roots. In the 1973 "Manifesto of Tiwanaku," the Kataristas classified social hierarchies as a continuation of the colonial situation, which made Indians "foreigners in their own land" (Albó 2008a; Escárzaga 2012a). Their influence swelled throughout the period of military dictatorship, especially once the military–peasant pact disintegrated following the 1974 massacre of campesinos in the Cochabamba valleys. The Kataristas eventually split into two separate factions, one that worked with the government (making indigenous activist Victor Hugo Cardenas vice president in the first Gonzalo Sánchez de Lozada administration) and another more rebellious and radical path led by peasant leader Felipe Quispe.

The Kataristas' message of cultural revivalism began to have an impact on national peasant organizations. In 1983, Bolivia's largest peasant union, the CSUTCB, published its own manifesto, which featured ethnic demands for the first time, including the demand for amendments to the constitution to recognize Bolivia as a multicultural and pluri-ethnic nation[9] (Ticona, Rojas, and Albó 1995: 42). The traditional left, led by the miners, was vehemently opposed to these kinds of ethnic demands, which they considered to be irrelevant or, worse still, dangerous, as they represented a form of "false consciousness" that obstructed class unity and revolution (Escobar 2008; Harris and Albó 1976). However, just as ethnicity became an important force in national peasant politics, workers' unions were declining in organizational strength as a result of the neoliberal onslaught on labor.

Lowland indigenous peoples also began to organize throughout the 1980s, creating the Confederation of Indigenous Peoples of the Bolivian Orient (CIDOB) in 1984. CIDOB came to national prominence in 1990 when it staged the "March for Territory and Dignity." Eight hundred men, women, and children walked over 1,000 km to La Paz from Trinidad to demand territory, autonomy, and special rights that would allow them to maintain their ways of life as indigenous peoples. There was a high level of media interest in the march, and it pressured the government to classify over 1.5 million hectares of land as "indigenous territories" over the objections of local ranchers and loggers (Albó 2008b: 41–42). Aymara communities in Bolivia's southern highlands also pursued a more autochthonous form of organization, and made efforts to reconstruct the ayllus through their organization, the National Council of Ayllus and Markas of Qullasuyu, or CONAMAQ as it is known by its Spanish acronym, which formed in 1997 (Albó 2008b: 54–56; Stephenson 2002).

This ethnic upsurge was not restricted to the Aymara altiplano and indigenous lowland territories, but gripped the entire nation. Scholars have noted that over the past twenty-five years there has been an explosion of cultural affirmation in Bolivian society at large. Throughout the 1990s, ever-increasing numbers of people reclaimed an indigenous identity, including those who lived in urban areas, did not speak an indigenous language, or even belong to a recognized indigenous group (Goodale 2006). In the 2001 census, an unprecedented 62 percent of the population recorded themselves as indigenous. These are the people who support Morales and the MAS: the poorest two-thirds of society including slum dwellers, workers, peasants, and of course the coca growers. The important issue to make clear here, then, is that the term *pueblos originarios*, or first peoples, places the emphasis on the legitimacy of political claims, rather than expressing some kind of racial essence (Canessa 2006).

Morales capitalized on this emerging ethnic identification. Andrew Canessa (2012a: 18) has argued that in contemporary Bolivia, "indigeneity is the foundation of a new nationalism." And yet, while the MAS government has used indigenous history as a means to reinforce alliances with social movements and to claim legitimacy, it has not always acted on behalf of indigenous people. Over the past ten years, the government has bypassed its own prior consultation laws and repressed indigenous mobilization against the state's large-scale infrastructure and extractionist projects (Canessa 2014; Fabricant and Gustafson 2011; Rossell Arce 2012). Nancy Postero (2017: 5) argues that "indigeneity has been transformed in Bolivia from a site of emancipation to one of liberal nation-state building."

The Glorification of the Sacred Leaf

As we have seen, historically the people who migrated to the Chapare identified themselves as peasants or workers, they mobilized around class-based discourses, and, lacking any regional history that they could claim as their own, there was no further elaboration of collective self-identity (García Linera, Chávez, and Costas 2004: 383–457; Gutierrez Aguilar 2014: 74–78). This all changed in the mid-1980s, when impending antinarcotics legislation (Law 1008) threatened to outlaw coca plantations in the region.

Given the mounting success of identity-based movements elsewhere in Bolivia (and Latin America more broadly), not to mention the diminishing power of the left, it is hardly surprising that union leaders consciously opted to pursue a form of indigenous politics. Deborah Yashar (2005: 189–90) writes: "The cocaleros saw the positive reception gained by the Kataristas and started to frame their struggle as one about indigenous rights. They banked on the perception that an ethnic struggle would resonate more powerfully than one for production alone. Hence they shifted their prior class-based rhetoric to one about indigenous traditions and pride." Likewise, Nancy Postero (2017: 6) notes how, as leader of the coca unions, Morales "originally emphasized class distinctions and anti-imperialism rather than ethnic demands, but during the multicultural 1990s, Morales gradually 'Indianized' his position, making indigeneity a central part of his public persona and political agenda."

In 1992, as part of the events marking five hundred years since the Spanish conquest, or "the invasion" as it is referred to by indigenous activists (Hale 1994), Evo Morales met with indigenous leaders from elsewhere in Latin America, including Nobel Prize winner Rigoberta Menchu from Guatemala. According to anthropologist Xavier Albó (2008b: 60), Morales drew inspiration from these international leaders and introduced the vocabulary of indigenous rights to the union movement, including the slogan "five hundred years of indigenous resistance." The notion that the coca farmers self-consciously pursued indigenous politics is no secret. A Bolivian film charting the life of Evo Morales, titled *Evo Pueblo* (Antezana 2007), which was shown at Bolivian cinemas, makes much of this issue. One hour into the movie, a coca union leader says to Morales: "Listen to me Evo, I was thinking about how we can expand our struggle, and I said to myself, the cocaleros, well we have to do something so that people recognize us as an indigenous movement. . . . What do you think?"

Being recognized by others as an indigenous movement was no simple task, however. The Chapare campesinos' status as an uprooted multicultural population meant that they were patently unable to claim any cultural heritage as traditional coca growers, in the way that the Aymaras in the La Paz Yungas could (coca has been grown in the Yungas of La Paz for centuries and was classified as a legal traditional coca growing zone under Law 1008). The Chapare farmers sidestepped the issue of their lack of indigenous credentials by focusing their attention on the coca leaf instead. Coca leaf went from being something that had previously been totally irrelevant to public self-identification, to being the "millennial coca leaf," absolutely entwined with the self-conscious presentation of an indigenous movement (García Linera, Chávez, and Costas 2004: 438–42). While coca always had sacred value, it was only in the 1980s that it became part of the collective identity of the union. By defending the *hoja sagrada* (sacred leaf), coca growers could make demands against the state without having to present themselves as authentically indigenous (or for that matter admit their true motivation for growing coca). For example, the 1993 Machu Picchu Manifesto, drafted by the Council for the Defense of Coca (CAPHC by its Spanish acronym), of which Evo Morales was the president, states that:

> The eradication of the coca leaf would be, for our Andean people, death. Because for us coca is everything: our material survival, our myths, our cosmo-vision of the world, the happiness to live, the word of our ancestors, the constant dialogue with the Pachamama, our reason to be in this world. In sum, the fight for the revaluation and defense of the coca leaf synthesizes all of these demands that today give meaning to our lives and without which there will be no future. *It is the symbol and the representation of our identity.* (CAPHC 1993; my translation)

This message of cultural activism is echoed in contemporary federation documents. For example, Federación Trópico's 2012 statutes affirm that "Coca leaf is our cultural patrimony, it's sacred, and the symbol of the Andean culture of the Aymaras, Quechuas, and all the first peoples of the entire country" (FETCTC 2012: 12). And the union membership card has "Long Live Coca, Death to Yankees" emblazoned on the back of it. The novelty of mobilizing under the banner of "sacred coca" is exemplified by the fact that Fausto Reinaga (1969: 100, 127), a pioneer of Bolivian indigenism and the founder of the Bolivian Indian Party (PIB), was vocally opposed to coca, which he characterized as an "opium of the masses" and as a "vice" (equivalent to alcohol) that "subdues the revolutionary spirit of indigenous peasants."

Indigenous activists have a long history of using public performance and spectacle to make themselves visible to national and international audiences (Conklin 1997; Turner 1995). To make the sacred status of coca explicit to the wider world, Chapare peasant farmers have organized a range of events including coca chew-ins, folk music festivals, and annual coca fairs in the cities (Healy 1997). Members of the coca union undertake public rituals in which coca plays a highly visible role (such as the beauty contest we saw at the beginning of this chapter), award garlands of coca to visiting dignitaries, and even run courses on how to cook with coca.

Within the Chapare, Radio Aurora has been absolutely essential for the "politicization of the cultural" (Alvarez, Dagnino, and Escobar 1998). A mural painted on the station's wall summarizes the editorial line well: it depicts an old man wearing a ch'ulo (a traditional Andean hat), his check bulging with coca; beneath is written the proverb: "For us the coca leaf is the culture of our ancestors . . . For them it causes insanity and idiocy." The union leaders and reporters who speak on the radio reiterate a standard message. These interlocutors place the Chapare within its global context. They point out how unjust it is that their native coca has been eradicated by troops serving foreign interests. They explain that coca is sacred and is definitely not cocaine. If only it was legal, they say, then the rest of the world would also be able to benefit from this special leaf. The DJs broadcast national music, and the lyrics of many of these songs refer to coca and its importance to indigenous culture (Bigenho 1998). The coca growers' anthem (which is broadcast several times a day) is a song called "Kawsachun Coca" (Long live coca); the chorus goes: "The coca leaf, they won't touch it, because it is native and it's esteemed. Long live coca—Death to Yankees." Another song rhymes "go home Yankee" with "get out of the Chapare."

In the hands of the Bolivian coca growers, culture represents a powerful political tool. By articulating the coca farmers' material demands (the right to grow coca) with a broader cultural and ethnic nationalist dimension, sacred coca offered the peasants a moral justification allowing them to reach out and form alliances with other sectors including workers, peasants, and even members of the urban middle classes (Gutierrez Aguilar 2014: 84; Laserna 1999; Sanabria 1999). Support for the coca farmers and their party became so formidable in the 1990s that former President Sanchez de Lozada admitted, "Our big problem is that the Bolivian people are against narco-trafficking but they are for these farmers" (Sanabria 1999: 553).

The coca farmers' ability to rally public opinion on their behalf can be traced to two factors. First, coca use is widespread and is considered an essential daily requirement for many people; thus in Bolivia we see strong sentiments of what Paul Gootenberg (2016) has referred to as "coca nationalism." Defending coca meant standing up against the United States and the deeply unpopular neoliberal policies. Second, the coca–cocaine trade brought in hard currency; thus U.S.-backed crop eradication sent shock waves throughout the entire economy and came to be viewed not simply as an attack on peasants living in a remote area of the country, but rather as an attack on everyone's livelihoods (Sanabria 1999). In this context, coca leaf can be viewed as an empty signifier (Laclau 2005), tying together diverse demands under a potent banner of anti-imperial resistance.

While noting the union's success at mobilizing coca as an ethno-nationalist symbol, it is important to bear in mind that the union does not have a monopoly over its symbolic capital. In Latin America there is a long tradition in which ostensibly indigenous cultural forms have been appropriated for nation-building projects (Bigenho 2006; Flores-Galindo 1987; Mendez 1996; Rowe and Schelling 1991), and coca is no different. Over the years, various presidents following anti-coca policies have worn a lacquered coca leaf as a badge on their lapel (Healy 1997), and the Bolivian pavilion presented coca leaf with great pride at the 1992 World's Fair in Seville.[10] In a similar inversion, during the years of forced eradication, the coca federation played on existing beliefs that came from the mass media about their dangerous character and the threat they posed to the existing order, while concomitantly trying to dispose of these images. On occasion the coca federation even explicitly acknowledged that coca leaf goes to make cocaine and used the threat of planting more coca in order to gain leverage over the government (Healy 1997). Further Raquel Gutierrez Aguilar (2014: 82) notes how in numerous forums, interviews, and public appearances, coca growers argued that they should be allowed to grow coca because Bolivia was committed to the free market and they had found a highly profitable productive niche.

Building a political identity rooted in sacred coca has obviously benefited the agricultural union, allowing it to build bridges with other movements. However, the focus on coca has proved double-edged: it works as a unifier, but it is also strongly connected with cocaine in national and international agendas, making the farmers vulnerable to the "war on drugs" (and terror). The ambiguous status of coca is amplified by some cocaleros, who publicly accuse other cocaleros (in the Chapare or in other more "traditional" coca growing regions such as the Yungas) of only growing coca for the drug trade.

The Yungas de Vandiola

In late September 2006, members of the security forces entered the Vandiola region to uproot coca bushes. The local population attempted to block them from entering what they claimed was a legal "traditional growing area" (Bolivia's antidrug Law 1008 permits two hundred hectares of coca in this region). In the disturbance that followed, two peasants were shot and killed. The local population eventually overpowered the militarized police and held them hostage for two days (*La Prensa* 2006). Soon after this incident the human rights ombudsman visited the community to verify what had happened. A shaky video made by the commission pans around to show the basic houses made from nylon tarps and roughly cut wood. The camera then focuses on the cache of arms the peasants had confiscated from the militarized police, and ends with a close-up of the two dead bodies. Following this, the video provides a series of testimonials from local farmers, who decry the violence meted out by the security forces. A union leader faces the camera and stresses that the Vandiola coca growers are not at all like their Chapare counterparts, but are "proper natives" who should be allowed to grow coca. Referring to a map, the leader indicates that the conflict took place in a traditional area where coca cultivation is legal. He acknowledges that if they had been growing coca further to the east (in the national park), that would be illegal and would not be traditional. He says, "We are in the traditional zone. We are in the Yungas, comrades. We are natives. We live here, we are not Chapareños [people from the Chapare]." The connection between place, identity, and legitimacy is striking.

While the Vandiola farmers claimed that this was an unprovoked attack, UMOPAR (the militarized police force) officials maintained that the peasants ambushed them with help from foreign mafias. The Morales administration accepted the security forces' portrayal of the confrontation, and characterized the incident as "a premeditated and planned attack by drug traffickers" (*Opinión* 2006a).[11] Following the incident, Radio Aurora sided with the government and broadcast negative messages about the Vandiola farmers, with the announcer repeatedly referring to them as drug traffickers. The announcer declared: "The laziest has three hectares, but some have sixteen! Imagine what that would be worth? With that kind of money I would probably go crazy . . . they have never fought for the right to grow coca, they just sat there quietly while we suffered, turning their coca into *mamita dolares* [money], you know? The white factory [cocaine production]! But now their coca is being eradicated, they don't like it, and they claim it's a traditional area!" In this narrative the allegation that Vandiola farmers are involved in cocaine production is used as a way to demonize and delegitimize them.

I was at home helping my landlord Don Jose Meneses pack dried coca to be sold at market. Jose was up to his waist in a sack jumping up and down to compress the coca. As we worked we listened to the breakfast show on the radio, and yet again the announcer spoke at length about the Yungas de Vandiola. Don Jose nodded in agreement: "They are not real cocaleros," he told me. "They are not organized like we are. Vandiola is at altitude; the coca in Vandiola can only be harvested once every six months and the leaves are far thicker. . . . You can't chew that coca. It is only good for one thing, dancing on!" With this Don Jose was telling me that Vandiola coca goes directly to the maceration pit to be transformed into cocaine (here dancing refers to the act of stomping the coca leaves). Doña Mercedes put her head around the kitchen door. "See what they do in Vandiola? It hurts me what they do with our poor little coca!" Doña Mercedes's comment was clearly for my benefit; she wanted to distance her community from the connection to cocaine production.

Seven years later, in November 2013, I attended the first-ever meeting that bought together diverse subfederations from the Yungas de Vandiola region. The meeting was held against the backdrop of yet another violent conflict between coca growers and government eradication forces, but this time in the Apolo region close to La Paz (a lower-altitude zone that is not recognized as legal under Law 1008) (Castellón 2013). In her opening speech, Vandiola coca union leader Silvia Cruz recalled the deaths of 2006, and referred to the dead as "martyrs." She went on to repeat the same arguments that were made in the video, including the fact that the Vandiola coca growers have been present in the region since long before the designation of the area as a national park. The proof she offered was that their coca plants are old (*macho cocas*), bequeathed "from our grandfathers and our grandfather's fathers." She said that given their long-term residence in the region, they should be respected as a "traditional area" with special rights to grow coca. Cruz did not miss the opportunity to deride the Chapare farmers, whom she classified as *gente nueva* (new settlers). She pointed out that all of the Chapare coca goes to drug trafficking; "Chapare coca has lost its cultural value," she said.

It is not just Vandiola coca growers who verbally attack the Chapare. Leaders from the Association of Coca Producers of the Yungas of La Paz (la Asociación de Productores de Coca de los Yungas—ADEPCOCA) have also repeatedly stated that Chapare coca is only fit for cocaine production. In 2017, the president of ADEPCOCA, Franklin Gutiérrez, told Bolivian journalists, "Everyone knows that the production from the Chapare does not go to traditional consumption, for chewing. This coca is larger and thicker and hurts the tongue." He went on to say, "Our coca [from the Yungas] goes for the *pijcheo* [to be chewed], to drivers, workers, miners, and others who consume our leaf. The leaf from the Yungas is sweet, it's purer, you can chew it" (Burgos Gallardo 2017). But as coca production in the Yungas has expanded to become the most important in the country, inevitably a considerable amount of it is used for cocaine production (Farthing and Ledebur 2015: 14).

The examples above show how coca is used as a political football. The coca growers from Vandiola, the Yungas of La Paz, and the Chapare all maintain that their coca is sacred and that it is "the emblem of our identity." However, they also claim that coca produced in rival areas is not sacred and is only intended for cocaine production. This process of othering constitutes an attack against the rival regions' legitimacy. The fact that coca growers support anti-coca policies when they are carried out in other regions clearly undermines their alleged unconditional commitment to the native shrub. This schism reveals the political and economic motivations behind the manipulated coca identity, namely that the Chapare coca growers present coca as sacred and therefore untouchable in order to defend their economic interests.

Conclusion

Coca is undeniably important to the Chapare coca growers; people genuinely see it as sacred and an essential part of their daily life. And yet historically coca was not important for determining social identities in the Chapare. Indigeneity as an avenue for political action only became important in the 1990s, and was a powerful way for the coca growers to critique U.S. domination exercised through drug war policies. To this day, indigeneity has continued to be an important trope for the farmers because it allows them to speak about their common interests without having to invoke what they cannot openly admit—that much of the coca they produce feeds into the drug trade. For the coca farmers, then, a claim to indigeneity is at heart a demand to have their livelihoods respected and to live free from oppression. It is not a demand for cultural rights.

Some commentators consider the sudden appearance of farmers mobilizing around indigenous identity in the Chapare as a fraud; the cultural traditions they lay claim to are considered to be invented and therefore fake (see, for example, *El Día* 2012a; Gómez 2006b; Paulovich 2013). This is a gray area; arguably, the coca growers' deployment of millennial coca has been invented for political ends. But, as Eric Hobsbawm (1995) has astutely pointed out, all traditions were invented at one time or another, and so the fact that they were invented recently does not make them any less authentic (see also Sahlins 1999). In this case, the people who are doing the inventing are the same Quechua and Aymara speakers who have suffered a long history of racism, injustice, and violence at the hands of a white(er) mestizo elite.

Anthropologists have long argued that ethnicity is best thought of as a relational concept rather than the sum of distinct "authentic" properties, something that can only ever be observed "on the margins" (Astuti 1995; Barth 1969; Cohen 1967). The same lessons hold true for modern indigenous identities as well. Marisol de la Cadena and Orin Starn (2007: 4) state that "indigeneity emerges only within larger social fields of difference and sameness; it acquires its 'positive' meaning not from some essential properties of its own, but through its relation to what it is not, to what it exceeds or lacks." If we avoid essentialist notions of indigeneity, then we can see it principally as a rights discourse. Thus, as Andrew Canessa (2008: 355) has argued: "A claim to indigeneity is a claim to justice based not simply on historical priority but a sense of historical injustice." From this perspective, we can understand how, for the coca growers, indigeneity is not defined by a deep history of blood and soil; rather, it is rooted in postcolonial identities and a shared struggle against the domination of foreign and national elites, embodied in the idea of the sacred coca leaf.

Moving away from debates over authenticity, it is important to ask about the implications of the shift from a politics based on class to one based on ethnicity. Žižek (1997) has urged leftists to recognize the futility of particularistic struggles over identity that leave intact global processes of capital accumulation. For Bolivia's coca growers, identity politics is a very limited tool for advancing their rights: it depoliticizes people, as they have to hide their real economic or political interests. The implications of this are clearly illustrated in the case of the Yungas de Vandiola: identity politics creates a situation where people compete to be the most authentic, the most indigenous, and the most believable of all. Ultimately, they end up disempowering one another and drawing attention to their own fragile political identity. This is counterproductive given that both sets of farmers have very similar interests, namely the continued right to cultivate coca.

5. Community Coca Control

In November 2013, I was traveling in a pickup truck with German Siles, the person responsible for the economic development wing of the state coca monitoring institution, the Economic and Social Development Unit of the Tropics (Unidad de Desarrollo Económico y Social del Trópico de Cochabamba—UDESTRO). German complained that even with the MAS in power people still saw him as the enemy. "They [the coca growers] call us the Wolves . . . but it's not like that, we are there to help." UDESTRO's mission is to regulate coca production in the Chapare (including coordinating the eradication of illegal plantations) and to encourage peasant farmers to grow crops other than coca. German told me that it was a difficult task; "for them coca is monumental, it's sacred, it's everything, they died to defend it. So how can I suggest alternatives?" Later that same day at a union meeting where German was scheduled to give a talk about GPS technology, a group of peasants joked with him. They told German that their coca was infected with a terrible disease; when he inquired further, they responded, "UDESTRO . . . the plague is UDESTRO!" They fell about laughing and patting each other on the back. While this was a joke, there was a more serious message behind it that German understood only too well: the peasant farmers were unhappy about the limits imposed on coca cultivation.

On coming to power, President Morales widened the break with the U.S.-backed antidrug strategy (which focused on the forced eradication of coca leaf and the criminalization of coca growers) that had begun in 2004 under President Carlos Mesa. The new policy, often referred to as "coca yes, cocaine no," draws on the coca growers' own distinction between coca leaf and cocaine. On the one hand, the strategy legalized the cultivation of a small amount of coca leaf in specific zones, encouraged the coca unions to self-police to ensure growers did not exceed this limit, and envisioned the industrialization and export of coca-based products. On the other hand, the government vigorously pursued drug traffickers and attacked cocaine production. The overriding aim of the policy was to reduce harm to coca grower communities.

The new approach, which has been hailed by drug policy reformers, has shrunk coca cultivation and has had various positive impacts, including dramatically cutting human rights violations and allowing some coca growers to diversify their sources of income (Grisaffi 2016; Grisaffi and Ledebur 2016). A *New York Times* (2016) editorial recently concluded that Bolivia's drug strategy is "showing more promise than Washington's forced-eradication model." But while the new strategy has achieved a great deal, as the comments made to German suggest, not all coca growers are happy about it.

This chapter describes how peasant farmers who depend on coca for their livelihoods have experienced a range of coca control policies. The first section outlines the harms associated with U.S.-backed crop eradication and the failure of U.S.-financed development programs to offer peasant farmers realistic alternative livelihoods. The chapter then introduces Bolivia's new coca control strategy in more detail and considers grassroots assessments of it. The conclusion reflects on the challenge Morales faces in balancing grassroots demands for the right to subsistence with his commitment to the international community to cut coca and drug production.

Crop Eradication

Bolivia has always been beholden to external powers, be they the Spanish, the British, the International Monetary Fund, or the United States (Bulmer-Thomas and Dunkerley 1999; Drake 2006; Fernández 2004). But nowhere is Bolivia's contemporary lack of sovereign control more evident than in the domain of antidrug policies, which have largely been dictated from Washington (Grandin 2006: 215–18). In 1986 the United States launched the Triennial Plan, which focused on crop eradication and interdiction operations in Bolivia and Peru. In July of that year, the United States sent six Blackhawk helicopters and 160 U.S. military personnel to assist Bolivian law enforcement to destroy drug labs ("Operation Blast Furnace"). Shortly after, in 1988, the Regulation of Coca and Controlled Substances Law, known as Law 1008, was passed by the Bolivian Congress under heavy U.S. pressure. According to David Herrada (a coca farmer and member of Congress), "the law arrived to Bolivia written in English, it had to be translated."

Coca eradication initially got off to a slow start. Bolivian President Jamie Paz Zamora compensated growers at a rate of US$2,000 per hectare eradicated (Painter 1994: 89–90). Cash payments eventually had to be stopped, however, because they encouraged coca cultivation. Cocaleros would use the compensation to invest in land and plant more coca so they could receive yet further payouts. During Gonzalo Sanchez de Lozada's (1993–97) first administration, eradication was also undertaken at a slow pace, and reduction efforts were based on dialogue with the unions and compensation in the form of agricultural credits and other forms of development assistance. De Lozada resisted the U.S. embassy's calls to carry through with forced eradication because he worried that facing up to the Chapare unions risked derailing his plans to sell off the few remaining state-owned enterprises (Hylton and Thomson 2007: 98).

Things changed in 1997 when Hugo Banzer (a former military dictator) and his Acción Democrática Nacionalista (ADN) party came to power on a platform of restoring national dignity by tackling the coca–cocaine issue head on. On entering office, Banzer implemented a no-holds-barred eradication policy, known as the Dignity Plan (Plan Dignidad), with the intention of destroying the entire Chapare crop by 2002, and resettling one-third of the Chapare population (around 15,000 union members) outside of the region[1] (Ministerio de Gobierno 1997: 50). The policy was driven by the U.S. embassy, which threatened to withhold badly needed aid if the plan was not adopted (Vazualdo 2014). Over the following years, the government doubled the number of police and military in the Chapare region and enacted what Raquel Gutierrez Aguilar (2014: 86) has described as a "systematic terror policy," abusing, intimidating, and in some cases killing civilians.

When Banzer became ill and the office passed to his vice president, Jorge Quiroga (2001–2), the drug war intensified. On November 27, 2001, the government issued Supreme Decree 26415, which prohibited the drying, transport, and sale of coca planted in the Chapare. The law stated that "anyone who is caught transporting or selling coca will be imprisoned for eight to twelve years" (Gutierrez Aguilar 2014: 87). The closure of what had previously been legal coca markets provoked violent clashes between peasants and government forces in the Chapare, but also in the city of Cochabamba (Amnesty International 2003). The protests of January and

February 2002 (which occurred in the Cochabamba suburb of Sacaba) are remembered as the Coca War, which Morales has described as more important than either the gas or water wars because "by defending coca we defended our sovereignty" (*Los Tiempos* 2016).

The escalation of the drug war in Bolivia took place in the context of the U.S.-led "War on Terror." Youngers (2003) argues that following the 2001 attacks on the World Trade Center in New York, Washington-based policy makers linked the war on drugs and the war on terror into a single offensive.[2] The Bolivian government soon adopted this vocabulary too (*Los Tiempos* 2003). For example, at a speech at the United Nations in New York, the then president of Bolivia, Jorge Quiroga, qualified drug traffic as the "Siamese twin of terrorism" (Morales 2001), and on another occasion Quiroga drew comparisons between the coca growers in the Chapare and Al-Qaeda (*La Patria* 2001). Tackling the perceived terrorist threat in Bolivia became a priority of the U.S. embassy. In 2004, the Bureau of International Narcotics and Law Enforcement Affairs doubled the security assistance for Bolivia, citing "security for drug eradication and interdiction operations" and "equipment and training for the Bolivian army's new counter-terrorism unit" (Ledebur 2005: 177).[3] It is telling that the Chapare coca unions have never appeared on the U.S. State Department's list of terrorist organizations, however (Isacson 2005).

U.S. involvement in Bolivia's drug war in the early 2000s severely undermined national sovereignty. Farthing and Ledebur (2004) note, "In the Chapare, the U.S. government trains, equips and funds all anti-drug units." Officers in charge of coca eradication took part in regular training programs in the United States, where they were encouraged to identify with U.S. values and interests (Gill 2004). And a local newspaper reported that antinarcotics police, military officials, and public prosecutors received a "gringo" bonus of up to 3,000 bolivianos (around US$400) a month, which was paid directly through the Narcotics Affairs Section of the U.S. embassy (*Opinión* 2006b). The U.S. Drug Enforcement Administration (DEA) shared a base with local antidrug forces in the Chapare, and closely supervised them. Control was so tight that Bolivia's fleet of Huey helicopters (donated, maintained, and fueled by the United States) could only be operated under the supervision of the U.S. embassy. Finally, until 2002, the U.S. embassy operated its own paramilitary unit (the Expeditionary Task Force), an organization the human rights ombudswoman in Bolivia classified as "mercenaries" (Ledebur 2003).

The Dignity Plan dramatically reduced the amount of land under coca cultivation in the Chapare, and was hailed by the United States as a significant victory in the war on drugs.[4] However, claims of success were premature. An unintended side effect of repressing coca production in the Chapare was a 400 percent increase in the price of coca and the rapid expansion of coca production in the Yungas of La Paz (Jackson et al. 2003: iii). Drug war gains came at a heavy human and economic cost. Eradication denied peasant farmers their only source of income, leaving many struggling to survive. Cocaleros remember that at this time there was no money to pay for food, health care, or education. "It was so sad, we were so poor that all the children ever had for lunch was a stale bun," lamented my landlady Doña Mercedes. Dr. Godofredo Reinicke, a medical doctor and the human rights ombudsman for the region during Plan Dignidad, confirms that between 1997 and 2003 the cocaleros suffered from an increase in malnutrition and preventable infectious diseases. In light of these harsh conditions, some opted to abandon their land altogether. They moved to the peripheral areas of the city of Cochabamba, where they found work in the informal economy.

The drug war justified repressive policing in the Chapare. During fieldwork I collected countless interviews charting the abuses suffered by coca growers at the hands of the security forces. Adriana, a young mother with two small children, recalled how, when she was only sixteen, a group of soldiers entered her house; they knocked her to the floor and were about to rape her when her father burst in to stop them. She told me, "Here, more than anything, the women suffer violent sexual assaults from the Leos" (short for "Leopards"—a reference to the militarized police). Others told me of houses being torched, the military throwing tear gas canisters into school classrooms, arbitrary detentions, beatings, and extrajudicial killings.

Over the period 1997 to 2003, 53 coca growers were killed, 631 were seriously wounded, and over 4,000 were incarcerated on little or no evidence under the terms of the draconian Law 1008 (Medrano 2017). Given the impunity of the armed forces, the harsh measures prompted reprisals, which in turn left 27 police and military dead and 135 wounded (Ledebur 2005). Human Rights Watch, which had conducted a study of human rights violations in the Chapare in the mid-1990s, and the UN Human Rights Committee voiced concerns over violent crackdowns, the use of excessive force, and unlawful violence against coca growers (Farthing and Ledebur 2015: 17). Perhaps unsurprisingly, the government's policy of "zero coca" in the Chapare came to be seen locally as "zero cocaleros." In a 2011 interview, union leader Emilio Choque, recalled this troubled time: "At that time, I remember, there was no peace here. The government kept saying 'the Tropics have to stop planting coca,' but what they really meant to say was, 'we have to get rid of all the cocaleros.'"

The Failure of Alternative Development

While the bulk of U.S. funding was dedicated to eradication and law enforcement, the United States also invested money in alternative development initiatives. Between 1982 and 2001, the U.S. Agency for International Development (USAID) spent an estimated $229 million in Bolivia[5] (GAO 2002). Initially, USAID invested in the highlands and valleys to try to prevent people from migrating to the Chapare, but by the late 1980s the focus had shifted to encouraging peasant farmers to grow legal crops instead of coca. The crops promoted by USAID included bananas, coffee, palm heart, passion fruit, pineapple, black pepper, and timber. However, with few exceptions coca growers claim that U.S.-led initiatives did little to improve their livelihoods because the technical and commercial aspects of the crops were not appropriate.

Coca has several comparative advantages as a cash crop: it grows like a weed in places where other crops do not (on steep slopes, acidic soil, and at altitude), it reaches maturity after only one year, and it can be harvested once every three to four months, providing the family with a regular source of income. The work of planting and maintaining coca involves both sexes of all ages (see figure 5.1), and the main tools (including a machete, digging stick, and a backpack-mounted crop sprayer) are cheap and widely available in rural areas. Coca has a high value-to-weight ratio; this is important because many farmers live far from the nearest road and therefore have to carry produce long distances on their backs (see figure 5.2). Most importantly, while the price of coca varies considerably, there is always a guaranteed market for it.[6] As Doña Apolonia Bustamante, a coca grower and union leader in her forties, told me, "Coca is our subsistence; it allows our children to study and pays for our clothes, visits to the doctor, and our food."

In contrast to coca, crops such as bananas, citrus fruits, and palm heart require a substantial initial investment, agro-chemicals, and large tracts of land close to the road in order to be profitable, making them unviable

Figure 5.1. A girl helps her mother to dry coca leaves in the sun. Photo by author.

Figure 5.2. Man walking to his farm, which has no road access. Photo by author.

Figure 5.3. The lack of bridges in the Chapare means that trucks often have to cross rivers on boats. Photo by author.

for most coca growers. Other substitute crops, such as coffee and cacao beans, take a long time to mature, so dividends appear only after several years. As U.S. assistance was conditioned on the prior eradication of coca, many farmers went bust before they could harvest their substitute crops and were faced with the decision of either replanting coca or going hungry (Farthing and Kohl 2005; Lupu 2004; Toranzo Roca 1990).

The most serious limitation for crop substation projects, however, was the lack of markets for tropical products. The domestic market for fruit is saturated, and so prices are very low (in 2006 a hundred oranges would frequently sell for less than a dollar wholesale in Cochabamba), and the international market for cash crops is notoriously vulnerable to dramatic shifts in price. Moreover, the small-scale producer, located in a landlocked country with (until recently) poorly maintained roads, cannot seriously be expected to compete with the production from countries that have long been established in these markets (see figure 5.3). Given the lack of viable markets, people complained that it often made more sense to let the substitute crops rot in the fields than to go to the expense and effort of harvesting them. As one middle-aged female peasant farmer said: "We have oranges . . . thousands of oranges, but you can't do anything with them. We take them to the market and they don't sell; sometimes you invest all of your money in transporting them to the city, but you don't even make back what you paid out. That's no way to live!"[7]

USAID-financed projects ignored best practices in development strategy by refusing to work with the coca growers' unions or the municipalities, which have been run by the coca growers' unions since 1995. Rather, USAID set up their own parallel "associations of producers." To gain access to development assistance, peasant farmers first had to join an association and agree that they would no longer grow coca and denounce their neighbors who continued to do so. This inevitably generated conflict within coca grower communities. Union affiliates identified the members of USAID-backed associations as traitors who were working against the interests of their organization. Fights between the two sides (which sometimes meant fights between neighbors) were common.

Highly paid external consultants designed and administered USAID projects, and this provoked resentment. Cocaleros complained that most of the money destined for their communities was spent on overhead for the workers, including wages, cars, hotels, and offices. In a 2006 interview, Epifanio Condori, the director of the coca growers' radio station, explained the role and functioning of alternative development in the region: "I always spoke about alternative development on my radio show. Let's say of the twenty million dollars that they supposedly sent to the Tropics of Cochabamba, well, they did nothing with it! They threw away the money on things that were not useful . . . 80 percent went on their salaries and 20 percent stayed here . . . we would have been better off if we had administered the money ourselves!"

USAID has a long history of intervening in Bolivian politics on the pretext of "economic development" (Field 2016: 32), and projects in the Chapare seemed to follow this pattern (Laserna 2000). Coca union leaders came to the conclusion that USAID intended to break the union organization through a strategy of divide and rule. One leader said, "We realized that the Yankees were trying to make us fight between comrades." Another told me, "the NGOs gave out money to corrupt the people; they are dictators, they think they know it all." And Feliciano Mamani, the mayor of Villa Tunari, explained, "The NGOs came here to destroy the unions." From the 1990s onward, coca union members regularly burned, ransacked, or destroyed USAID facilities, equipment, and alternative development farms and plantations. In 2008, the coca unions decided that they would expel USAID from the Chapare, a decision that was supported by the region's mayors and President Evo Morales. USAID subsequently closed all operations in the Chapare, and the coca growers erected a sign on the main highway that read "Territory free of USAID" (AIN 2008). On May 1, 2013, Evo Morales expelled USAID from the nation entirely for allegedly fomenting divisions within the country's social movements with the aim of destabilizing his government (Achtenberg 2013).

Whereas USAID had a poor track record, the European Union had more success. In contrast to U.S.-driven initiatives, the Europeans recognized the advantage of working with the union structure and town halls (Grisaffi and Ledebur 2016: 8–9). The EU initiative was designed on the premise that the only way to cut dependence on coca is by reducing poverty and improving services. In 1998, when U.S.-backed forced eradication was in full swing, the European Union launched its municipal strengthening program (known as PRAEDAC by its Spanish acronym), which directed almost US$6 million to the Chapare municipalities to help them execute public works (Farthing and Kohl 2005: 191). Not only did PRAEDAC provide much-needed infrastructure improvements; it also enhanced the legitimacy of the state in the region. Feliciano Mamani, mayor of Villa Tunari, explained: "Before, alternative development was conditioned on coca eradication. In contrast, PRAEDAC has supported the municipalities unconditionally and has been open to participation and [community] control. This means that PRAEDAC respects the population and our local leaders" (EuropeAid 2014). Supporting this assessment, an independent evaluation found that EU cooperation in the Chapare "has enabled government institutions to shift the dynamics of their relation with civil society organizations" (Calcopietro et al. 2014: 5). In this way, PRAEDAC created a credible foundation for what was to come next, community coca control (Grisaffi, Farthing, and Ledebur 2017; Grisaffi and Ledebur 2016: 9).

Community Coca Control

In October 2004, a government eradication team killed two coca growers, which contributed to massive social unrest in the Chapare. To calm the growing tension, the Carlos Mesa administration (2003–5) accepted a long-standing demand of Chapare coca growers—the right for each family to cultivate a small plot of coca, known as a cato (1,600 square meters).

The agreement ended violent confrontations between police and farmers immediately. The so-called cato accord was initially designed as a temporary measure; however, on entering office Morales adopted the cato system as the cornerstone of his coca control strategy.[8] Morales informally increased the previous cap on coca cultivation from 12,000 to 20,000 hectares nationally; this allowed for an additional 7,000 hectares of legal coca in the Chapare and a further 1,000 hectares of coca in the province of Caranavi in the department of La Paz (UNODC 2015: 43). This has since been increased to 22,000 hectares under the new coca law launched in 2017, with 14,300 hectares now permitted in the Yungas and 7,700 in the Chapare (AIN 2017). The government remains committed to the eradication of coca outside of the designated zones, and troops routinely eradicate over 11,000 hectares annually, far exceeding government targets (UNODC 2016b).

In order to gain a cato, each union member is required to obtain a land title, register for a biometric ID card, and have their cato measured and logged by the state coca monitoring institution, UDESTRO. These data are compiled on a database and synced with satellite data, the land registry, and on-the-ground GPS measurements, making it one of the most complex drug crop monitoring systems in the world (Farthing and Ledebur 2015). Building on this infrastructure, it is then up to the local-level unions to exercise internal controls (referred to as "social control") to ensure that farmers respect the one-cato limit. As discussed in chapter 3, the concept of social control draws on forms of pre-Hispanic indigenous community organization to privilege collective over individual rights.

Coca control is a shared responsibility, which involves the entire community. Each base-level union organizes regular inspections of coca plantations; commissions are formed of local members and often include people from neighboring communities. Members of the sindicato use a combination of persuasion and coercion to achieve compliance. In many cases, to avoid sanctions, community members eliminate coca plants in excess of the cato limit before the commission arrives (Grisaffi 2016: 158–60). If people continue to plant excess coca, the local union forbids the member to replant for a period of a year, which, because of maturation time, effectively means two years without any coca income.

The farmers have good reasons to police one another; they believe that if coca cultivation is restricted, prices will go up. As one man explained, "We work less, but earn more." The policy then builds on the concept of the "limited good"; this is the idea, outlined in chapter 3, that there is a limited number of good things in the world, and if an individual does better, it comes at a cost to everyone else. People are motivated to stick to the rules as a result of their understanding of the importance of reciprocity and a commitment to place and community. There are external pressures as well. If a sindicato is thought to be not adequately policing itself, the entire community can lose their right to grow coca for a period of a year (Farthing and Kohl 2014: 136). Finally, peasant farmers recognize that if they cannot make the strategy work, they risk a return to forced eradication.

As a result, pressure to honor the agreement is intense. One man explained that under the old policy, when the military pulled up his coca, he could replant without any immediate repercussions. "Before, when we planted the coca and they ripped it up, we would replant and they would rip it up again." However, he said that today it's *jodido* (really harsh): "everyone knows how much coca you have and they don't want me to get rich at their expense." The threats are real; by 2014 more than 800 growers in the Chapare had lost their cato for breaking the agreement (*Opinión* 2014).

The second level of compliance comes from UDESTRO. Its staff (a civilian force) conducts routine visits to farms, and if they find more than a cato of coca, they schedule the removal of all of the family's coca by the Joint Task Force (a military unit). As each sindicato knows when to expect a revision, union members uproot all excess coca in advance; thus UDESTRO's presence rarely generates conflict. Moreover, the majority of UDESTRO's workers are sons of coca grower families, and as a result, they are viewed as compañeros (comrades). As Doña Yolanda, a female farmer in her late fifties, explained, "They understand that we depend on coca. We can talk to them; if there is a problem, then we can find a solution." As is evident from Yolanda's comments, the integration of union members into the state apparatus has enhanced the state's legitimacy in the region. The director of UDESTRO is himself a coca grower, and he is required to give regular reports at federation meetings. The degree of coca union control over UDESTRO was vividly illustrated to me when I attempted to solicit an interview with him in November 2013. The director agreed in principle to be interviewed, but he told me that I would have to obtain permission from the general secretary of one of the six coca federations before he would speak with me.

The state has not surrendered control to the unions entirely, however. There is still a militarized unit called the Surazo Force (a section of the Joint Task Force) that will forcibly eradicate coca when union members are not compliant. Today, eradication is generally not accompanied by violence, however. Leyla, one of Radio Aurora's reporters, explained, "Before, we were all terrified of the security forces; but now, it is not like that. Now there is communication, we have reached an agreement. If they have to eradicate coca, then we let them, but now they respect our rights."

Alongside control efforts, the government has prioritized economic development. In 2006 the Cochabamba Tropics was declared one of Bolivia's five new "special economic zones," where taxes are lowered and public investment is prioritized (*El Deber* 2016). Since then, the region has benefited from high levels of state finance, including the construction of roads, hospitals, schools, factories, a university, and even a state-of-the-art opera house. The government built an international airport in Chimore (a small town located in the center of the Cochabamba Tropics), and an ammonia and urea processing plant in Bulo Bulo (located on the eastern edge of the region). The US$844 million price tag of the urea plant represents Bolivia's largest-ever single investment.[9] The MAS administration has also provided farming communities with access to mechanized tools such as rice-husking machines and tractors, established cold chains for dairy produce, and built fruit juice, honey, paper, and coca processing factories. As a result of government programs, coca grower families now have access to cheap loans and state-built housing, and they count on a scholarship program to assist young people to study at a university (including abroad in Venezuela or Cuba).

Government initiatives (such as the fruit juice processing plants) have expanded the market for local produce. According to one European Union evaluation, "alternative agricultural production has increased substantially and a number of promising productive chains have been created" (Calcopietro et al. 2014: 50). Some Chapare farmers are making the most of these opportunities and are successfully diversifying their sources of income. To give but one example, the government has promoted fish farming in the Chapare.[10] One woman explained that her fishpond (which was built with assistance from the local town hall) provided twice the income of a cato, and said that she was considering abandoning coca altogether (Grisaffi 2016: 161). Families can earn up to $7,250 annually from fish farming; once overhead costs are factored in, this leaves $5,800 for the farmer (*Los Tiempos* 2017a). This is a significant sum in a country where GDP per capita is just over $3,000 (World Bank 2017). Thus, some farmers have come to describe coca as a savings account or a safety net, rather than their main source of income.

The control initiative also demonstrates Bolivia's commitment to addressing the international community's concerns about coca cultivation for the illegal market. The government has built a factory in the Chapare to process coca-based products, such as teas, solutions, candies, syrup, and flours for export. However, UN drug control treaties remain an obstacle to establishing a legitimate international coca-based industry, and the domestic legal market cannot soak up Bolivia's current coca production. As a result, the factory runs well below capacity (*Los Tiempos* 2014a) and is referred to locally as a "white elephant." A recent EU-funded study (CONALTID 2013) suggested that Bolivia only requires 14,000 hectares of coca to satisfy legal demand, but current production is over 23,000 hectares.

The Morales administration came under heavy criticism in 2008 when it decided to expel the U.S. Drug Enforcement Administration (DEA) for allegedly conspiring against the government (Quiroga 2008). The DEA had been operating in the country for thirty-five years and was a key component in the U.S. war on drugs. Against this background, the MAS government has been eager to show the international community that it is committed to tackling the drug problem, and it has taken an uncompromising approach to enforcement.[11] In spite of the decrease and eventual cessation of U.S. funding for counter-narcotics operations (all U.S. funding ended in September 2013), the Bolivian security forces have increased the seizures of illicit drugs and the destruction of drug laboratories in recent years. During Morales's first five years in power (2006–12) the police seized 187 tons of cocaine, a massive increase compared with the fifty-six tons confiscated on the DEA's watch between 1999 and 2005 (*La Razón* 2013). Of course, the meaning of these data is open to interpretation; it could be that enforcement operations are more effective, but equally it could also mean that more cocaine is being produced (or at least trafficked through Bolivia from Peru). Nevertheless, the point still stands: the Morales administration has demonstrated the political will to combat the cocaine trade (Youngers and Ledebur 2015: 9–13).

Grassroots Assessments

In 2014 I was asked to write a report on Bolivia's coca control program for a drug policy research organization. Aware that high-level leaders might downplay grassroots concerns, I sought out base-level members who I knew could be counted to speak candidly about the issue. I found that farmers were torn;

on the one hand, they thought that things had got immeasurably better; the violence and abuses of the drug war were seen as a thing of the past and the local economy had started to grow. People told me how in the past they never had parties but now they were commonplace. Others focused on their increased ability to consume; one man told me "before, they [peasant farmers] only ever used to drink *chicha* [home brew], but now they drink [bottled] beer and rum." In this context, drinking beer and rum is a clear indication of higher levels of disposable income. Others focused on how their neighbors had replaced their rusty bicycles with Chinese-built motorbikes and carried out home improvements. And yet, while noting that things had gotten better, many people nevertheless complained that the cato was inadequate and the government had not done enough to diversify the economy.

I met Don Fernando Lazo outside his house, polishing a beat-up Toyota that he had recently bought to run as a taxi. Fernando invited me to sit with him and chew coca, and he soon warmed to the issue. "Look, Tomás, coca is everything here. Just like your job is to teach, our job is to plant coca," he said. Fernando explained that in the tropics people value coca because it is resistant to disease, has a high price, and can be harvested once every three to four months: "People are used to it; they are accustomed to the regular income." Fernando also stressed the importance of coca to local culture: "You know that the Tropics of Cochabamba is a *zona cocalera* [coca-growing zone]; we don't want to lose our cultural identity." He stated that from his perspective the union should not talk about legal coca and illegal coca because "all coca is sacred, so all coca must be protected." Here Fernando mobilizes ideas about indigeneity to justify to me (an outsider) why restrictions on cultivation are immoral. In a pithy statement, he made clear the disillusion he felt with the current policy: "It's true, with the cato the price [of coca] has gone up, but still people miss it." He explained that before a person might have up to five hectares of coca and "they are the ones complaining now." He concluded by telling me that some lambast Evo for being a "damn idiot."

Fernando was keen to impress upon me that a cato does not generate sufficient cash to support a family. To prove his point, he listed all of his outgoing costs including food, health care, transport, and overhead (tools and agro-chemicals) and set them against his coca income of around $200 per month. "A cato will not cover everything; maybe if you are frugal and have no family . . . maybe . . . but even then it won't cover everything." I countered that the government's position has always been that the Chapare farmers should find alternative crops to supplement their coca income. Fernando looked unconvinced; from his perspective the same barriers exist to accessing markets as before. Fernando had tried other crops including pineapples, achiote, oranges, and papaya, but he assured me that the income generated by these crops was minimal. He was considering fish farming, but as yet had not got around to it.

Fernando then spoke of his children, both of whom were born in the early 1990s (members of the so-called generation 1008, after the antidrug legislation). They are now married with children, and they want land and a cato of their own. However, these ambitions remain unfulfilled. Over the past ten years the value of land in the Chapare has increased dramatically as a result of land titling and legalized coca, making it unaffordable for as-piring farmers. Moreover, the number of catos in the Chapare is capped at 40,000, and the federations will not allow sindicatos to register new mem-bers. Hence, the only way to acquire a legal cato is if it is reallocated from another person, something that does not happen often. Fernando worried that his children would have to move to the city and seek work there, but without a university-level education he knew it would be hard for them to find a decent job.

If there was discontent in the main colonization area, it was even more pronounced in remote regions far from the main road. Between 2006 and 2008, I made several visits to Isiboro Secure (where the agricultural colo-nization zone merges into the TIPNIS national park) to help Radio Aurora's technicians install a booster station. While there I met Samuel Pozo, a local grower and sindicato leader. Samuel explained that in Isiboro, most cash crops will not grow because of the steep slopes and sandy soil, and the roads and bridges (if they exist) are woefully inadequate, making the area impassable for weeks at a time during the rainy season. Given the harsh conditions, local farmers like Samuel argue that they should have the right to grow two catos of coca per family. They see this as fair payback because, in the local narrative, it was the Isiboro farmers who put up the stron-gest resistance to government eradication programs in the past. Samuel explained: "We were the warriors in the battle to defend coca, we have the most martyrs. . . . Morales promised us a hectare of coca, but all we got is this lousy cato! What did we bother fighting for?" (Morales never officially endorsed unlimited coca cultivation; even so, many grassroots members I spoke to were of the opinion that he had made this commitment.) As I spoke with Samuel, helicopters thundered overhead deploying troops to eradicate coca plantations in the nearby national park (where under the new policy coca cultivation is still illegal). Nodding toward the helicopters, he told me: "Now it seems that our own federation wants to . . . a bit . . . to harm us. . . . The federation is giving more priority to other areas, no? But here, they have given us almost nothing. I don't know what the federation is thinking because we are going to feel it hard because we have helped the struggle a lot, no?"

There was talk in the Isiboro sindicatos that they should split from the union to establish their own federation that could better represent their interests. There was even a push to make Isiboro a separate municipality. Local union leaders had gone as far as submitting all the relevant paperwork to the constitutional court in Sucre. Samuel described this as a "dream of a forgotten place." Finally, and most significantly, Samuel explained that on several occasions coca farmers in Isiboro had faced down government troops (the Joint Task Force) on eradication missions and expelled them from the region.[12] I tried to push him further on this issue, but he, along with others, was reluctant to speak about it in any depth. Samuel ended our conversation with a warning. He said, "Thanks to coca we are in power, but coca could also bring this government down." With this he was expressing his sincere disappointment with the MAS, and the potential for coca farmers to withdraw their support. Several other union leaders and even municipal officials used the same formulation during the period of fieldwork.

Given the emphasis the union and the MAS put on "bottom-up control," we might reasonably expect people to voice their concerns about the cato accord at union meetings. However, this was rarely the case. Base-level members describe the regular consultations with government ministers and the president as "a waste of time," a "show" designed to placate them rather than to offer any real alternatives. Farmers evidently felt that when it came to coca, they had no meaningful role to play in generating policy. Most told me that coca policy comes "from above" and explained that it is micromanaged by Morales himself.

The data on coca cultivation show a decline in the Bolivian coca crop, from 31,000 hectares in 2010 to 20,200 hectares by 2015, representing a 35 percent net reduction (UNODC 2016b). This in turn has led to steep increases in the price of coca, making Bolivian coca the most expensive of the three coca-producing countries (for comparison, see UNODC 2016a, c). This indicates that the policy is working, and yet many coca growers I spoke with assured me that, while they respected the cato, "nobody else does." I was told, "everyone has more than a cato," and "they [other coca growers] are ambitious, so of course they plant more." One man told me "some [people] still have three hectares [of coca], but they hide it deep in the jungle."

It was true; I knew people who played the system. Most who broke the rule simply planted additional coca on the same piece of land and hoped that nobody would notice (inspections carried out by UDESTRO are intermittent, so it is possible to do this, and I heard that some unions make pacts that they will overlook production above the cato limit). Others have attempted to subvert the regime in more subtle ways, for example, by splitting their ten-hectare farms into two smaller plots and registering the extra plot in another family member's name, thus affording the farmer two legal catos on what is essentially the same piece of land. Some have bought up additional land in distant sindicatos. As these catos are often registered under the names of dead relatives, they are referred to as "ghost catos" or "*catos fantasmas*."[13] Farmers have also encroached into the national park areas (TIPNIS and Carrasco) to set up additional (illegal) plantations.

Land and Legibility

Throughout the 1990s, the Bolivian government made efforts to carry out land titling in the Chapare through the National Agrarian Reform Institute (Instituto Nacional de Reforma Agraria—INRA) with financial support from USAID. Scholars have been very critical of such programs; both Timothy Mitchell and Alan Gilbert highlight the problems land titling can provoke, including an increase in landlessness and stratification in poor communities as land becomes a marketable commodity (Gilbert 2002; Mitchell 2005). For these reasons, the coca unions have always resisted land titling programs (as historically campesinos have throughout highland Bolivia).[14] Leader Gualberto Chavez explained: "USAID had a different vision [from our own]. They only wanted to give us a land title if we reduced our coca plantations; we worried they would take our land away." Leaders were also concerned that land titling would undermine the union's authority, which, as we saw in chapter 3, is rooted in its control over land. Those who followed through with the procedures to gain official land titles were classified as enemies of the movement and were expelled from the grassroots unions.

Attitudes toward land titles changed with the MAS victory and the launch of the cato, however. To be eligible for a cato, farmers first have to acquire a land title, and grassroots unions have participated actively with engineers from UDESTRO to measure plots and collaborate in mapping processes. This has not been without its problems, however. Boundaries have never been precise, and so the act of mapping generated considerable conflict between individuals and communities. But more significantly, coca growers told me that as a result of land titling, the sindicato has lost its teeth. Over the period 2013–14, I sat through many union meetings, and I noticed that both leaders and union members were far more cautious about following through with sanctions than they were during my first fieldwork stint in 2005 to 2007.

For example, in 2014 I attended a meeting of Sindicato Aurora, where the members were debating how to punish Doña Ellie, a woman in her early fifties who had violated sindicato authority by moving the boundary markers during the land titling process. In this way, Doña Ellie had gained an extra patch of land at her neighbor's expense. Doña Ellie refused to pay compensation and acted aggressively toward other members of the sindicato. At the meeting, which was convened to solve this issue, Don Julio Salinas (the general secretary of the sindicato) told the members: "Look, I am not scared [to order her coca to be ripped up as punishment]; if you all decide that that is what we should do . . . then let's do it. But it is up to you [the rank and file] to make the decision. I don't want everyone saying 'Don Julio made us do it.' It has to be a decision of the bases. I don't want to be the only one to go on trial!" There was an extensive debate, but by the end of the meeting the members had come to no firm decision and opted to leave the issue until the following month.

Later, while walking home, I asked my friend Giovanni (a former leader) about why the sindicato was unable to act decisively. He explained: "Look, Tomás, you can't do anything anymore. Now when we cut down coca or confiscate land it always brings problems—we are trapped by the very same laws that we made." Giovanni was alluding to the fact that because individual members now have their own land title they also have legal protection from the state. As such, some leaders are unwilling to follow through with sanctions (such as the confiscation of land) for fear of criminal prosecution. Giovanni explained that this in turn had led to problems of discipline, and disorganization. He said that levels of participation in meetings had declined over the past five years, that people were less willing to pay their dues, and that turnout for rallies and other political events seemed to be lower.

But if the union's ability to control the rank and file had diminished, the state's power over the union seemed to be getting stronger. In *Seeing like a State*, James Scott (1998) argues that it is in the nature of the state to make society "legible," and therefore amenable to its control. States have pursued a range of techniques to know their subjects and territories, including the establishment of land surveys and population registers, and the invention of freehold tenure, among other things. With the roll-out of the cato program, the Chapare has been made "legible" in Scott's terms.[15] The state now knows exactly who owns land, how much coca individual farmers have, and where it is located. And just as Scott suggests, this knowledge can be used to control the farmers, and by extension the union. This is not a hypothetical discussion, but a very real concern. Coca growers told me that with the cato they were "held to ransom" by the government. Don Carlos, a coca grower in his fifties, explained: "It's [the cato] a double-edged sword; sure it gives us a bit of money, but it is used to control us. The state gives us the cato, but the state can take it away too." Others voiced similar concerns, stressing that the cato can be used by the government as leverage over the union. There have been cases where UDESTRO (the state coca monitoring institution) has ripped up coca plantations of union members who have opposed the MAS, an issue I return to in chapter 6. There is a clear tension, then, between local self-governance as described throughout this book and the expansion of citizenship rights in Morales's Bolivia.

Conclusion

Morales faces a problem: he cannot say in public what he knows only too well, that an unknown (but potentially significant) amount of coca produced in the Chapare is used for cocaine production. When it was just the union, this fact could be overlooked, but once in government the MAS and the union had to tackle this issue head on. Morales has to walk a difficult line, controlling coca while simultaneously discussing how it supplies the domestic legal market, even going so far as providing the region with a factory to produce coca-based products to absorb production. But there is an inherent duplicity here, one that suits the coca growers, but only so far.

The hope of the MAS leadership was that the long-term consolidation of the cato would appease the rank and file, but it clearly fails to achieve that aim. For people who only ever spoke about coca as something that is sacred and that should be valued and protected, the cato represents an inadequate compromise. Base-level members complain that it does not generate enough money; they are angry when their illegal plantations are eradicated by government troops, and they say that there has been insufficient investment to offset the impact of limited coca production.

But if people are unhappy about the policy, they lack the language to articulate their concerns. If they were to talk about real material politics, they would necessarily have to publicly acknowledge the illegal basis of their livelihoods. Coca policy, then, exposes the weakness at the heart of the MAS project. Morales promised that he would decolonize the state and the economy. However, when it comes to coca (arguably one of the government's more important campaign issues), the government's hands are tied. International frameworks outlaw coca leaf and call for its eradication. As a result, Morales could never fulfill the demands of his bases, because while he bends the framework, he cannot act completely outside of international conventions.

While the cato accord might frustrate coca growers, looked at from the outside it is a great success. Bolivia's community coca control program has proven to be a cost-efficient and less violent alternative to the forced eradication of coca. The new approach has shrunk coca cultivation to the lowest levels recorded since 2003 (this is so because even if individuals plant more than a cato, they still have less than they had in the past), cut the number of coca farmer deaths and injuries linked to forced eradication, and allowed some coca grower families to diversify their sources of income. The result is a program that multilateral organizations including the Organization of American States, the European Union, and the UN Development Programme consider to be a success (Calcopietro et al. 2014: 48, 60; OAS 2013: 6; UNDP 2016: 13). The Johns Hopkins–Lancet Commission on Drug Policy and Health explains that the "Bolivia example is a rare case of meaningful participation of drug crop farmers in planning and implementing programs meant to benefit them" (Csete et al. 2016: 1467).

The United States has remained resolutely opposed to the program. Every year since 2008, the United States has repeatedly blacklisted Bolivia for noncooperation with its unilaterally determined drug targets. This has denied Bolivia access to trade benefits accorded under the Andean Trade

Promotion and Drug Eradication Act (ATPDEA), which had previously supported jobs by allowing microsuppliers to compete in the U.S. market. Kathryn Ledebur of the Andean Information Network argues that, "As Bolivian coca production holds steady at the lowest rate in the region, without widespread conflict, and the country strengthens regional antidrug cooperation efforts, the U.S.' unilateral 'F' grade [in the certification process] for Bolivia appears contrived and unconvincing" (Ledebur 2016). The fact that Peru and Colombia remain "certified" only goes to show that certification is a political act as opposed to a reflection of ability to tackle coca and drug production.

6. The Unions and Local Government

The role coca grower unions play in administering their local communities is not carried out in self-contained spaces. The next layer of governance affecting coca farmers is the municipal government, with its headquarters in the region's larger towns. This level of government was established as part of the Law of Popular Participation in 1994 and encompasses the entire country. The town hall, which oversaw development in Aurora, was based in Villa Tunari, about a twenty-minute drive from the village along a cobbled road, hand-built in the 1990s.

In the Chapare at election time, all of the houses along the main road fly the colors of the MAS (blue, white, and black); other parties are simply not welcome. Doña Guillerma Sanchez, a veteran leader in her late fifties, told me that in the 1970s and 1980s the peasant farmers were mindless: "We would vote for anyone if they bought some bags of sugar and a [campaign] T-shirt." But now, she says, "If they [other parties] come to campaign here, then we burn their flags and their T-shirts; we chase them out." Guillerma went on: "In the Chapare there are no other parties; sympathizers for other parties don't exist. Almost 99 percent vote for the MAS. There are always a few blank votes, but that would only be 1 percent, and that's just because people have made a mistake."

The data support Doña Guillerma. In 1999 the MAS (running on a combined ticket with the United Left) took 59 percent of the vote in the Villa Tunari municipal elections; this rose to 87 percent in 2004, and 100 percent in 2010 and 2015, with a high voter turnout (García and García 2012; *Los Tiempos* 2015b). Thus, ever since 2004 the mayor and all councilors in Villa Tunari municipality have belonged to the MAS party. Equally impressive results were registered in the region's other municipalities. In the 2010 municipal elections, the MAS took Entre Rios with 100 percent, Chimore with 100 percent, Puerto Villaroel with 88 percent, and Shinahota with 77 percent (García and García 2012: 349).

From an outsider's (read: Western) point of view, such one-party rule at the local level could be seen as antidemocratic. In *On the Political*, Chantal Mouffe (2005: 29), drawing on Carl Schmitt's "friend–enemy" distinction, argues that politics always has a partisan element, and "for people to be interested in politics they need to have the possibility of choosing between parties offering real alternatives." Mouffe further states that, "if we want people to be free we must always allow for the possibility that conflict may appear and to provide an arena where differences can be confronted. The democratic process should supply that arena" (Mouffe, cited in Castle 1998). Mouffe's understanding of politics in terms of agonistic relations (the space allowed for opposing and often conflicting positions) has been taken as an ideal yardstick for measuring the health of a democracy. For example, in recent debates on the postdemocratic turn, scholars have decried what is seen as a loss of adversarial contest between left and right in European politics, and the way informed debate has been replaced by an emphasis on technocratic administration. Politics is said to have been hollowed out and homogenized (Mair 2013), leading some academics to talk of a global "crisis of democracy" (Nugent 2012: 281) or even "post democracy" (Crouch 2004).

This emphasis on antagonism and conflict as a precondition for true democratic engagement, however, is more Western-centric than is often assumed. A first aim of this chapter is to explain how the case of the coca growers tells a different story. For them, homogeneity of opinion and uniform outcomes cannot be equated with dictatorship or so-called post democracy (or both). There are other reasons why the coca growers produce these astonishing results in their municipal elections (with the MAS often achieving 100 percent of the vote), and this chapter addresses those reasons. Central to the story I am telling is what coca growers refer to as "social control"; this is the core principle that any political decision is acceptable only if it is proposed by the bases and is supported by an absolute majority. Hours if not days of debate and scrutiny go into making a consensual decision, and the importance of this work is continually reiterated. As we will see, social control can also take more violent dimensions; this chapter shows how people do not shy away from physical means of forcing leaders into compliance.

The value coca growers place on consensus over conflict, on majority vote over partisan politics, and on direct control over secret ballots does not mean that people are totally aligned with the decisions of the unions or the town halls, however. On the contrary, people often complain that they are not happy with the state of affairs. A second aim of this chapter, then, is to understand when and how dissatisfaction arises and what this means in the context of grassroots democracy as it is lived out and envisaged by coca growers. I show that discontent surfaces when leaders fail to respect the will of the bases. This is usually the case when practices of favoritism or corruption (otherwise common and widely accepted as an inevitable part of political life) are perceived to be channeled in favor of groups or individuals who are not considered to be "one of us," that is, the majority bases. What produces dictatorship from a local point of view, then, is not the absence of contestation, but rather a lack of compliance with the will of the absolute majority. Again, we can see that this is a very different view of democratic engagement from the predominant understanding in Western societies, sketched out above.

In this chapter, I first trace out the importance of social control at the level of the sindicato and how it scales up to inform the practice of the entire union. I then describe how the assembly-style democracy of the peasant union is superimposed onto the town halls. Just like a union leader, public officials, including mayors and councilors, are expected to enact the decisions of the bases, or lead by obeying. However, as we will see, with distance from the sindicato (where kinship ties predominate), the power of grassroots members to exert social control over their leaders steadily decreases, which leads to criticisms of autocracy and dictatorship. Throughout this chapter we will see that there is a disconnect between how social control should work in theory and what actually happens on the ground.

Assembly Culture

At the local level, the MAS is said to operate as an extension of the union. In the words of union leader Doña Guillerma (introduced above), "If we vote for the MAS that means we vote for ourselves." In order to understand how the MAS functions, then, we first need to understand how decisions are made at the level of the sindicato. Here I examine the monthly meeting held in Aurora, which is representative of the meetings held by each base-level union across the region in terms of its format, style, and the kinds of issues that are discussed (regular meetings that involve the entire community are common in the rural highlands and valleys of Bolivia).

Sindicato Aurora holds its meeting on the first Friday of every month in a barn on the outskirts of the village, a building made from cinder blocks topped with a tin roof. The walls are covered with murals depicting Che Guevara, Evo Morales, Tupaj Katari, and Bartolina Sisa, alongside slogans such as "Coca, Power, Territory," "Long live coca, death to Yankees," and "MAS-IPSP." Aurora is one of the larger sindicatos, with approximately 150 affiliates (there are equal numbers of men and women registered as members). The participants sit on plastic garden chairs or wooden benches, but some women prefer to sit on the floor, where they can stretch out and nurse babies or crochet. Equal numbers of men and women participate in the meetings; women normally sit together on one side of the room and men opposite. There is a warm feeling among the participants; for them this is a day without work and an opportunity to see friends. People chat with one another and share coca leaf, which they chew. A few women set up stalls outside to sell fruit, drinks, and fried snacks.

Each sindicato is led by a general secretary, followed by a treasurer and supported by six to eight subsecretaries responsible for coca, social issues (including health and education), agricultural production, sports, external relations, and roads. Members of the committee sit behind a desk in front of a chalkboard at the far end of the barn. The treasurer sits apart at a separate desk. When describing the structure of the sindicato, local farmers often drew similarities to government. My landlord, Don Jose, put it this way: "The general secretary . . . well, he is like the president, and the secretaries are his ministers, and we [the rank and file] are the members of Congress . . . it's just like the government but on a smaller scale."

At least one member from each affiliated household is expected to attend the meeting and to participate in what the coca growers refer to as vida organica (organic life). Don Jose soon worked out that I was enthusiastic about meetings, and so he would send me along on his behalf. In order to verify that all affiliates are present, a register is called at the beginning and at the end of each meeting. If the meeting turns out to be particularly long, the general secretary calls for the door to be locked to ensure that nobody leaves ahead of time. Any affiliate who is not present (or represented) incurs a steep fine. The concern with attendance reflects the coca growers' belief that resolutions are valid only if the decision has been made with the direct participation of all community members. The coca growers put an intrinsic value on political participation, which they describe as a moral duty that everyone must fulfill.

The meeting begins with a reading of the minutes of the previous month's meeting, followed by reports from the various secretaries who head diverse commissions. The larger part of the meeting is dedicated to routine administrative issues, such as encouraging members not to fish with dynamite, organizing a local fiesta, problems with flooding, or deciding how many days of communal work will be spent to open a new road or to maintain the cemetery. These are all important issues that have a direct bearing on the daily life of union members. One of the most hotly debated segments of the meeting is always the report of the treasurer, who discusses the sindicato's finances and collects fines and membership fees. The sindicato often hosts visitors (including local health workers, teachers, or a technician from the town hall), who give presentations on topics relevant to members. Along with routine matters, base-level sindicatos also discuss issues of national importance. Over the course of my fieldwork, I witnessed debates on topics as diverse as the maritime limits between Peru and Chile, Evo Morales as the head of the G77 plus China, the state of Fidel Castro's health, and the launch of Bolivia's first telecommunications satellite. These conversations are driven by the desire for their leader to take these grassroots perspectives to the higher-tier federation meetings so that they might feed into government policy.

During the meeting, members can ask for *la palabra* (the word) and speak for as long as they wish. They normally begin by introducing themselves and affirming the positions of all previous speakers on a similar topic, often repeating what others have said verbatim. The aim of this discursive style is to emphasize respect for others, but also to build consensus. The coca growers use the verb *consensuar* (to reach consensus) to describe this process. Indeed, when there is an important matter to be discussed, the leader will introduce the topic saying, "We are going to have to work hard to consensuar this one." Don Angel, a union member in his fifties, described the process in the following way: "All members have the same rights and obligations. They can make a proposal, ask to speak, or make a criticism. On the basis of this we make our decisions, and from that the resolutions."

There is an assumption that common ground can be reached and that the decisions that a sindicato arrives at represent the collective will of the population. Even so, meetings are often characterized by heightened emotion. I witnessed angry altercations, tears, laughing, shouting, and at times threats of violence. Sometimes meetings would get out of hand. On these occasions, it is up to the general secretary to impose order. The leader would occasionally invoke my presence as a reason why members should "behave well": "Look, Tomás is here taking notes! Do you want him to go back to his country and tell them that we have bad manners? That we make women cry? Calm down, compañeros!"

Building consensus takes a long time; meetings that start early in the morning often continue late into the afternoon (and even the night). Given the discursive style, growers sometimes complain that the conversations simply go around in circles. When meetings are perceived to be dragging on, the executive committee will face outright rebellion. People call for a *cuarto intermedio* (a short break), or *hora* (time/end). However, while participants might become frustrated with the process, they still see debate as vital work. People who do not pay adequate attention, passing the time dozing, snacking, or chatting with friends, are roundly criticized. Consensus cannot always be achieved, however, and the sindicato puts off difficult decisions to future meetings so that people have an opportunity to negotiate with one another in private spaces where deals can be struck. As we will see, this is the first of many examples of the contrast between assembly culture as an ideal and what actually happens in practice.

Chapter 3 described how the sindicato has the power and authority to sanction its members. In private, some coca growers explained that the reason the sindicato appears to "think with one mind" is as a result of what they referred to as "enforced conformity." Some of my informants worried that if they did not go along with the dominant position, they would be victimized and sanctioned. One older man told me, "If I said that I am not *conforme* [in agreement] with what they say, they would denounce me as a right-winger, or as one of the opposition. That could bring me problems." In other words, the assembly culture of the unions does not allow for the possibility of conflict or, in Mouffe's terms, agonism. Rather, as we saw in chapter 3, anyone who breaks with the status quo is classed as an enemy and punished.

When it comes to making a final decision, the coca growers hold a public demonstration of support known as a *voto aclamativo* (public vote). The methods employed by the sindicato include raised hands or the *fila* (line) system; the latter, which is used only to select leaders, requires sindicato members to line up behind their chosen candidate; the candidate with the longest line wins. The reasons the coca growers prefer public voting systems to private ones are twofold. First, it prevents fraud, as everyone can bear witness to the process. Second, public voting makes people accountable for

Figure 6.1. The Union Police secure the path for Vice President
Alvaro García Linera on a visit to the Chapare. Photo by author.

the decisions they make, reflecting the coca growers' overriding concern
that decisions should be participatory and sovereign. As a result of public
voting systems, people often vote unanimously for a given person or position. Thus, in the Chapare, voting does not operate in the way liberal think-
ers would suggest. It has nothing to do with free choice; rather, the way
people vote reflects their ideal of what it means to be a good person and to
honor long-standing commitments to one another.

The democratic principles outlined above are strictly enforced. At larger-
scale meetings or rallies, the unions select an ad hoc police force from their
own ranks to ensure that people respect the assembly culture (this has nothing to do with the system of community justice outlined in chapter 3). The
Policia Sindical (Union Police) wear an armband or a T-shirt (with "Union
Police" printed across the back) to identify themselves and are armed with
a long stick or water pistol (see figure 6.1). Anyone who falls asleep, talks
over others, drinks alcohol, or attempts to leave a meeting early will be rep-
rimanded and most likely squirted with water or hit on the head with the
stick. The members of the police force take this task seriously, and high-

level union leaders frequently had to remind the volunteer force not to act too punitively (there have been cases of syndical police severely beating members). The police force exists only for the duration of the event (at most three days, the time it takes for a congress to run its course) and will disband afterward. When the force is next required it will once again be summoned into existence, but this time with a new configuration of volunteers.

Participation

At meetings, interactions are overwhelmingly characterized by an ethic of respect, and yet not everyone participates equally in debate. Male ex-leaders typically dominate conversations. These so-called elders (*los antiguos*) make their status known by wearing the leader's uniform of dark flannel trousers and a blue polo shirt embroidered with Federación Trópico and the MAS party logo.[1] The elders, who are defined by their length of residence in the area and the leadership roles they have assumed, are deferred to because they are thought to have more experience in how the community has resolved a similar problem in the past, thus setting a precedent that must be followed. Richer members of the community also have disproportionate influence in the discussions. This is because wealthy individuals (by local standards) are often godparents to other members of the sindicato and might also be sponsors for community initiatives (such as the sports team, parties, and so on). Being a godparent puts them in a hierarchical position vis-à-vis others, and as one farmer put it, "You can't contradict your padrino (godfather), you can only agree with him." The same person went on to say, "money dominates in the sindicato."

Research has shown how social movements (even those with democratic and egalitarian intentions) might reproduce racism and gendered forms of oppression found in the dominant society (Gledhill 2004). The coca unions are no different in this respect. Women participate actively in the sindicato and assume leadership roles; however, their voices are not always accorded the same weight as those of the men. On several occasions I witnessed women being talked over, hushed, or ignored when they spoke. Doña Maria Ledezma, a leader in her thirties, told me: "At the beginning, when the women were only recently entering into politics, there was a lot of machismo, they [the men] ignored us. They said 'women should stay at home to cook and look after the children,' but since 1994 the women have also been organized, and we have gone breaking these chains day by day." Here Doña Maria is referring to the establishment of the Women's Federation, which was set up with the aim of ensuring that women are represented in leadership positions and to assure women access to land[2] (Agreda, Rodriguez, and Conteras 1996: 40).

Doña Maria explained: "Now we have men's and women's organizations; it used to be that no women went to the congresses, but now we go as the 'women's organization'; we are part of the presidium, and automatically the woman has to be vice president and the man the president." As Doña Maria explains, things have improved, and women are now on the presidium; but as she notes, they are only ever the vice president. The female cocaleras I spoke to said that there have been advances in terms of their political participation; however, they stressed that men continue to sideline them and do not realize that they have additional responsibilities, specifically care work, which means that they might arrive late to meetings or be unable to fulfill their union duties. Doña Maria stressed: "The truth is there is always discrimination; now it's less than before, but the treatment is not the same. The men are jealous [of women's leadership positions]."

Finally, male sharecroppers and farm laborers who attend meetings on behalf of the landowners were also ignored in debate. I was told, "If you are not a full member [i.e., own land], then you don't even have the right to speak." Thus, while there is a normative assumption that all union members will participate actively and equally in the union, in point of fact, gender, wealth, ownership of land, and prior experience (being a leader or ex-leader) qualify the strength of an individual's voice.

Leadership

All members of the sindicato, including men and women, have the opportunity to serve their community by taking on a leadership role (although this right is restricted to landowners).[3] Leadership positions are graded, from low-level offices such as the secretary of sports right up to *dirigente* (general secretary of a sindicato). A leader who is successful at the sindicato level (the lowest instance of the union) might then climb the union career ladder to occupy a position on the executive body of a peasant central or even the federation. For example, Evo Morales started his union career as the secretary of sports for his local sindicato and went on to become the head of the Six Federations (a position he has held onto for over twenty years).

When I asked people, "What makes a good leader?" I was told that he or she had to be conscientious, responsible, capable, honest, and a good orator, but more than anything, dynamic. This emphasis on being dynamic is because the leader's primary role is to lobby the federation and town hall to ensure that their sindicato receives its fair share of resources and public works. The leaders also shoulder the burden of ensuring the economic well-being of the community, that justice and order are maintained, and that the sindicato is well represented at central- and federation-level events (including participation in rallies, protests, and demonstrations).

A leadership role is generally considered to be an onerous responsibility, involving a lot of hard work for no pay. Leaders complain that they spend all their time at meetings or the town hall and have no time to work in their fields—a common complaint of movement leaders elsewhere in Bolivia (Lazar 2008). Some leaders told me that as a result of the hard work they put into the union they were impoverished. However, while the leaders stress hardship, a union career is also perceived to be a source of self-betterment. Through the experience of leadership, people gain oratory, intellectual, and organizational skills. This is particularly important in an area where many older people have no more than a primary-level education.

In 2006, Don Raymundo Para, a leader in his early thirties, told me: "We consider the union life like a school, we teach ourselves. . . . I always say that thanks to the union organization I have learned something, at least to speak; at least I have learned that." The belief in the union as a route to self-improvement was widespread in the Chapare. I came across several communities where union leaders had produced brief pamphlets about unionism bearing titles such as *Universidad Alternativa* (alternative university) and *Educación Sindical* (union education). The leaders command a high level of respect within the community, and, as we have seen, they maintain an advisory role once their tenure has expired. In Gramsci's terms, the leaders are "organic intellectuals" in that they organize and articulate the feelings and experiences of the rank and file and bring into being new modes of thought and understanding of the world (Crehan 2002: 133).

When the Chapare was militarized in the 1990s and early 2000s, people were reluctant to assume leadership positions because being a union leader meant putting oneself in harm's way. In those days, dirigentes were expected to be at the front of the marches and road blockades, and they were hunted down and arrested by the militarized police on suspicion of narco-terrorism (Dangl and Ledebur 2003; Ledebur 2003). Today, however, being a leader is a far more attractive proposition. As a man in his thirties put it, "Before, nobody wanted to be a leader, but now, with the government, well, it's good to be a leader. Now people want to do it." While there is a strong element of public service involved in being a leader, it also brings with it a range of personal benefits. Being a leader provides the opportunity for travel to meetings, which is paid for by a modest allowance from the sindicato (from the perspective of grassroots members, leaders are always traveling around, having a good time, and getting drunk "with our money"). Leaders might also broker deals with local companies that work for the sindicato (for example, logging or construction companies), which might be worth several thousand dollars. It is widely assumed that leaders will take a small cut of these deals (within limits, such low-level pilfering is tolerated, as it is seen as fair recompense for the hard work the leader has put in). But most significantly, with the MAS in power, some consider a leadership position to be a stepping-stone to a well-remunerated government job (known locally as a *pega*), or at the very least an opportunity to build relationships with powerful local figures such as higher-tier union leaders, municipal councilors, and the mayor. Gaya Makaran (2016) has discussed how Morales and the MAS continue to rely heavily on the distribution of patronage to buy political support.

Elections for grassroots leadership positions are held annually, and there is no limit on the number of times an individual can hold a post. In the Chapare, people do not put themselves forward for a leadership position; rather, the community "names" them. It is very difficult to turn down a nomination without good reason (such as being seriously ill or experiencing a family loss). Quite apart from losing face, if a person is named for a post and turns it down, they incur a significant fine. Most current leaders insist that they never wanted the burden, but that the members of the community had demanded it of them.

When I first arrived in the Chapare, I was under the impression that the community simply selected the most competent person for the job. However, it soon became clear that sindicato elections are characterized by a degree of horse trading. Kinship groups and friends make pacts to ensure that the person they support gets the position. Having an ally as the leader is beneficial to grassroots members, as it is hoped that he or she will prioritize their needs over the needs of others, for instance, by taking their side in a dispute, fast-tracking any bureaucratic procedure, or turning a blind eye to excess coca cultivation.

This type of deal making is not evidence that the democratic principles of the union have somehow been corrupted, however; as discussed in chapter 3, each member is expected to put the needs of his or her kin group and close allies above those of others. Favoritism, then, is built into the system. Preferential treatment is tolerated (if not expected) at the grassroots so long as it is not exaggerated and does not contradict communally shared goals. This links to the broader anthropological argument that corruption is never an absolute phenomenon, but rather depends on whose point of view you look at it from (Gupta 1995). For those on the inside, it makes sense; it's all about honoring commitments to kin and allies. But for those on the outside, that is to say those who are excluded from networks and the benefits they bring, personalized politics is considered something negative and corrupt.

When a leader is officially installed, they take a vow in front of the entire community. With one hand on their heart and the other raised in a clenched fist, they commit that they will not steal, lie, or be lazy (*ama sua, ama llulla, y ama quella* in Quechua). This solemn occasion reflects one of the most important elements of sindicato democracy: the emphasis that the bases put on holding their leaders directly accountable, a process they refer to as social control. If a leader is deemed to be acting inappropriately, the bases have the right if not the duty to impose a punishment or even force them out of office. I heard of leaders facing sanctions for the embezzlement of funds, the corrupt allocation of land, and for not adequately following the will of the bases. The overriding principle is that leaders enact the decisions made by the rank and file; they follow, they do not lead. Grassroots control of leaders is emblematic of local democracy across the Andes (Starn 1992; Ticona 2003), but it is also a feature of the organization of indigenous communities in Latin America more broadly (Gossen 1999: 261; Nash 1997a: 264).

Leaders and rank-and-file members are committed to grassroots control as an ideal that should be worked toward. Leaders described their role as limited to being a "guide," in order to "orient" the bases; I was told that "we [leaders] are only ever a spokesperson; if we do not do what they [the rank and file] say, then they can knock us down," and "the dirigente makes proposals, but it is the bases who decide yes or no. Without his bases the dirigente can't do anything." In a 2014 interview, Doña Segundina, then the head of the women's federation, explained: "I am just like any other woman; I don't feel

Figure 6.2. Grassroots delegates, union leaders, and members of the municipal government participate in a regular meeting of the Six Federations where they evaluate the performance of their leaders. Photo by author.

like a leader. They can throw me out if I cheat them, that's the strength of the people."

The form of social control found at the grassroots informs the organization of the entire union. Thus, in spite of the hierarchical structure of the Six Federations, the location of the decision-making power resides with the base-level members. In theory, it is they who deliberate and come up with proposals, which then rise through the tiers to the federation's executive committee, where they are clarified, turned into policy, and then voted on (see figure 6.2). One ex-miner turned coca grower in his mid-fifties explained the deliberative process: "In our meetings we make proposals; these go up to the central and then after to the federation, national confederation, and even the government. Of course, here, often we just speak directly to the president [Evo Morales]." This assembly-style democracy of the peasant unions is critical in structuring how Chapare municipal governments function.

In February 2014, while I was attending Aurora's monthly sindicato meeting, the leader, Don Julio, told the rank and file that over the following week they would be renewing subscriptions for the MAS party, and that everyone was expected to register. Julio said, "Bring your *peons* [farm laborers], bring your great-grandma, bring anyone who is of age [old enough to vote]!" Although he added (perhaps for my benefit), "of course, this is voluntary, but those who do not register, well, we are going to assume that you are members of a different party." Given that a common denunciation is "you are one of the opposition," Julio's comment can be interpreted as a threat. Later that same day, several farmers told me that they expected there would be a check at the next meeting, and anyone who had not renewed their membership in the party would receive a hefty fine. One farmer told me in a critical tone, "we have to be *MASistas* [MAS supporters]; if we don't then *multa* [fine]!" There is a total overlap, then, between membership in the union and membership in the MAS party.

The 1994 decentralization law that formed the municipalities called for grassroots organizations to supervise local administration. This was done through the *comités de vigilancia* (oversight committees). These committees were to be composed of representatives from local, grassroots organizations, and charged with overseeing municipal expenditure. The committees were empowered to cut funding to local government if they found that funds were being misused or stolen, giving them real power (Faguet 2003). When I began fieldwork in 2005, oversight committees operated in the Chapare; however, they were never considered that important because the coca union oversaw every aspect of municipal government.

The coca unions choose candidates from within their ranks to stand for public office. Mayor Feliciano Mamani explains: "Not just anyone can say, 'I am going to be a mayor, or a councilor or a member of Congress.' No way! First the organizations have to choose their leader; they say who is going to stand for election." The candidate is generally a person who already has significant leadership experience within the coca federations. For example, Don Leonardo López was a municipal councilor when I carried out my first period of fieldwork in 2005. He explained that he had been a sindicato leader for several years before progressing to become the leader of a central. Eventually, he was selected to stand as a councilor at a meeting of the

Figure 6.3. People queue to vote in the national election. Photo by author.

entire federation. He said, "Like that step-by-step we take on more responsibility. You can't do it all of a sudden! We always manage this organically,
according to the capacity of each person."

We have already seen that within the sindicato it is useful and desired to
have allies in leadership positions; this is also true at the municipal level.
Those with links to the mayor or a councilor utilize them to ensure that their
community gets access to services, to see that public works are executed in
a timely fashion, and even to get jobs in the town hall (such as dump truck
driver, chauffeur, or security guard). Thus, just as in the sindicato, when it
comes to choosing public officials, there is a great deal of backroom dealing. Leaders of diverse centrals gather together to agree on a candidate in
return for future favors. Once the federation has settled on its candidates,
they still have to win the position by participating in the municipal election,
which is referred to as the *segunda elección* (second election). However, as
far as most candidates are concerned, the segunda elección is more of a
formality than a serious competition, because the coca federations have so
many votes at their disposal that the candidate they endorse will inevitably
win (see figure 6.3).

While the coca growers unions marshal a large voting bloc, they are not complacent. State-run elections for public office are conducted via secret ballot, and so occasionally the sindicatos will hold a practice vote before an election. At the monthly meeting, mock ballot papers are circulated and members are required to cast their vote under conditions similar to those at the polling booth. Once this task has been completed, the leader will go through each ballot in turn to explain whether it has been filled in correctly. A correct vote is a legible vote, but more importantly it is a vote for the MAS candidate. Practice voting is deemed necessary because many older coca farmers are illiterate, and so leaders fear that members might accidentally vote for the "wrong" party.

In Office

In the Chapare, when the MAS wins the municipal election, it is not the party that wins but rather the coca union. This is because, as a result of the hegemony the coca growers enjoy, they have been able to impose their own forms of decision making onto municipal government (Guimarães 2009). For example, each municipal councilor is elected with a deputy who, in theory, should replace him or her if the main candidate is unable to fulfill his or her duties. This is established in law across Bolivia; however, the coca growers subvert this system by always rotating the councilors halfway through their term (irrespective of whether the principal candidate can undertake their duties or not). Councilor Porfilio Ortiz explained: "Come what may, we have to swap roles." According to Porfilio, this is done to aid transparency, but also so that more people can develop administrative and leadership skills. In addition, by effectively doubling the number of people who hold office, more base-level communities can be represented at the level of the municipality. Porfilio told me: "Each sector has its space inside the town hall; that means each sector feels more represented." Porfilio refers to this system as *gestion compartida*, or shared administration, something that "is not up for discussion." The emphasis the union members put on sharing responsibility harks back to the traditions of rotating leadership found in the ayllus (see chapter 3).

Mayors and councilors think of themselves primarily as union leaders. Mayor Feliciano explained: "We come from the unions, and we can never forget that." Once in office, the role of the mayor and the councilors is to carry out directives that come directly from the coca federations. Councilor

Porfilio explained: "In the municipality we manage the administration, but only with the agreement of the population. The bases know everything that we are doing. They take the decisions about what they want. All we do is to approve it, and then the mayor executes the work. The bases are always evaluating the work we do, that's why we are always in the assemblies [union meetings]." When I asked Councilor Emiliana Chavez about the relationship between the bases and the town hall, she explained: "It's the social organizations that run things more than anything. We are selected by our organizations, and so we have to go to all the [union] meetings; that's what they want. They control us; they closely follow the work that we do."

Union leader Eddy Matos put it this way: "If the mayor makes 5 percent of the decisions, we [the unions] make 95 percent." The degree of control exerted over public officials is reflected in the fact that they pay a large chunk of their salary to the union (20 percent for councilors, 40 percent for mayors), and officials are expected to provide regular reports on the progress of their administration—a commitment Mayor Feliciano describes as "sacred." Feliciano told me: "Every month we inform the federation's general assembly what we are doing and how it is going. According to the law, we also have to give a public report as well, but we only do that once a year." Clearly for Feliciano, his priority lies with the union; the yearly official report is more of an afterthought. Alongside their duty to attend federation meetings, Mayor Feliciano and the councilors regularly attend sindicato-level meetings, fiestas, and sports and cultural events. On these visits, public officials observe protocol by participating in drinking, dancing, and speech making.

While the mayor is present at union meetings, the reverse is also true. The general secretary of the federation is a constant presence at the town hall. Don Oscar Comacho (the general secretary of the federation) would sit next to the mayor at most public meetings and answer questions and make suggestions with equal weight. Given that the town halls double as meeting places for the coca federations, union members are in constant contact with local officials. Just as in the sindicato, if the bases detect misconduct or contempt for union authority, then in theory they have the power to sanction the mayor or councilors. This could take the form of a fine, public humiliation, or removal from office. In practice, however, this rarely happens. I heard of several instances (from neighboring coca union–controlled municipalities) where the unions had to put up with unpopular councilors and even a mayor because there is a tacit acceptance that removing a public official would create a media storm that would reflect badly on the national MAS party. This illustrates yet another example of the disconnect between theory and practice.

It is not just the mayor and councilors who are beholden to the unions, but the functionaries as well. The federation's statute declares: "the advisors and workers in the town hall should honor our principles." The document states that it is preferable that the town hall hire "professionals who are of peasant extraction and members of the Federation." In reality, however, most administrators, accountants, lawyers, and engineers who work at the town hall are middle class, university educated, and drafted from the city. Even so, these workers are subject to the same checks as their elected colleagues. The union's statutes state: "the advisors and workers should be evaluated every three months at federation meetings" (FETCTC 2012). The federation reserves the right to fire anyone who works at the town hall and whom they deem is not working in accordance with their principles.

The expectations of grassroots unions about what the town hall can deliver are often unrealistically high. Mayor Feliciano told me: "The sindicatos want everything, and they are impatient. They don't understand that processes have to be gone through; sometimes there just isn't the money for the projects they want." As a result, the relationship between the coca unions and municipal government can be tense. For instance, in 2010 a peasant subcentral laid siege to the town hall for two days straight, demanding that work on a sports stadium be completed (it was a year behind schedule). Such events were by no means uncommon; base-level sindicatos frequently resorted to direct action tactics to ensure that they got what they wanted from the town hall. Reflecting on such issues, Councilor Emiliana Chavez commented: "At times the dirigentes can be really tiresome, a real pain in the ass."

While the coca growers have benefited as a result of their control over the town hall, those who live in the Chapare but who are not aligned with the coca federations, including small business owners in the towns and lowland indigenous groups (the Yuquis and Yuracarés), say they are excluded from access to municipal resources. The hotel owners complain that no money has remained to develop tourist infrastructure in the town. And leaders of lowland indigenous groups told me that the town hall prioritizes "projects for the cocaleros," while their communities lacked basic services (municipal functionaries vigorously denied this charge, however).

So far we have seen how assembly culture informs democratic practice within the union and how this has been superimposed onto municipal government, making the town halls an extension of the movement. However, with distance from the sindicato (where the close ties of kinship predominate), controlling leaders becomes more difficult. The following case study of a municipal election in the neighboring municipality of Shinahota illustrates the importance the rank and file attach to holding leaders accountable, but also the impossibility of achieving direct control all of the time.

The Shinahota Election

Shinahota is a bustling market town about a forty-minute drive from Aurora. The town is located on the main road through the Chapare that connects Santa Cruz and Cochabamba. Huge trucks roar past carrying goods from east to west, and vice versa. Drivers often stop for a few hours to visit the town's many karaoke bars and restaurants. Five-story-high buildings (built in a style known locally as coca baroque that imaginatively combines Greek columns, blue mirrored glass, and iridescent green tiles) tower over wooden shacks and makeshift stalls selling watermelons, toothpaste, and DVDs.

In the run-up to the 2015 municipal election, the local federation (Federation United Centrals) had to decide who would stand for mayor. At a general assembly (held in the local sports stadium), nine of the union's thirteen centrals backed Lidia Poma, an experienced leader and former head of the women's federation (giving her 3,450 votes), and the remainder lent their support to the incumbent mayor, Rimer Agreda (with 2,800 votes). In spite of the bases' overwhelming support for Lidia, Evo did not accept this decision, and blocked her nomination, backing Rimer instead. The reasons why Evo did not want Lidia are unclear, but according to a high-level union leader, "Evo said he couldn't work with her." Another person told me that Morales was angry about Lidia's vocal stance that the government should do more about addressing the fusarium plague that was killing the Chapare coca crop[4] (Pearson 2016).

I was not present for what happened next, but Freddy Cajias, a long-standing friend and local union member, filled me in on his version of the story. Shortly after the selection for the mayoral position, Morales attended a meeting at the headquarters of the Six Federations (which is located very close to Shinahota). Over five hundred farmers gathered outside the building to protest Morales's decision to overrule Lidia Poma's nomination (put another way, they were exerting social control). Morales refused to speak with the protestors, and several hours later, when he attempted to exit the building, hundreds of angry farmers kicked his car and threw stones. Four coca growers were subsequently arrested and imprisoned on charges of "endangering the president's life" (*Los Tiempos* 2014b).

In the face of strong opposition, Morales withdrew his support for Rimer and proposed a third person, Matilde Campos, to stand for mayor on the MAS ticket (Antezana 2014). This was not sufficient to ease tensions with the rank and file, however. Morales's lack of respect for union authority infuriated some union members. In this climate of dissatisfaction, a group of dissident coca growers registered a new electoral front called UNICO (United for Cochabamba) to contest the municipal election (this party was first established by Claudia Delgado, a former MAS deputy). Initially, there was a great deal of enthusiasm for this new party, and according to Freddy, it looked as if UNICO would gather enough support to take the town hall. However, as the elections grew closer, support for UNICO dwindled. In the end, the MAS won with 66 percent of the vote. UNICO took 28 percent and gained one councilor, and the MNR took 6 percent. While this was clearly a safe win for the MAS, it nevertheless represented a slump in support when compared with results in the neighboring municipality of Villa Tunari, where the MAS won the 2015 election with 100 percent of the vote (*Los Tiempos* 2015b). In the context of MAS hegemony in the Chapare, UNICO's 28 percent of the vote is significant.

Jonny Rojas, a local journalist, told me that more people would have voted for UNICO, but they were worried about the repercussions. People understood that a MAS-dominated town hall would cut funding to any locality that explicitly sided with UNICO (it is common for voters in Bolivia to hedge their bets in this way; see Lazar 2004). What made these threats all the more acute was the fear of surveillance. I was told that union leaders circulated rumors that secret cameras had been installed in the voting booths. It is not clear whether this was true (it most probably was not true), but people did genuinely worry about it. Jonny was planning to write about the local election for a national news outlet; however, a group of union leaders came to his home and threatened to burn it down if he reported the story.

In April 2015, not long after the municipal elections, the Six Federations held an extraordinary general meeting where union leaders loyal to Morales decided to punish the ringleaders of the UNICO mutiny. According to press reports, Don Leonardo Loza (the general secretary of the Six Federations) told the delegates: "Two things can never be forgiven: corruption and the betrayal of the [political] instrument." It was decided that the ten affiliates who had "betrayed" the movement by mobilizing in favor of an "enemy" party would be expelled from the federation and would lose their right to grow coca[5] (ERBOL 2015b). Leonardo Loza stressed that going forward the union would pass resolutions to ensure that members could not use the organization to advance alternative political agendas ever again. Union leaders insisted that this was an "organic decision," that is, a decision determined by the rank and file (*Pagina Siete* 2015b).

Zenon Escobar was one of the UNICO militants who had had his coca eradicated on the federation's command. In a 2015 interview with the Bolivian press, he said that the decision to sanction him did not come from the bases at all, but rather from union leaders. "The leaders decide and the base complies. It was the leaders who decided that all of us who were opposed to the MAS would lose our coca." He claimed that there was a climate of fear in the Chapare, and that the leaders threaten anyone who challenges them[6] (Fides 2015). Meanwhile Limbert Condo, coca grower and now councilor for UNICO in Shinahota, told the press that he receives constant threats and that the union members who have contact with him suffer intimidation and have been ejected from union meetings (ERBOL 2015a). The human rights ombudsman, Rolando Villena, waded into the debate, stating that he was concerned about the sanctions against coca union members, and called on Morales to overturn the decision (ERBOL 2015a).

When I asked grassroots union members back in Aurora their opinion on the Shinahota elections, most (although by no means all) were critical of the way Morales had handled the situation. One older farmer told me, "We don't kneel before Evo! It [the selection of the mayor] was the people's decision, it has to be honored." Another recalled that in his inauguration speech Morales had said that he would lead by obeying; "why then doesn't he let the candidates the bases chose go to the elections?" Union members saw Shinahota as yet another example of how the electoral victory of 2005 had altered relationships of power within the union. Base-level members argued that they had been sidelined in favor of a more top-down approach to governance. One farmer explained: "The leaders, in reality they submit to Evo Morales. Evo says something and then they have to do it . . . if not, then they lose his favor, they are no longer his friends. That's how he manages things." Another told me, "The leaders who get on [rise up the union career ladder] are those who are most aligned with the MAS." Grassroots members used words like "ambitious," "opportunistic," and "self-interested" to describe those higher-tier union leaders who are uncritically loyal to the governing party.

Some farmers complained that bottom-up control of the union no longer meant anything. For example, when I asked a friend if I could accompany him to his local sindicato meeting, he confided: "Tomás, it would be a waste of your time, there is no debate at the meetings anymore. The leaders, they just do propaganda for Evo, it's just Evo, Evo, Evo!" and "You cannot criticize Evo or give a point of view, you are only allowed to say yes, everything comes from above." One of the most telling signs was the shift toward private (using an urn) instead of public (raised hands) voting systems to select candidates for higher-tier union positions. When I asked why this was the case, one female coca grower explained: "Well, it's a political step isn't it? People are worried, they think he [the candidate] is going to be important, so they have to protect themselves from reprisals."

Conclusion

The coca growers subvert "normative" (read: Western) ideas about democracy and how it should be enacted (see Nugent 2008). For the coca growers, full membership in a political community is dependent upon the exercise of political rights and social obligations that far exceed the right to vote. Their assembly culture prioritizes personal relationships, face-to-face interactions, consensus building, and the direct accountability of leaders to their community. Even voting, which liberal theorists like Joseph Schumpeter or Robert Dahl consider to be the defining feature of a functioning democratic system, is not an exercise in abstract free rights; rather, coca growers use voting as an opportunity to make their allegiances clear.

We have also seen how the assembly culture of the unions does not allow for the possibility of contrasting positions, or in Mouffe's terms agonism, which she considers to be a central feature of Western democracy. Indeed, from the perspective of many coca farmers, when the organization is working well, "all are in agreement." Anyone who transgresses commonly held ideas and values risks being ostracized, sanctioned, and even expelled from the organization. The most important element of the coca growers' assembly culture is that leaders should follow the will of the bases—they should "lead by obeying." At the grassroots level, where kinship relations predominate, the rank and file exert powerful control over their leaders. In theory, this form of social control is replicated throughout every instance of the union. The grassroots sindicato should control the centrals, and the centrals control the federation, which in turn controls the town hall.

Throughout this chapter we have seen that practice often falls short of theory, however. At the grassroots level, deals are struck in private, women's voices are marginalized, and at the level of the federation cabals preselect candidates for positions in public administration. While it is tempting to see this as a failure of the grassroots form of democracy, we might more accurately say that such behavior is written into the political structure of the union. Personalized links cut across the sindicatos, and, as we saw in chapter 3, it is precisely these connections that make it work. But what makes it function at the grassroots is also what gives rise to the contradictions at the higher levels of the union. Politics continues to be personalized, but as the scale increases the stakes get higher and more people come to feel excluded from these networks—leading to an escalation of tensions evident in the Shinahota election.

The unions have always been autocratic and coercive. So the fact that "everything comes from above" is not in and of itself all that surprising. It is not the autocratic control that is noteworthy here, then; rather, it is who it is directed at, how it is done, and what its consequences are. In the case of the Shinahota election, Morales clearly broke with the will of the bases, and this betrayal was evident for all to see. Previously, the unions only had to control their local union leaders, councilors, and mayors, but today they have a president and other national leaders to worry about. It would seem that the popular perception is one of distance and alienation, and these criticisms are narrated through tropes of selfishness and amorality. From the point of view of rank-and-file members, some leaders (particularly those at higher levels) are no longer committed to fulfilling their duties to the rank and file, but rather are self-interested and are rewarded for acting in this way (see also Makaran 2016: 40).

In sum, coca growers are not committed to the abstract ideals of a Habermassian public sphere, whereby citizens participate on equal terms in rational debate, geared toward the formation of public opinion, which then becomes the authoritative basis for political action (Habermas 1989). Rather, they want their leaders to serve them, to repay their debts and satisfy their material demands, even if that means excluding others. When they feel they are excluded from networks and the benefits they may bring, it is then that anger mounts and claims of "autocracy," "betrayal," and "dictatorship" arise.

7. The Coca Union's Radio Station

Throughout the 1990s and early 2000s, the mainstream media repeatedly targeted the coca unions, presenting them as criminals, drug traffickers, and terrorists. Headlines included "The government has Evo's date book with addresses for the FARC and ELN" (illegal armed groups in Colombia) (Vegas 2002), "Morales is not a valid interlocutor" (*El Diario* 2001), and "Drug trafficking [in the Chapare] breeds terrorism" (*La Patria* 2001). Coca growers were acutely aware of how this media presence damaged their movement. In a 2006 interview Fernando Ochoa, then the general secretary of Federación Trópico, told me: "They [the media] turned the other pueblos originarios [first nations] against us. Everyone hated us, because they considered us to be drug traffickers, narco-guerrillas." Evo Morales too denounced the media as his "worst enemy" (Fuentes 2006).

This raises the question: If the national media are at the service of elite interests, then how have ordinary people come to construct a coherent image of the lives, values, and practices of other marginalized groups and classes? Put another way, how was an alternative hegemony built from the bottom up? These questions were answered eloquently by Don Andreas Solano, a union leader in his fifties, who alerted me to the importance of radio. He told me: "The radio is not a luxury, it's a tool for work . . . without radio there is no orientation, there is no communication. Practically, without radio it is as if we don't have an organization."

While the mainstream communications media are controlled by elites, the same technology can also provide the tools for social movements to advance their own vision of politics and society. Information and communication technologies have been appropriated by a wide variety of marginalized subjects. Arabs and Berbers challenging French rule in Algeria (Fanon

1967), indigenous peasants in Chiapas (Nash 1997b), antiglobalization protestors in the United States (Juris 2012), and prodemocracy activists in Egypt (Howard and Hussain 2013), to name but a few, have used radio, film, but also the Internet and social media for internal and external communication. The literature suggests that alternative media serve a dual function for activists. Primarily, it provides the infrastructure to enable them to communicate with one another, and in turn this can facilitate collective action. But it also permits social movements to broadcast their own messages in response to the exclusion experienced within the dominant public sphere (Downing 2001; Wilson and Stewart 2008).

Alternative media, then, allow for the formation of what Nancy Fraser calls a "subaltern counter public sphere," that is, "parallel discursive arenas where members of subordinated social groups invent and circulate counter-discourses to formulate oppositional interpretations of their identities, interests and needs" (Fraser 1992: 123). Scholars have used Fraser's ideas to explore the nexus of culture and politics in contemporary social movements globally (Cody 2011), including the indigenous rights movement in Bolivia (Albro 2005; Himpele 2008; Stephenson 2002).

Of all the possible media technologies, radio stands out as being particularly suitable for poor and marginal people. Radio waves penetrate even the most remote rural areas; it is low cost for the producer and consumer, accessible to illiterate populations, and has locally significant content. From the very first day I arrived in the tropics I noticed that radio was a constant presence. Radios could be found strung on the handlebars of bicycles, tucked into backpacks, and hung on trees. Homes, shops, and taxis all had their radios blaring, and all were tuned to the same station, Radio Aurora. This is because it puts out the strongest signal in the region, but also, as the farmers frequently told me, "it's ours," "we paid for it"; what is more, they simply didn't trust any other source of information.

Given the pervasive presence of radios and the way that they accompany solitary peasant lives, I argue that radio offers possibilities for contributing to the loyalty and cohesion of the union.[1] Drawing on Benedict Anderson's (1991) work on nationalism, I suggest that the daily experience of listening to the same radio station has enabled the coca growers to achieve and maintain a common understanding of who they are and the problems they face. Radio builds solidarity with strangers and makes the union bigger than the sum of its parts. It is hardly surprising, then, that on coming to power the MAS government attempted to control Radio Aurora. In what follows, we will consider how the station was established, the role it plays in supporting union activity, and the way it was hijacked by the governing party. First, however, we examine Bolivia's mainstream media and the way it excludes and marginalizes oppositional voices.

Bolivia's Precarious Public Sphere

We cannot carry on putting up with the absurd, criminal action of this government. We cannot permit these hordes of drug addicts, these miserable cretins, to expose us to such danger. When they descend like vultures on their prey, then we will see that we, the respectable citizens of Santa Cruz, are exposed to attack. But by then it might be too late. They are going to put our backs against the wall and execute us in the most brutal fashion. Are we going to wait for them to come to murder us?

It was July 2007, and I was sitting in the studio of Eastern Radio, a small commercial station operating in the city of Santa Cruz. The radio presenter, Arturo Negron, was giving his daily afternoon broadcast, which he described as a "service to the people." Arturo is a vocal supporter of the anti-MAS autonomy movement in the eastern lowlands. Arturo's anti-Morales diatribe went on; he characterized the government and its supporters as monkeys, murderers, criminals, rats, and liars. While Arturo's views are extreme, analysts noted that during the first MAS administration the majority of Bolivia's newspapers, magazines, and radio and television stations "denied Morales's legitimacy and stripped him of authority" (O'Shaughnessy 2007: 67).

Bolivia's broadcast media is owned by a handful of ex-politicians, business owners, and transnational corporations (Torrico 2008). For example, Bolivia's leading television network, UNITEL, is controlled by Osvaldo Monasterio, who, besides being one of the largest landowners in Santa Cruz, also has interests in banking and enjoys close ties with opposition political parties. Monasterio was even a member of Parliament during the de Lozada administration (Velasco and Fernandez 2007). What makes this worrying is that there appears to be very little distance between ownership and editorial control. The Bolivian commercial media take sides, and news coverage is characterized by errors in quality, accuracy, and analysis (Archondo 2003; Cajias and Lopez 1999; Cano 2007; Gómez 2006a). Moreover, with few exceptions the mass media has by and large ignored the concerns of peasants, indigenous people, and other protest voices (Goldstein and Castro 2006: 59–62; Torrico and Villegas 2016).

The coca growers are aware of the media bias and the damage it does; even so, rank-and-file union members are fanatical about commercial television, particularly the Colombian and Mexican TV soap operas that are shown every evening. My landlord was a self-avowed *novelero* (addict of soap operas) and would rush to finish work every day so he would be back in time for the show he was following. When I began fieldwork in 2005, most people did not own a television set, and access to electricity was limited. People would gather at bars and shops, where the owners would set up a small TV run by a generator. Watching people watch TV was enlightening; the viewers represented what Ien Ang (1996) refers to as the "active audience." Every time that Manfred, Quiroga, or any of the other representatives from the traditional ruling parties appeared on the screen, the audience would respond by spitting on the floor, booing, and shouting. The right-wing opinions of the commentators on the news program *Telepaís* were heavily criticized, and whenever the UNITEL tag line was repeated "UNITEL . . . where the news is," the audience would respond in unison "where the lies are!"

Early media theory posited a top-down model of transmission. Building on Gramsci's theories of how hegemony functions, members of the Frankfurt school argued that the mass media actively works to undermine class-based politics by transmitting a set ideology that benefits dominant class interests (Horkheimer and Adorno 1997). Latin American theorists took this idea further, suggesting that the mass media contributes to the ongoing process of underdevelopment in the Global South (Beltrán 1975, 1980; Huesca and Dervin 1994; Mattelart 1979). Scholarship has challenged this top-down model, recognizing the agency of the audience. Stuart Hall (1977) has shown how people interpret media texts in imaginative ways: members of the audience might accept, reject, or even alter the intended meaning. Subsequent ethnographic research has confirmed this point (Abu-Lughod 1993; Ginsburg, Abu-Lughod, and Larkin 2002; Michaels 2002).

It is clear from the example of the coca growers watching television that while there is persuasion from above, there appears to be minimal consent from below. Even so, that does not mean that we should overemphasize the role of the "insurrectionary" audience and ignore the institutions and interests of the mass culture industry (Mazzarella 2004: 350). In today's "audience democracy," the media represent a crucial battleground for modern politics (Manin 1997: 218–26). The media shape the field of debate, and the way the media choose to represent or ignore a particular movement has a profound impact on the outcome of its social and political projects (Gamson and Wolfsfeld 1993; Hammond 2004; McCarthy, Smith, and Zald 1996). This leaves us with a question: How, then, did the coca growers build cross-sector alliances that allowed them to revolt? The answer, as we will see, is radio.

Establishing Radio Aurora

The miners were famous for their union-owned and -operated radio stations, which were set up, managed, and sustained by the workers, who gave half a day's salary every month toward operating costs. The twenty-six miners' stations, which began to operate from 1949 onward, drew their personnel from the union's ranks, and they were trained as technicians, journalists, and announcers. In times of political upheaval, the stations linked their signals together, which enabled the union leadership to communicate with one another in order to coordinate protest at a national level. One ex-miner turned coca grower explained: "The miners made proclamations, made their position against the governments known, no? So then, you could stir up the enmity, the hatred of the neoliberal governments and the military!" The achievement of the miners' stations including their role in capacity building, generating local content, and the sense of ownership they engendered in their communities is unparalleled (Gumucio Dagron and Cajías 1989; Kuncar Camacho 1989).

During the period of dictatorships (1964–82), the miners' stations sustained repeated attacks from the military, and on each occasion housewives, students, and workers defended the stations, sometimes with their lives.[2] Ricardo Pozo, a technician from the miners' station National Radio, remembers how the station was eventually silenced during García Meza's bloody coup, which heralded an era better known as the "cocaine dictatorship" (1980–81):

> It was 1980, and I was in National Radio. . . . The radio was used to call on the people to resist. The troops were advancing to the mining centers, to take them. It was the only place left where there was still resistance to the coup, no? The troops came in at dawn to Huanuni. The soldiers shot everyone, at anything that moved; women

and children died in their beds because their roofs were made of tin and they were shooting from planes. If you were at home, you died anyway. They went into National Radio and destroyed it. The equipment, it was a short-wave transmitter, a really big one, and they put dynamite under it and hand grenades in it, and they shot at it and ruined it. And everything else, the voice recorders, microphones, records, everything, they took it all.

During the coup, almost all of the miners' stations were destroyed. It wasn't until Bolivia's return to democracy in 1982, under the feeble Unidad Popular government of Hernan Siles Zuazo (1982–85), that the confiscated radio equipment was eventually returned to the miners. Ricardo was part of a team that was commissioned to reinstall the equipment, but many transmitters were never reconnected because by then mining in Bolivia was on its knees. The now infamous presidential Decree 21060, which would close down nationally owned mines, was just around the corner. Today the miners' stations continue to operate, but they are a shadow of what they used to be (Herrera and Ramos 2013).

In the Chapare, the mode of communication of the fledgling unions was more rustic than that of the miners. In every community, a representative was elected who was responsible for calling emergency meetings by either blowing on a *pututu* (a trumpet traditionally fashioned from a cow's horn) or visiting every homestead personally. This was fine for the organization of village-level activities, but to organize larger groups of people it was totally impractical, particularly when one considers that some affiliates live over eighty kilometers from the federation's main meeting place in Villa Tunari.

Throughout the 1980s, leaders of Federación Trópico made use of a local privately run station called Radio Amazonas to disseminate their messages. However, this relationship broke down in 1993 when the owner of the station accepted a significant amount of money from USAID and began to broadcast messages that coca was ruining the moral fiber of the country, and that large-scale agribusiness was the way forward for the Chapare. As a result, members of the coca unions identified the owner as an enemy. Don Grover Munachi, who worked as a reporter at Radio Amazonas for six months in 1992, told me that the director of Amazonas opposed the coca union: "He ignored the abuses of human rights; he just didn't talk about it, neither good nor bad. He told me, 'don't talk about it,' even though there were deaths. . . . 'Because the UMOPAR [security forces] will take my radio away.' . . . In the end we said, this radio wants to divide us and make us fight between comrades."

A plan to build a radio station was put forward at a general assembly of Federación Trópico in 1993, with the idea that "it had to be the same, in the tropics just like in the mines." A pro-radio committee was formed, which included Evo Morales as its executive. The committee made contact with Ricardo Pozo, who was still working as a radio engineer at the miners' station, National Radio. Ricardo sold the coca unions an enormous and very old AM transmitter, which was installed in the village of Aurora in 1995. However, it soon became obvious that the transmitter was not suitable; it was expensive to run, and the AM radio waves got lost in the dense foliage, meaning the station was able to broadcast only over a very restricted area. After several months of experimentation, it was deemed to be inadequate.

By the mid-1990s the coca grower leadership had developed an international presence and counted on the collaboration of support groups in Europe, Canada, the United States, and Latin America (Sivak 2010: 52–58). Avelino Mercado, a peasant leader in his seventies and member of the first pro-radio committee, explained how the union capitalized on these links: "Evo in those times went to Europe, he managed to get some help, no? He told people that they were hurting us. He traveled all over the world—and he was able to get a little bit of help. . . . We needed everything, equipment to go on air, antennas, something to pay the engineer, everything!" The committee raised US$25,000; much of it came from contributions from members of the union, with additional donations from international collaborators. The union bought an FM transmitter, which was installed in 1997. The station was named Radio Aurora: 27 de Junio (Radio Aurora: the 27th of June) to commemorate the Villa Tunari massacre. Just like the miners' stations before it, it was decided that the station would be funded, managed, and operated by members of the union.

The international links behind the radio station clearly irked U.S. agency workers on the ground. A 2003 USAID report notes that the "pro-coca radio station" was donated by "well-meaning, sometimes politically motivated European NGOs who seemingly do not make the connection between helping the poor, downtrodden, marginalized masses and the international drug trade" (Jackson et al. 2003: 66). From that point on, USAID made it a priority to either purchase or subsidize other local radio stations to counter the pro-coca movement[3] (Jackson et al. 2003: 66–67).

The Power of Radio

When I first arrived in the Chapare in 2005, poverty, poor infrastructure, and low levels of literacy combined to make radio the most important communications media in the region. Nonbrand radios could be bought cheaply in the local market towns, batteries were affordable, and people had all sorts of ingenious ways to recharge them including frying them in a pan or leaving them in the sun for hours on end. The 2001 census recorded that in the Villa Tunari municipality (with a population of 53,996 people), there were over 15,000 radios, but only 1,650 television sets and eleven public telephones (Mezza and Quisbert 2004: 109; PNUD 2005: 302). Every coca grower household I visited owned at least one if not two radios.[4]

At its most mundane, radio is important because it allows for the rapid dissemination of information between people spread over large distances. In the Chapare, travel is slow and expensive on poorly maintained roads. Until 2010 cell phone coverage was restricted to the largest towns, and even then the signal was unreliable and expensive, so when I began field-work very few people owned a cell phone. The radio was essential, then, because it allowed union members to communicate with one another directly. The program *Agenda Radial* (Radio Agenda) is key in this regard. It is aired three times a day (in both Quechua and Spanish) and is used to send short messages and urgent communications between union members. Messages are usually directed at groups of people, such as calls for urgent community meetings, notices about public works, invitations to parties, and other messages from the union leadership or municipal authorities. Even today, when most people have access to mobile phones, radio remains an important medium for everyday use—and *Agenda Radial* continues to be used to share messages.

The ability to spread messages quickly was essential during the darkest days of the drug war (1997–2003), when the radio was used to coordinate protests and to warn leaders about the location of the security forces. When I first visited the Chapare in January 2003, coca farmers were blocking the main road to demand an end to forced coca eradication and the release of jailed leaders. I noticed that each of the peasant farmers had a small radio on their person to keep them updated about the location of the troops. Farmers explained that this was useful because it allowed them to be prepared for when the UMOPAR would arrive. In a 2006 interview, Leyla (a reporter at Radio Aurora) explained: "Our job was really important; we had to keep them up to date, to let them know if they [the UMOPAR] were coming or they weren't coming. We were all scared, because when one of our compañeros dies, it hurts us in our hearts and we didn't want that to happen again."

Radio Aurora hosts several shows that offer spaces for audience participation including phone-ins and song requests. On Saturday mornings schoolchildren would dedicate songs to their classmates; on Friday night adults would chew coca together and send a message to an absent friend, and birthdays would be acknowledged. Emails and telephone messages would arrive at the radio station from other areas of Bolivia, and even from migrants working or studying in Venezuela, Cuba, and Spain. Programs that allow a degree of public participation are very important because this "ritual of communication" (Carey 1989) works on maintaining relationships, which, due to the relative difficulty of travel within the region and the expense of other communications devices, might otherwise be neglected. The fact that the radio gives voice to neighborhood-level discourse means that when people do meet up on market days or on public transport, they have things in common to talk about. In Stuart Hall's (1991: 35) terms, this sort of radio engagement makes the community "knowable" and "locatable." This is important because, as E. P. Thompson (1971) has argued, spaces where people can share gossip provide the germ for political action. In the Chapare it is the radio that creates this denser form of sociality.

The director would devote many hours to broadcasting speeches by established union leaders who are well versed in politics, economics, and international relations. Leaders would refer to this as "orienting the bases." Union members valued these discourses; indeed, farmers often described listening to the radio as a duty that they had to comply with or as an activity they are "dedicated to." The drive to listen comes from the fact if people are not up to date with the latest news, they are ridiculed at sindicato meetings for being lazy, stupid, or not committed. The private act of listening to the radio, then, forms an essential part of public participation in the movement. Don Camilo Limon, a farmer in his eighties, explained: "If it hadn't been for the radio we would still be like . . . like . . . little animals . . . like that . . . without communicating."

Radio Aurora's signal only covers a fifty-kilometer radius, and so alone, the station was never going to have very much impact on the cocaleros' standing in the wider world. However, at the margins of Bolivia's media community, religious, trade union, and cooperative radio stations endure. While all of them suffer from a lack of funding and a precarious legal status, they have amplified their impact by working together in networks. Educación Radiofónica de Bolivia (ERBOL)[5] is a community radio association that provides the infrastructure to make this possible. Using satellite and Internet technologies, ERBOL brings together thirty-five stations, making it one of the largest radio networks in the country (Camacho 2001: 168).[6]

ERBOL news features the voices of people who are normally locked out of the mainstream media, and broadcasts are presented in a mixture of Spanish, Quechua, and Aymara. Unlike the mainstream media, which floods the public sphere with advertising and has low credibility, the direct participation of small, unprofessional radio stations in the elaboration of news content means that the programming of the ERBOL network more closely reflects the range of public opinion and interests of the country's majority (Gómez 2006b: 197). The network provides one of the few national forums for the expression of indigenous-peasant, political, social, and economic aspirations, and allows marginalized groups to present their way of life and culture to a national audience in a way that others might understand, respect, and support.

To give but one example, during the period of forced coca eradication ERBOL allowed the coca unions to denounce the state's excessive use of force and to contest the government's narrative about the Chapare. Over the course of many interviews, Radio Aurora's director, Don Epifanio, told me engaging stories of how, via ERBOL, he would berate the police for abusing the farmers, provide alternative versions of stories circulating in the mainstream media, and deconstruct the image of the coca unions as a "narco-terrorist" organization. To illustrate the power of radio, Epifanio told the following story from 2002:

> The national news was on the television, and it said that the cocaleros had shot a policeman! Well, I immediately phoned up ERBOL and told them live on air, "No, it's a lie, it wasn't the cocaleros, it was the security forces, they shot one of their own by accident!" In response to the broadcast, the government said, "The correspondent from ERBOL in the Chapare is a liar, it was the cocaleros." So I said, "So then show us what type of bullet entered the body of the policeman and tell us if it was a bullet from a military weapon or if it was from the old Mauser rifles that the cocaleros use." They never said anything else, and that was the end of the story. From here we put out a different image of the cocalero.

The fact that Radio Aurora participates in national networks, and is therefore outward facing, imposes limits on what can and what cannot be said. There is a prevailing logic that broadcasts have to make the union look good, and any information that reflects badly on the organization is edited out of the broadcasts. To give but one example, when I asked Leyla if she would report on a violent conflict between two sindicatos that we had witnessed, she responded by saying "No, no, that is not a good idea. . . . In the end these are internal things, and if we did put that on air, well, it would be like giving information to the enemy; the opposition would be laughing at us."

ERBOL not only allows the coca growers to broadcast their own news, but also through this network they become familiar with the voices of other peasant communities, that is, people who are similar to them. In November 2005, I spoke to Don Avelino (introduced above). He told me:

> Now we have a powerful radio! In the mining centers, in Cochabamba, in La Paz, all over, we communicate with the radios of the other compañeros [comrades]. They know our situation and who we are, but also we know about them. We know what is going on with the women, with the miners, with the peasant brothers and sisters. We know . . . everything . . . at the national level. And like that we have been able to break it [the elite grip on power], because we are not alone anymore. We have united with the other social movements, and that has made us stronger.

Don Avelino indicated that he feels emboldened by the knowledge that they are not by themselves, but are part of a broader coalition, all fighting the same struggle. Avelino was by no means the only person to speak of the connective power of radio. Coca growers frequently expressed feelings of sympathy for the perceived injustices experienced by diverse groups they had heard about through ERBOL's news programs.

Community radio has allowed marginalized people (that is, people who are excluded from the mainstream media) to become aware of one another, and it has been essential for the formation of a "subaltern counter-public." This in turn has transformed relations of power, challenged status quo views, and empowered ordinary people to act. In early 2006, I asked Andres Gomez, the director of ERBOL's news programming, whether community-networked radio has enabled social protest. He looked incredulous: "Of course it has! Look, we now have an indigenous president!" He went on to say, "Many times they [business elites, politicians] throw the blame at ERBOL, that the Indians have risen up, that the Indians have started to take notice; they blame us for that. They even blamed us for bringing down the last government of Gonzalo Sanchez de Lozada!"

Taking Control

Once the MAS entered power, Radio Aurora's role changed from one of being belligerent and combative to toeing the line and promoting the government agenda. The tagline of the coca growers' station, broadcast every twenty minutes or so throughout the day, is "The sovereign voice of the Bolivian cocalero." This encapsulates the idea that the radio is run by and for the union. Everyone who worked at the station echoed this sentiment; they stressed that the principles that inform the union's assembly culture also underlie radio production. Grover Munachi told me: "The doors are always open, the policy is to let everyone speak," "it is the voice of the cocaleros," and "it is the voice of the people." The reporters also stressed that the radio was a tool to exert social control over union leaders, the town hall, and even the government. For instance, Leyla was asked, "Does this radio station belong to Evo Morales?" She insisted it did not: "This radio does not belong to Evo Morales! It is not his! . . . We do not always favor the government; if there is some information, or they have done something wrong, well, we have to say so, like a newspaper, as a communications medium, what the government is doing badly." However, contrary to what Leyla claims, it seems highly unlikely that the station will ever act as a watchdog over the MAS administration. To the contrary, as we will see, these days it appears to act as a propaganda machine.

As a result of grassroots pressure, Morales allowed prominent social organizations to put forward names for a handful of government ministers during his first administration. The Six Federations took this task very seriously, and after a protracted consultation with the bases they put forward the aptly named Oscar Coca to fill the role of vice minister of coca and development. However, soon after, at a rally held in the Chapare, Morales announced that Félix Barra had been offered the job. Not only had Morales ignored the choice of base-level members; he had chosen someone from the rival coca-growing region of the Yungas for a role that Chapare farmers thought should rightfully go to one of their own.[7] One leader commented, "¡Que macana! Evo hasn't respected our decision; the power has gone to his head!" Given the gravity of the situation, the director of Radio Aurora (Epifanio) broadcast grassroots concerns that Morales had shown contempt for union authority. He thrashed out the implications about the lack of accountability live on air and called on Morales to return to the Chapare in order to explain himself before the Six Federations. Epifanio's insubordination did not stop there; he also criticized Morales for continuing as executive general secretary of the Six Federations, reasoning that with Morales as the head of the union, the cocaleros would never be able to criticize the government. Given that Radio Aurora is owned and operated by the federation, Epifanio's call on Evo to respond to the bases was entirely legitimate; it represented a form of "social control."

There was no way that Morales could have heard the broadcast from La Paz, but through his Chapare networks, he found out. A few days later, Epifanio was summoned for a disciplinary hearing at the presidential palace. When Epifanio returned, he reported to me word for word what happened in the meeting. He was incredibly tense, so I assume that some of what he said was exaggerated. Epifanio told me: "Evo said to me, 'in the radio you can't say anything against the government . . . and certainly nothing against me. You are only going to talk well about this government. . . . You fall in line or you are going!'" In response Epifanio told the president: "This is not ethical, I am not a public relations man but a journalist, I cannot enter into this game." To which Morales allegedly said: "I have things under control there [in the Chapare], with my agents, they keep me informed about everything, about the leaders, about the radio, about everything. . . . I have everything under control." Epifanio's parting words were, "Mr. President, this is worse than a dictatorship."

It never was Morales's call to fire Epifanio. Such a decision has to be made through a process of deliberation with the bases. And so, once Epifanio was back in the tropics, the executive committee of the federation called a general meeting to discuss the future of the station. After two hours of debate in the Villa Tunari town hall, it was decided that Epifanio, along with the other six members of the radio team, would be fired. The union delegates accepted this course of action because they were reluctant to contradict Morales. As one man put it, "Evo is like our big brother, so we have to listen to him." What is more, the general secretary of the federation implied that if the rank and file accepted Morales's personal choice for a replacement director, then the government would fund the establishment of the federation's own local television channel (a project that had long been in the pipeline).

The next day it was overcast, and a light drizzle gradually soaked everything. It was also the day of the carnival in Aurora, an event traditionally organized by the staff at the radio station. On this occasion, the personnel did not feel like going out to lead the fancy dress parade or present the special programs that they had prepared for the day. Instead, they sat in the office, waiting in vain for a phone call to reinstate them in their jobs. By half past eleven in the morning, it was obvious that it was not going to come. Epifanio fired up the transmitter and entered the small studio. Live on air, he read out a statement, which had been signed by all members of the radio team. Don Grover and Sergio crammed around Epifanio in the studio.

In his soft voice, Epifanio explained that the previous day there had been a general meeting of Federación Trópico and that the majority of the delegates had voted to get rid of all of the personnel on the grounds that they were incompetent. This, Epifanio pointed out, was a sham: "The authorities have offered us no sound reason as to why all of the personnel have been fired. Indeed, on the contrary, the authorities have thanked each worker for the unconditional service that they have given to this communications medium." As Epifanio wound up the announcement, he said that the action taken against the staff was "a threat, and an attack against the right to free speech." After reading out his resignation letter, Epifanio collected his belongings and walked to his small cinder block lodgings. He did not want to bump into Evo Morales, who was scheduled to arrive at the radio station that very afternoon to *ch'alla* (celebrate) the new FM transmitter that the federation had recently bought.

Although many people were reluctant to openly criticize Morales for fear of being thought of as "disloyal" and branded an enemy, in private some grassroots members expressed anger about what had happened to Epifanio. Coca farmer Don Samuel Aguilar told me: "They [the leadership] speak so much about corruption and telling the truth, and look what happened to Epifanio! They fired him, and all he did was tell the truth!" In public, however, most people preferred not to talk about the issue. When asked, union leaders either answered an entirely different question or else mumbled that it was Evo's decision. The only person willing to address the true nature of the sacking was a female deputy senator for the Chapare, who casually told me that the coca growers got enough bad press as it was without having Epifanio speak "*huevadas*" (nonsense) about them.

Epifanio's replacement was Don Héctor Torrico, an experienced broadcaster trained in the miners' stations and later at NGOs in the city of Cochabamba. Héctor's reception in Aurora was difficult. Many people felt that it was his fault Epifanio had been fired. Moreover, he was an outsider who was taking over an important job in the union. This made some people suspicious. It was said that Héctor "is not 'organically of the MAS,'" and some classed him as an opportunist. It soon became clear why Evo had selected him: Héctor had no ties to the union, and his primary loyalty lay with Morales, whom he desperately wanted to please. Héctor was not shy about this; indeed, he often spoke about the radio as a stepping-stone to a job in government; he aspired to be the minister of communications.

Don Héctor's first job as director of Radio Aurora was to rehire some of the staff (excluding Epifanio) and to train new members to avert the closure of the station. He also cut ties to ERBOL (the community satellite network discussed above) because, in his own words, "ERBOL is too critical of the government." Radio Aurora now downloads and rebroadcasts the national news from the state-run radio network (Red Patria Nueva) instead. Radio Aurora had always been run on a shoestring budget; however, within three months of Héctor's arrival, the station underwent a rapid modernization, including the installation of a satellite link for the Internet, new studio equipment, and some time later a pickup truck. The staff could now call on local government agencies for favors, including the loan of equipment for special events, and when the radio station needed heavy work done, the director could request that the commander of the local military barracks send over a few soldiers to help out. Finally, in 2013, when Radio Aurora's radio mast was destroyed by lightning, the union mounted its antenna on Entel's telecommunications mast (the state-run telecommunications company) at no cost. Entel also became a sponsor of the radio station, with the staff kitted out in Entel-branded T-shirts. In short, the radio station, which had always prided itself on being sovereign, had become financially dependent on the state.

Today, the station promotes a progovernment message with no critical reflection. As a result, when union members listen to the radio, there is a gap between the ideological self-image of the union that is broadcast and the issues that they see as being important in their day-to-day lives. Many times I sat with coca growers listening to the radio when the broadcast urged the base-level members to grow less coca or to attend a protest or rally that had little to do with them. On each occasion, the listeners reacted by questioning the union policies and criticizing the executive committee for rushing through proposals without adequately consulting the bases. For many, the station is no longer thought to be the "sovereign voice of the Bolivian cocalero," but rather a MAS propaganda machine.

Radio Kawsachun Coca

Since coming to power, Morales has fought what he describes as the "scourge" of the mass media. In May 2007, Morales issued Supreme Decree 29174, which promotes the expansion of telecommunication services in rural areas where people lack ready access to news and communication media (Internet, phone, and broadcast coverage). This had a huge impact in the Chapare; by 2010 Entel (the telecommunications company nationalized by Morales in 2008) had installed several mobile phone towers across the region to provide reliable and affordable network coverage. The MAS administration has also improved the coverage and quality of the state-owned media, including Radio Illimani and the TV channel Canal Siete. The centerpiece of Morales's communications strategy, however, is the National Radio System of the First Peoples (Sistema Nacional de Radios de los Pueblos Originarios), a radio network that includes thirty-four stations in all nine of Bolivia's departments (states).

In October 2006, Morales addressed a large meeting of the Six Federations at the headquarters of the organization in Lauca Eñe. He said, "The media have humiliated us. They have lied about us. They call us drug traffickers, terrorists, the Taliban even! How can a drug trafficker be president? Now they say that I am incapable, stupid, crazy! The mass media are at the service of neoliberalism." Morales went on to justify the government's choice to build a brand-new radio station in the Chapare. "We are not putting in this radio to indoctrinate; no, we are giving it to the people to manage, to speak truth and to educate. If the millionaires can have their own television and radios, then we also have the right to have our own communication media! That is why we have set up Radio Kawsachun Coca!"

Radio Kawsachun Coca (Long Live Coca in Quechua) is a government-backed station, the largest in the First People's network, and is located only twenty kilometers from Radio Aurora. In theory, the station should function much like Radio Aurora, with the Six Federations responsible for its operation, funding, and management. However, all of the equipment still officially belongs to the state, and the station relies on the government for financial and organizational support. Union leaders told me they were struggling to convince the rank and file to pay for it.

Sergio Cayo (a reporter at Radio Aurora) and I first visited the station three months before its official inauguration in October 2006. The station boasts an enormous studio featuring the latest technology: live recording spaces, production facilities, and powerful transmitters, giving it the capability to broadcast to the entire state of Cochabamba. The scale of the project astounded Sergio—it eclipsed Radio Aurora; in fact, it was far better equipped than any commercial station that could be found in the city. Abel Pacheco, the provisional director of Radio Kawsachun Coca, boasted that it was going to "crush" Radio Aurora. Sergio responded by telling him that he was not afraid. "Radio Aurora already has a long history in the Chapare; it has won its audience, and they are faithful to it." But I don't think he believed his own words.

When I returned in 2013, Abel's prediction had become reality. Kawsachun Coca had indeed sidelined Radio Aurora. Many grassroots members who had traditionally been the audience for Radio Aurora admitted that they had switched stations, and now only listened to Kawsachun Coca. This was mainly because Kawsachun Coca's potent transmitter (and multiple booster stations) obliterated any other radio signal in the region, making it very difficult to tune in to Aurora. Also, people seemed to enjoy the well-produced entertainment programs, which were far more professional and slick than anything Aurora could manage. And yet, while people praised the station for the quality of its programming, when it came to the local news, grassroots members complained that it was just "propaganda for Evo" and that the station did not speak to their own experience. Epifanio (the former director of Radio Aurora), in a 2008 interview, characterized the new radio as a tool for propaganda. "The programs [on Kawsachun Coca] have to respond to the interests of the government and support the political instrument [MAS]. This radio has to be like that; it cannot be critical or make observations about the government. That way they are going to have a spokesman for the government here. This is outside the frame of community radio. Community radio should follow the sentiment of the people."

In 2007, I traveled to La Paz to meet with Gaston Nuñez (the minister for communication) to speak about the government's motivation for setting up these stations. Gaston sat behind a large desk; a colorful Wiphala hung on the wall behind him, flanked by portraits of Simón Bolívar and Tupaj Katari. He told me that the government had been obliged to set up Kawsachun Coca and the First Peoples Radio Network to fight against the tyranny of the mass media. He pulled newspapers out of drawers and showed me anti-MAS headlines to prove his point. I asked why the government had not simply invested in the community-run stations already present in Bolivia. Gaston responded, "The others . . . the ownership and control is diverse. . . . They are NGOs; they are people who are even related to the traditional political parties. We cannot be working with people who have acted irresponsibly in the past." He used words like "traitor" to describe left-leaning journalists who were not aligned with the government, panning organizations like ERBOL that had maintained a critical distance from the MAS government.

Conclusion

Union-owned and -operated radio has generated the kind of resources necessary for collective mobilization in the Chapare and further afield. Reporting on local events, orienting the rank and file, and providing a space for ordinary people to speak, share information, and reflect on their situation places the radio listener into a network of social relationships that lead to solidarity and self-assertion. I suggest that this quotidian public experience of the self allows what Benedict Anderson (1991) calls an "imagined community" to blossom. By steering clear of the big events, the spectacular and the extraordinary, we have seen how the weak ties that are generated by the everyday practice of listening to the radio are essential to the maintenance and functioning of the strong ties of the union structure. But while the radio helped the MAS come to power, it is now being used to control the union.

Two ideas about the principles governing local radio emerge from the ethnographic data outlined above. The first comes from Epifanio, who sees radio as a space for local actors to oversee the authorities. This fits well with the idea of social control outlined throughout this book. The second view, represented by Morales, suggests that the radio should serve the government's interests. Morales's intolerance of critical voices from within the ranks is clearly illustrated by his attempt to brand Epifanio as a traitor when he stood up for the interests of the rank and file, and the establishment of a government-run station in the tropics.

The MAS government's installation of a new radio station was ostensibly to counter the constant stream of misrepresentation coming from the mainstream press, but it also serves as an indoctrination mechanism for its supporters. The fear of overthrow was understandable during the right-wing rebellion in 2007–8, but seems like overkill now that the government has established a clear hegemony. In the Chapare, many people at the base level react cynically to the increase in state-controlled media and the state itself, even as (in the absence of a viable progressive alternative) they continue to vote for the government and see it as aligned with their interests.

At noon Don Edgar Jiminez took a break from harvesting coca leaf and sat down under the shade of an orange tree. He picked up his beat-up twenty-year-old radio, put it to his ear, and turned the knob. When it sparked into life, he flashed a grin in my direction. "They don't make them like they used to . . . this radio has been dropped, driven over, *carajo* [damn], it even knows how to swim!" Edgar took off his shirt and removed his dentures to make room for a wad of coca. He lit a strong hand-rolled cigarette (known locally as a *kuyuna*) and reclined against the tree. Thick blue smoke circled his head, and he smiled, obviously enjoying his pijchu (mouthful of coca).

The radio, balanced on his naked stomach, blasted out the tagline of Radio Aurora: "From the hottest lands of the Cochabamba Tropics a voice surges!" A song with the lyrics "long live coca, death to Yankees" crackled out of the speakers. The jingle ended with a voice-over booming with re-verb: "Radio Aurora, the sovereign voice of the Bolivian Cocalero." Following the jingle, a speech by Don Fernando Ochoa (then the general secretary of Federation Tropico) was broadcast. It was January 2007, and Fernando's discourse was designed to gather support for a mass rally to be held in the city of Cochabamba against the state's right-wing governor, Manfred Reyes Villa.[1] Fernando asked, "Who is Manfred?" He then answered his own question: "Manfred is the number one enemy of the people, the number one enemy of the political instrument, and the number one enemy of the Six Federations."

Don Edgar inhaled smoke and slowly breathed out; jabbing a fat finger in the air, he declared, "Listen to Fernando: he hardly even speaks Quechua, what an idiot! Who is going to pay for the transport to get there? Is Fernando going to pay? I don't think so." Edgar went on to complain that people used to mobilize because they wanted to; they would risk their lives to defend the right to grow coca leaf, but now, he says, "It's all politics. . . . We put Evo in Government . . . but what for? He keeps telling us to do things. What more does he want from us? They [union leaders] are useless; they just won't let us get on with our work. What do they call it when they oblige you to go, when they haven't even consulted the bases? . . . They call it a dictatorship!" With that he switched off the radio and told me that these days he preferred to listen to Radio Netherlands on shortwave instead.

This short vignette captures the central issue this book has attempted to tackle, namely the challenge of maintaining bottom-up control once the MAS came to power. The story of the coca growers and their movement provides a stark and dramatic lens to understand what happens when a grassroots movement takes state power, but then confronts international accords (and domestic opposition) that force a rupture between the elected government branch of the movement and the grassroots group that was the fundamental building block in getting it there. If we only employ the language of democratic representation, then Morales and the MAS look pretty successful. On MAS's watch the constitution has been rewritten, the political participation of disenfranchised people has increased, and Morales has made cogent arguments against rampant neoliberalism. But if we stop to consider what radical change actually means to the coca growers, then we see that grassroots ambitions have been frustrated.

In this concluding chapter, I pull together the data presented thus far to show how it is not enough simply to increase participation in politics and generate horizontal networks. The coca growers do not want abstract democratic ideals; rather, they want concrete payback in the form of more (if not unlimited) coca. But as we have seen, this ambition has been frustrated by factors that extend far beyond sovereign control. The main questions to be addressed in this concluding chapter, then, are: Could the coca growers have ever been satisfied, or were their expectations doomed to fail from the very beginning? And, from the coca growers' perspective, what needs to change for the MAS's experiment in democracy to function better?

Political Hope and Betrayal

At the grassroots level, coca growers have pursued a vernacular form of democracy that prioritizes face-to-face interactions, high levels of participation, consensus building, and holding leaders directly accountable. There is little space for dissent, and people who break with the status quo are punished. While liberal theorists might consider these practices to be the antithesis of democracy, for the cocaleros they represent the very highest form of political engagement they aspire to. This is because ideas about how democracy should be enacted are not enshrined in abstract codes and procedures, but rather are anchored in deeply held understandings of what it means to be a good person—what the coca growers refer to as bien cumplido (fulfilling one's duties). For instance, even voting becomes about much more than simply selecting a candidate; rather, it has to do with honoring ongoing reciprocal commitments and publicly affirming one's membership in a group.

From the very beginning, the MAS was established as an extension of the movement and was informed by the assembly culture practiced at the grassroots. With MAS's accession to power, the coca growers expected elements of the democratic practices found within the base-level sindicatos and town halls in the Chapare to be scaled up to become part of the official body of governance. According to their own logic, the national government should be subsumed by the unions, with Morales and his ministers enacting decisions made at their local union meetings. This much was made clear by the coca growers who, following Morales's election, declared that "all of us are presidents." With this they were staking a claim to a new form of citizenship, one that is built on constant engagement and compliant authorities, enshrined in the idea of "social control." However, with distance from the sindicato, where kinship relations and interpersonal commitments prevail, it is increasingly difficult for the rank and file to exert power over their leaders, and grassroots members soon felt as if they had lost control over the party they had set up.

Worse still, some coca farmers have come to experience the MAS in power as a form of domination. Don Edgar, who is mentioned above, complains that the leaders no longer speak for him and that their autocratic behavior represents a form of dictatorship. The union has a long history of sanctioning its members; coercion of this type was always deemed to be consensual because the union's goals were said to reflect those of each and every member. What is different today, however, is that sanctions are said to come from above, thereby breaking the link between the leadership and the bases.

The case study presented in this book illustrates the conflicts that emerge when electoral politics becomes the arena for realizing radical democratic ambitions. In so doing, it exposes the myth at the heart of the MAS, namely the model of direct democracy and bottom-up control that Morales and his aides have promoted as a rhetorical trope or aspiration designed to ensure the continuing legitimacy of the party, rather than a model that they enact in their current political practice. One coca farmer summed up the shift from opposition to government in the following words: "Before, we put stones in the road, now it's our job to pick them up." With this he was describing how in the past the unions would pressure government to meet their demands by blocking the road with stones, but with the MAS in power, the unions are obliged to support the government.

The rupture between the different levels of the union and the party stems from the fact that trade unions and governing political parties are very different types of beasts. The state requires sophisticated planning and administrative skills, and has to balance the interests and needs of a heterogeneous group of citizens. The coca union, meanwhile, is a relatively homogeneous group, and only ever aims to represent the demands of its members (Van Cott 2008: 175–209). The state, then, is an abstraction; it requires an abstracted idea of the citizens, the "imagined community" whom it can govern. But for the coca growers this abstraction does not exist. Rather, at the level of their sindicatos, governance is rooted in everyday social relations, and loyalty never really extends beyond the unions. The case study of the coca growers, then, points to broader problems that all movements face: namely, how grassroots ideas of governance can be scaled up to inform state practice without losing their radical identity and political ethics.

All of this could have been overlooked provided the coca growers' material concerns were addressed, but according to many grassroots members, they have not. This government has done more than any previous government in Bolivian history to address the needs of its impoverished rural and urban areas. But given the unrealistically high expectations that accompanied the MAS's accession to power, it is hardly surprising that some feel disillusioned. Base-level members have criticized the MAS administration's coca control policy (which restricts cultivation to one cato), which some say leaves them impoverished. They also note the limitations of government-led development programs in offering realistic economic alternatives.

While life has gotten immeasurably better with the MAS in power, from the perspective of grassroots members, the rewards have not been enough. Given how much hope the coca growers had in Morales, what explains the fact that he did not give them what they wanted? Why did he compromise on vital demands, such as coca production, and some would argue even actively betray the bases? And what, if anything, could be changed?

The Problem with Coca

The uncomfortable truth is that the Chapare peasants have used the traditional status of the coca leaf to defend their crops against forced eradication, while being aware of the fact that most of their harvest is used for cocaine production. As we have seen throughout the length of this book, any formal recognition of coca cultivation for illicit purposes is considered a taboo subject by the growers' unions, and it is never discussed at their meetings. Coca is only ever spoken about as something that is special and to be venerated. Indeed, some coca growers have even argued against differentiating between legal coca (a registered cato) and illegal coca (excess coca) because "all coca is sacred" and, as such, all coca should be protected (even if they also accuse coca growers in rival regions of growing coca for the illicit drugs trade).

Conventionally, trade unions and their parties defend labor rights, they take pride in their work, and they identify with the product of their labor. Of course, the Chapare agricultural unions take great pride in coca leaf, but there is an important issue that is always left unsaid, namely their dependence on the illicit cocaine trade as a market for their crop. As a consequence, neither the coca unions nor the MAS has ever been able to adequately (or truthfully) represent the farmers' economic interests. While in opposition, union leaders could channel discontent into a potent argument about indigenous identity and defending national sovereignty, but once in power this narrative fell apart as the reality of governing a country set in.

Morales is no longer solely accountable to the unions; he has to govern for all citizens and abide by international frameworks, and this means that he has been unable to satisfy the coca growers' key material demands relating to coca production. At the international level, coca leaf remains a restricted substance under current UN treaties (despite the government's 2013 victory in obtaining the right to consume coca leaf domestically). Thus, the MAS government has had to advance a policy that, while acknowledging the importance of coca to Andean culture and venerating the sacred leaf, simultaneously limits its cultivation to one cato per member. Over the past ten years, Morales has on occasion turned the security forces against coca growers to achieve this goal (sometimes with violent consequences, as was the case in the Yungas de Vandiola). Some farmers perceive restrictions to be harmful, as they depend on coca cultivation as a means of livelihood and social mobility.

The feeling of betrayal did not emerge when Morales came to power, then; rather, it was written into the story from the very beginning. The case of coca exposes the weakness of Morales's project of reinventing the state, because even when it comes to coca he cannot act autonomously, but is beholden to supranational frameworks. Today when Morales meets with union members in the Chapare, he no longer litters his speeches with phrases that justify coca, nor does he finish them with the slogan "Long live coca! Death to Yankees!" Instead, he is much more likely to urge the rank and file to restrict cultivation to the cato. In this way, and in contradiction to his previous strategy, Morales downplays the association between coca and Andean tradition. Indeed, during a public address at his birthday party in October 2013 (which was held in the Chapare with union leaders), Morales said that the call "long live coca" is now outdated, and that "maybe now we should say long live pineapples, long live oranges . . . or long live *palmito* [palm heart]."

While there might be dissatisfaction at the grassroots, coca growers are unlikely to withdraw their support from Morales and the MAS, however. The coca growers were among those who campaigned and voted in large numbers for the "yes" vote in the 2016 referendum (which would allow Morales to stand for a fourth term). They did this in spite of the limitations of Morales's program. This is because they know that the alternative would be far worse. More than anything, they fear a return to forced coca eradication, with the concomitant downward spiral of violence and poverty. This, then, is a politics of pragmatism rather than a utopian movement.

Coca growers know that if a right-wing (pro–United States) party got into power and turned against them, it is unlikely that they would be able to mount the kind of resistance they mustered in the past. One senior leader explained that it would be difficult to convince the rank and file to mobilize once more, because next time around the growers would know that the payback would only be a cato, so "why would they bother?" Besides, he noted that now the state is so integrated into the daily life of the Chapare residents (including the fact that all coca growers now have official government land titles and biometric ID cards) that it would be easier for the state to crush dissent. As noted, the farmers are now legible to the state and therefore more amenable to its control.

The case study provided in this book is unique because, unlike other social movements, the coca union is dedicated to an activity that is fundamentally illegal (but not immoral from the coca growers' point of view). Even so, it provides a clear example of the difficulties on the part of politicians of ever meeting the material demands emanating from their bases, particularly in an environment where supranational frameworks limit sovereign control. Radical movements all over the world face these problems every day, namely how to reconcile big ideas with the mundane realities of governing and everyday life (Feuchtwang and Shah 2015; Koch 2016; Shah 2014). This, then, raises the question: What needs to happen to ensure that the coca growers' demands are better met going forward?

Alternative Policy Proposals

As it stands, Chapare peasants have few options but to grow coca, as it is one of the few crops that give them a reasonable rate of return (this is particularly true for those who live in more isolated areas). Consequently, if the status quo is maintained, the peasant farmers will always be outlaws and vulnerable to repressive policing. There are two ways out of the current impasse, however. The first approach is to decriminalize the coca plant at the international level, thereby allowing Chapare peasants to produce coca for the legal market. The second approach is to assist the peasant farmers to develop realistic sources of income that do not rely on coca cultivation.

The coca growers' unions argue that if coca were legal, then they could export it in the form of coca teas, liquor, flour, and other semi-industrialized products. In Colombia, coca-based products are increasingly popular, and coca use in Peru and Bolivia is undergoing a renaissance. No longer an ethnic preserve, coca is being consumed in geographical areas (the Peruvian coast, the Bolivian lowlands where the city of Santa Cruz has emerged as a major market) where it was previously unheard of, and is being used by social groups (students, urban workers, the middle class) who, only a generation ago, would have found it too "Indian." In Chile, Paraguay, Argentina, and Brazil, and even in Europe and North America, small markets for coca products are emerging, although often in semi-clandestine forms (Henman and Metaal 2009: 21). In January 2017, Bolivia announced that it would export coca tea to Ecuador and Venezuela (*Pagina Siete* 2017). But the Chapare farmers hold out most hope for China. From watching TV, they know that the Chinese drink tea, and they assume that they would be able to export massive volumes of coca tea to the country, a topic that is frequently discussed at union meetings. When Bolivia hosted the G77 plus China meetings in 2014, coca growers from the Chapare set up stalls in the Santa Cruz airport and in the city's central plaza to promote legal coca-based products to the delegates (ANB 2014).

The drug policy debate is shifting, especially in Latin America. The regional debate focuses on the failure of current policies to achieve their desired objectives and the high cost of implementing supply reduction efforts in terms of violence, corruption, and institutional instability. Leaders from Mexico, Guatemala, Brazil, and Colombia have proposed initiatives including decriminalizing drugs for personal consumption, reducing penalties for drugs offenses, creating corridors for the transit of illicit drugs (so they can move unhindered to the market without destabilizing the entire region), and increasing expenditure on harm-reduction programs. Latin American leaders have also called on the United States to do more to stem the flow of money (and arms) that drives production (Collins 2014; GCDP 2016; Mathieu and Niño Guarnizo 2013).

This is not just talk; some countries have taken unilateral steps toward drug policy reform (see contributions to Labate, Cavnar, and Rodrigues 2016). In December 2013, Uruguay became the first country in the world to legalize and regulate the production, marketing, and consumption of cannabis. Even the United States has taken steps toward reforming drug laws. Since 2012, legal, regulated cannabis markets have been approved in nine states, starting with Washington, Oregon, Colorado, and Alaska, and nineteen more have legalized its use for medical purposes. Even so, modification of the international drug conventions is slow. Any recourse to legalizing coca will be contested, as was the case when Bolivia attempted to amend the Single Convention to permit traditional coca chewing within its territory (Jelsma 2016: 21).[2]

With Donald Trump in the White House, the reform drive will likely suffer a setback, however. The Trump administration appears to be committed to bringing back the harsh antidrug rhetoric and polices of the 1980s and 1990s. Trump has proposed building a wall along the United States' border with Mexico, with the aim of cutting drug smuggling (all experts agree that it will be ineffective), and during a speech before law enforcement officers in February 2017 Trump vowed to be "ruthless" in the fight against drugs.

To this end, he named Jeff Sessions, a renowned conservative drug warrior, as his attorney general (Ingraham 2017). The 2018 budget called for a boost in spending on the military and security on the border, while at the same time demanding deep cuts in essential foreign development aid and diplomatic initiatives (Gomis 2017).

Given the difficulty of legalizing coca at the international level, a medium-term strategy has to focus on the implementation of viable, sustainable livelihoods that dissuade people from relying on coca in the first place. This means increasing state presence through the expansion of roads, schools, and health clinics, and providing farmers with loans, credit, and know-how to diversify their production. Perhaps most importantly, the government needs to ensure that there are markets for non-coca tropical agricultural products through the expansion of processing plants located in coca-growing regions, for example. Many of these elements are being implemented by the MAS administration, but, according to farmers, still not enough is being done. If the United States provided support for such initiatives (without making assistance dependent on the prior eradication of coca, as was the case in the past) and worked with (as opposed to against) the coca growers' unions to implement programs, then much more could be achieved. European Union–led initiatives in the Chapare provide a productive model in this regard (Grisaffi, Farthing, and Ledebur 2017; Grisaffi and Ledebur 2016: 8–10).

In December 2016, MAS activists approved the candidacy of Morales for the 2019 elections, this despite the fact that in February of that year Bolivians voted to deny him the right to run for a fourth consecutive term in a national referendum.[3] Morales welcomed the party's decision, saying, "If the people decide it, Evo will continue" (*Economist* 2017). The fact that Morales is indicating that he wants to overrule the constitution (first ratified in 2009) might not be the worst thing from the coca growers' point of view. As we have seen throughout this book, rules are there to be negotiated or even broken. The bigger challenge going forward, rather, is how a new Morales government would address the central paradox that this book has identified, namely finding a way out of the impasse that places people at the risk of criminalization for pursuing their livelihoods.

In Bolivia, policies aimed at tackling the illicit drug trade are to a great extent dictated by an international agenda. Thus, even if grassroots ambitions for alternative democratic practices were realized (including the emphasis they put on consensus building and holding their leaders directly accountable), the government would never have been able to fully satisfy the coca growers' material aspirations, because their livelihoods are intimately tied to an economy that is internationally outlawed. Unless there is radical change at the international level, then, the Chapare coca farmers will always be on the wrong side of the law.

NOTES

INTRODUCTION

1. In 2004 (the year preceding Morales's historic win), only 23 percent of the Bolivian population reported that they had any confidence in political parties, making them the least trusted institution in Bolivia. In 2005 the proportion of people who reported being satisfied or very satisfied with democracy stood at only 24 percent (Seligson and Moreno 2006).

2. Subcommander Marcos was the leader of the Zapatista movement in Chiapas, Mexico, who stepped down in 2014.

3. In 2007 the MAS administration created the National Coordination for Change (La Coordinadora Nacional por el Cambio—CONALCAM) to bring together the heads of Bolivia's social movement organizations with the president, his ministers, and congressional leaders in order to discuss government policies.

4. The concept of grassroots control over leaders was institutionalized in a new constitution adopted in 2009, which enshrines the idea that social movements should oversee government spending and policy as well as public contracts with private companies, something that draws on largely essentialized indigenous community concepts of *social control*. According to Farthing and Kohl (2014: 42), the emphasis on social control in the constitution is as a mechanism to battle corruption. The concept underlies areas as diverse as ensuring health program quality to limiting coca cultivation. The extent to which processes of social control are actually applied is debated, however (Anria 2010, 2016a; Mayorga 2011: 97; Postero 2010; Wolff 2013).

5. Evo Morales is the executive general secretary of both Federación Trópico (the largest and most militant of the Chapare coca unions), and the Confederation of Coca Unions in the Cochabamba Tropics, referred to as the "Six Federations."

6. At a 2006 meeting of all six coca federations, Morales stated, "not only Evo is President, the six federations [coca unions], all of us are presidents compañeras and compañeros" (speech at the closure of the VIII Congress of the Six Federations. La Coronilla, Cochabamba, February 14, 2006).

7. García Linera insists that "governing from below" requires power to be concentrated in the president (Svampa and Stefanoni 2007: 161).

8. Social movements aligned with the MAS have demonstrated outside Bolivia's Congress to put pressure on legislators to pass MAS-sponsored bills, specifically those on agrarian reform and the new constitution. In 2007 MAS supporters (including the coca growers) used protest in an attempt to force the governor of Cochabamba (Manfred Reyes Villa) to resign, going as far as setting the prefecture on fire (Albro 2007: 357). Reyes Villa was ousted in a 2008 recall referendum.

9. *Caudillismo*, which Wolf and Hansen (1967) argue emerged during the tumultuous post-independence years, is an entrenched aspect of political practice in Latin America and can be observed in a range of settings from unions to government (Gledhill 2000: 111–14; Poole 2004; Starn 1992: 105–6).

10. When union members complained that they could not get close to Morales, they were describing how his security detail would form a protective human wall around him.

11. Presidents were removed from office before the end of their term in Argentina (2001), Bolivia (2003 and 2005), Brazil (2016), Ecuador (1997, 2000, and 2005), Honduras (2009), Paraguay (2012), and Venezuela (2002—although Chavez was back in office forty-seven hours later). In addition, there were several unsuccessful efforts, including an attempt to unseat Evo Morales in 2008, which was led by large landowners in Bolivia's eastern lowlands, with tacit support from the United States (Fabricant 2009).

12. Cocaine involves two distinct products, powder cocaine and cocaine-base products, which are commonly referred to as "crack" (in reference to the "cracking" sound it produces when heated). Powder cocaine is expensive in the northern consumer markets; it is normally inhaled, and its use is often associated with upper-middle-class urban consumers. Crack, meanwhile, is a solid form of cocaine that is smoked; it is cheaper, more intense, and is associated with high levels of street crime (Bourgois 1995).

13. From 2006 to 2010 the amount of cocaine consumed in the United States decreased by approximately 50 percent. Experts argue that this was because consumer preferences have shifted to other drugs including marijuana (which has now been decriminalized in more than twenty states) and methamphetamines (Caulkins et al. 2015).

14. The largest retail markets for cocaine in 2013 were the United States (whose 47 percent market share is worth an estimated $40 billion), followed by Western and Central Europe ($34 billion, or 39 percent of the global market) (UNODC 2016d). Cocaine is flowing south too, as demand increases in South America. Brazil's estimated 900,000 users represent the single largest market in South America (Gootenberg 2016).

15. Daniel Mejía (2015) estimates that the cost of eliminating the amount of coca needed to produce one kilogram of cocaine in Colombia is about US$240,000, more than double the price of one kilo of refined cocaine in the United States.

16. As a result of the "balloon effect," although the amount of land under coca cultivation in Peru, Colombia, and Bolivia fluctuated between 1987 and 2008, the total coca acreage in the Andean region as a whole remained remarkably stable, at around 190,000 hectares (Youngers and Walsh 2010: 3).

17. In 2000 the United States and Colombia jointly launched Plan Colombia, a multibillion-dollar "aid" package (80 percent of which was destined for the police and military) with the stated aim of reducing narcotics production by half within six years and to regain security in the country (Mejía 2010). The extent of the project was so

vast that it made Colombia the third largest recipient of U.S. foreign aid by the end of the 1990s.

18. In Lima, which is located on the coast far away from coca-producing zones, coca use is limited, although over the past ten years coca consumption has increased in coastal areas (Gootenberg 2016).

19. Revenues from hydrocarbons and mining increased as a result of higher commodity prices on the global market, but also because of the MAS government's decision to insist on a greater share of the rents in the hydrocarbons industry, currently centered on natural gas.

20. The Afro-Bolivian population are the descendants of slaves who were bought to Bolivia to work in Potosí's silver mines during the colonial period.

21. The 200 to 500 meters figure refers to the main agricultural area of the Cochabamba Tropics; some parts of Chapare, such as Colomi are much higher.

22. The 2001 census indicates that in the municipality of Villa Tunari (where I conducted fieldwork), 70 percent of respondents learned to speak in Quechua as a first language and 81 percent of the population self-identify as Quechua. The remaining respondents said either that they did not identify as indigenous (11 percent) or that they consider themselves Aymara (5 percent) or another indigenous group (3 percent) (PNUD 2005: 302).

23. It is estimated that Bolivians consume approximately twenty thousand metric tons of coca leaf annually, equivalent to approximately 14,000 hectares of production (Burgos Gallardo 2017).

24. Given its medicinal properties (including its power to alleviate altitude sickness), functionaries of the United Nations and the U.S. State Department have enthusiastically sipped on the coca tea offered on arrival at Bolivia's main international airport, located 4,000 meters above sea level (Henman and Metaal 2009: 22).

25. Contrary to dominant narratives, Allan Gillies has argued that Bolivian politicians pushed back against the United States–led "Andean Initiative" in the late 1980s (Gillies forthcoming).

26. Law 1008 also considered the Vandiola Yungas in Cochabamba and the Franz Tamayo Province in La Paz as "traditional zones," but did not stipulate how much coca could be grown there (Farthing and Ledebur 2015: 16).

27. Law 1008 makes a distinction between illegal and "transitional" zones. In illegal zones, coca has to be destroyed immediately. Transitional zones (of which the Chapare is one) were subject to crop substation programs. The law required Bolivia to eradicate a minimum of 5,000 hectares per year (Farthing and Ledebur 2015: 16–17).

28. Crop eradication in the Yungas regions was always done at a slower pace, partly because of its status as a traditional area, but also because the hilly topography and limited access roads meant that peasants could more effectively defend the region against police incursions (Crabtree and Chaplin 2013: 106).

29. The new coca law nearly doubles the area for legal cultivation from the 12,000 hectares allowed under Law 1008 to 22,000 hectares. It legitimates the existing 20,000 hectares of coca fields that were permitted under the 2004 cato accord and adds a further 2,000 to satisfy demands from coca growers in the Yungas of La Paz (Farthing 2017).

1. The Rise of the Coca Unions

1. Laura Gotkowitz has drawn attention to the important role agricultural unions played in promoting the 1952 revolution, a sector of the population that has traditionally been overlooked as historical actors in Bolivia (Gotkowitz 2007).

2. The COB brought together workers' unions from Bolivia's mines, the small manufacturing sector, peasant farmers, indigenous peoples, and some middle-class sectors. Its leadership was always drawn from the militant miners' unions, however.

3. In the early 1960s, USAID armed peasant militias to assassinate left-wing leaders of the miners' unions (Field 2016: 32).

4. At first there were only five coca federations. Federation Yungas split from Federación Trópico in the early 1990s. Growers in Yungas Chapare claimed that they lived in a "traditional area" and hoped to gain special rights under Law 1008. These special rights were never granted by the state, however.

5. The six federations of coca producers are affiliated with the Unified Confederation of Campesino Unions of Bolivia (Confederación Sindical Única de Trabajadores Campesinos de Bolivia—CSUTCB) and the Bolivian Syndical Confederation of Intercultural First Peoples Communities of Bolivia (Confederación Sindical de Comunidades Interculturales Originarios de Bolivia—CSCIOB), which was formerly known as the Bolivian Syndical Confederation of Colonizers (Confederación Sindical de Colonizadores de Bolivia—CSCB).

6. The women's federation exists only as an executive committee; it does not have its own grassroots sindicatos, however (Arnold and Spedding 2005: 94–98).

7. Morales joined forces with Filemón Escobar, a controversial ex-Trotskyist mining leader. Escobar had moved to Cochabamba after the mine closures and the defeat of miner resistance, and increasingly adopted a pro-indigenist political stance (see Escobar 2008).

8. Maria Clemencia Ramirez (2010: 84) has drawn attention to how in coca-growing regions of Colombia normal civil and social rights are suspended. The "state of exception" is a government mechanism used to legitimize military actions against civilians and thereby achieve long-term institutional stability; with reference to Agamben, she describes it as "a technique of government."

9. The Law of Popular Participation (LPP) called for the establishment of oversight committees (comités de vigilancia) to provide "social control" over municipal administration and thereby limit corruption. It also empowered local grassroots organizations to participate in the planning process. Each territorial unit (known as a Territorial Base Organization, or OTB) was able to define its own needs for public spending, which were articulated through the Annual Operative Plan (Plan Operativo Anual—POA).

10. The outcome of decentralization in Bolivia has been mixed: in some regions the reforms entrenched long-standing inequalities as mestizo elites came to dominate municipal politics. However, the picture is quite different in regions like the Chapare, where well-organized peasant movements took control of municipal governance and ran it for their own benefit. In the Chapare this has meant investing state funds in previously neglected rural areas, including providing basic infrastructure such as roads,

drinking water, and sanitation, but also the construction of health clinics and schools (Albó 2002a; Albó and Quispe 2004).

11. Organizations at the founding conference of the political instrument in Santa Cruz included La Confederación Sindical Única de Trabajadores Campesinos de Bolivia (CSUTCB), La Confederación Sindical de Colonizadores Bolivianos (CSB), La Confederación Nacional de Mujeres Campesinas Indígenas Originarias de Bolivia "Bartolina Sisa" (CNMCIOB-BS), and the Six Federations of Coca growers of the Tropics of Cochabamba.

12. In Ecuador, with the election of Lucio Gutierrez in 2002, indigenous leaders who had been involved in the general strike and coup that removed Mahuad from office in 2000 were able to join the national government as cabinet ministers. The indigenous movement then saw its moment of triumph fade away into accusations of corruption and patronage as they struggled to make the transition from outsiders to insiders (Collins 2004). Meanwhile, on its accession to power in 2003, the Brazilian Workers Party established a well-differentiated political organization that worked autonomously from its social base (Hunter 2010).

13. No coca union leaders were offered ministerial posts. After Evo Morales, the next most important Chapare coca grower in government is Felipe Caceres, the vice minister for social defense.

14. Even Morales's right-hand man, Vice President Álvaro García Linera (an elite public intellectual), was widely thought to be "not one of us" and therefore not to be fully trusted. Rank-and-file members disparagingly referred to García Linera as "the wife of Evo" and were of the opinion that as a result of his undue influence, the union's more radical proposals had been watered down. In the words of Doña Maria, a leader in her thirties, "In my opinion . . . it was Álvaro who has weakened Evo's position against the transnationals. He made the nationalization softer, more in their favor."

15. Colonialism is used to refer to a state of mind, language, and culture. Decolonization, then, is an attempt to promote a different kind of thinking and approach to state building along indigenous lines (Escobar 2010; Quijano 2007; Walsh 2010).

16. Significant cash transfer programs include the Bono Juancito Pinto, a payment for school attendance; Juana Azurduy, for pregnant and lactating mothers; and Renta Dignidad, a universal pension.

17. An IMF study argues that reductions in inequality and poverty have been driven by income growth at the bottom end of the income distribution (Vargas and Garriga 2015).

18. Bolivia's Gini Index decreased from 0.60 in 2004 to 0.47 in 2014 (World Bank 2016a).

19. Right-wing forces occupied state institutions, closed down airports, and shut down gas pipelines to neighboring countries. Large agribusinesses cut food supplies to the west of the country (where support for MAS is strongest), and key military commanders told Morales they would not obey orders to crush the rebellion. Phillip Goldberg, U.S. ambassador to Bolivia, flew to Santa Cruz to meet with Rubén Costas, the state governor, and one of the leaders of the autonomy movement, during this tense period. Morales subsequently expelled Goldberg (September 2008), declaring him persona non grata for having "conspired against democracy and Bolivia" (Fabricant 2011).

20. Critics have argued that when it comes to natural gas, Bolivia still lacks adequate technical and administrative capacity, energy self-sufficiency, and full-fledged economic sovereignty (Kaup 2010).

21. The no vote (against reelection) took 51.3 percent of the vote and won in all of Bolivia's major cities; meanwhile, the yes vote (in favor of reelection), which took 48.7 percent, prevailed in rural areas and urban peripheries, MAS's traditional heartlands (Achtenberg 2016).

22. There are competing arguments about why Morales failed to secure a victory in the 2016 referendum. The winners claim "the people have spoken," while the losers argue that there was a dangerous misinformation campaign orchestrated by the right (and paid for by the United States). The truth likely lies somewhere in the middle (Gustafson 2016; Stefanoni 2016).

23. Bolivia's economy relies mainly on natural gas exports, which have halved in price since 2014. In 2017 Bolivia is expected to earn $2.1 billion from gas sales, just a third of what it made when prices were high. The IMF estimates that in 2017 GDP grew 3.9 percent, far below the peak of 6.8 percent in 2013. Further, the IMF has warned that Bolivia's overvalued currency is hurting producers of goods besides raw materials (*Economist* 2017).

24. A survey undertaken in 2010 found that 45 percent of farm owners in Villa Tunari municipality would "occasionally" make use of a paid laborer (CPDI 2010: 132).

25. In the Chapare, people (particularly young men) use nicknames to refer to one another. However, for ease I have anonymized informants by using standard Bolivian names.

2. The Lowest Rung of the Cocaine Trade

1. A 2015 news article reported that the police destroyed 2,433 coca paste workshops in the Chapare in 2014 (de los Santos 2015).

2. The website of the Bolivian Special Anti-Narcotics Police Force (Fuerza Especial de Lucha Contra el Narcotráfico—FELCN) records that in 2016 it confiscated almost thirty tons of cocaine in Bolivia (FELCN 2017).

3. *Lejia* is the name of the alkali used to activate the coca. There are several forms of it available; *lejia dulce* (sweet lejia) is made from the ashes of burned vegetable matter, which is mixed with cane sugar and anise.

4. There are clear parallels between Spanish promotion of coca and the way British industrialists encouraged sugar consumption among Britain's working classes during the nineteenth century to provide them with a cheap source of calories while they labored in the factories (Mintz 1986).

5. In 1904 the Coca-Cola Company removed the cocaine alkaloid from its product, but to this day it continues to use de-cocainized coca leaf as a flavoring agent for its formula.

6. Under the terms of the Single Convention, Bolivia's reaccession could have been blocked if sixty-one ratifying parties to the Convention objected.

7. It took over ten years for the MAS administration to approve the new coca law, because an entitled group of growers in what Law 1008 designated the Yungas "tradi-

tional zone" opposed any legalization of cultivation in the Chapare. Initially, the new coca law was going to permit only 20,000 hectares—but an additional 2,000 hectares were permitted to stave off rebellion (Farthing 2017).

8. Ironically, the landowning elites who came to control the cocaine trade in the 1980s emerged as a direct result of U.S. government advisors promoting the formation of an export-oriented agro-industrial sector in the eastern lowlands during the 1950s (Mesa, Gisbert, and Mesa 2003: 664).

9. The practice of dividing plots of land among children meant that the plots steadily decreased in size until they were no longer large enough to support a family.

10. Coca growers are permitted to commercialize a very small amount of coca privately.

11. The amount drug processors will pay for coca leaf varies in line with market conditions, including how much coca is available and the supply of precursor chemicals to process cocaine.

3. Self-Governing in the Chapare

1. https://www.youtube.com/watch?v=cfsuUdQpYJo.

2. Speech made by Evo Morales, September 10, 2013, Villa Catorce de Septiembre, Chapare.

3. Godparenthood, or *compadrazgo* as it is known locally, is a form of fictive kinship, whereby a senior member of the community takes responsibility for the education, religious development, or marriage of a more junior partner. The relationship implies a commitment and duties on both sides. For instance, the godparent of a marriage (normally the person who pays for the church ceremony) has the responsibility to check on the young couple and police any untoward behavior. In turn, the couple owe their godparents regular visits, invitations to eat together, and offers of assistance as and when needed (see Spedding 1998).

4. The 2009 constitution legitimizes the practice of community justice for minor crimes and dispute resolution. The constitution does not permit the use of violent punishments (Hammond 2011).

5. In the Chapare's larger villages and towns, the sheriff's position is not necessarily tied to the union, but rather he is elected by the town's civic committee (town council). In all but the very largest towns, the civic committee is composed of people who are also members of the union.

6. In cases of compensation, the claimant has to pay a 10 percent fee to the sindicato (which goes into the community's coffers). This is far cheaper for the claimant than if they were to take the case to an official lawyer.

7. Reciprocity is not only enacted between humans. In peasant communities, offerings of food, alcohol, cigarettes, and blood to the Pachamama (a female earth deity) maintain harmony with the supernatural world and ensure continuity in the returns from crops and flocks (Bolton 2002; Harris 2000b).

8. Here I am referring to Marcel Mauss's observations on the nature of the gift, in which he shows how the triple obligation—to give, to receive, and to return—helps

to create and maintain particular social relations of power and hierarchy within any society (Mauss [1954] 1990).

9. A landowner does in fact benefit from loaning a neighbor or friend land. The person who borrows the land puts considerable time, effort, and resources into clearing the dense foliage and trees (known locally as monte) and planting crops, making the land apt for cultivation in the future.

10. Coca is also repackaged for practical reasons. Coca leaves get hot and humid and can spoil if left too long in a sack.

11. The process of mobilization mirrors the segmentary political systems observed by Evans-Pritchard (1940) in Nuerland.

12. Penelope Harvey and Hannah Knox (2015) have examined how infrastructure facilities (such as roads and public buildings) are symbols of modernization in the Andes.

4. From Class to Ethnicity

1. In urban contexts the word *cholita* is often used pejoratively.

2. Marisol de la Cadena has argued that women are always deemed to be "more Indian" than men (de la Cadena 1995).

3. In the Chapare many women do not wear the pollera. When I asked my friend Leyla if she would wear a pollera, she replied, "No, that is for people who are more from the countryside." See Mary Weismantel's *Cholas and Pishtacos* for a discussion on the link between traditional dress, class, and indigeneity (Weismantel 2001).

4. There is no Quechua nation per se; rather, it is a linguistic group.

5. Ex-mining leader Filemon Escobar vehemently opposed Harris and Albó's argument that the miners were in some way opposed to the indigenous peasant groups (Escobar 1986).

6. I do not want to give the impression that the relationship between coca growers and lowland indigenous peoples such as the Yuracarés is always negative. Yuracarés have settled in coca grower communities (and vice versa). The sense of ethno-racial difference is by no means absolute (Sturtevant 2015).

7. In 2009 the MAS government advanced a plan to put a Brazilian-financed 300-km-long paved road through the middle of TIPNIS to connect the cities of Cochabamba and Trinidad. The road would first pass through several coca grower communities in the Chapare (including the village where I was living), and the farmers had high hopes for it. Some built extra rooms on their houses so they might operate as a motel; others set up small shops; and one peasant subcentral several miles down the road even gathered together to construct a gas station. However, the road project was put on hold in 2011 as a result of pressure from lowland indigenous groups who staged a national march to highlight their concerns over the road's environmental and social impacts. The march was subsequently violently repressed by members of the security forces. Indigenous mobilization against road construction only served to highlight coca growers' conviction that the lowland indigenous groups represent a barrier to development. In a 2013 interview, Don Porfilio, a coca grower leader and municipal councilor, explained that the road had been a "dream" of the coca growers for a long time, but "the indi-

genas [indigenous people] got in the way." He assured me it was absurd to think that the "Yuras" (short for Yuracaré, used to refer to indigenous groups) would not want a road; rather, he insisted that it was foreigners and NGOs who had "manipulated" them and encouraged them to protest in a bid to destabilize the MAS administration. "They [indigenous groups] want development, just like we do. They plant bananas, oranges, and achiote; how are they going to sell those products without a road?" He continued, "A road would be good for them, there would be more movement, more sales, more development." When the government temporarily stalled construction of the road, the unions took matters into their own hands. Besides sending a permanent delegation to Sucre in an effort to repeal Law 180 (which has stalled construction on the road), the coca growers started work on opening the road themselves, contracting machinery and workers to improve the section running up to the border with the TIPNIS park.

8. At the same time that he was pushing through multicultural reforms, de Lozada also rushed through the law of capitalization (a gloss for privatization), which gave the go-ahead for the sale of the state's oil and gas, energy, telecommunications, national airline, and rail companies (Kohl 2002).

9. Observers have commented that, despite advancing a pro-ethnic agenda, the CSUTCB is nevertheless characterized by a tension between leftist, worker-based ideologies and a more "ethnic" set of demands recognizing the indigenous status of the majority of its members (Postero 2017: 28).

10. Personal communication with Penelope Harvey, July 4, 2007.

11. Human rights activists involved in the case confirmed that they had found no evidence of drug trafficking in the affected communities. Moreover, it turned out that both of those killed were not foreigners at all, but rather local residents (AIN 2006).

5. Community Coca Control

1. The farmers targeted for resettlement were the members of Federación Trópico, the largest and most militant of the six coca federations.

2. Sarah Radcliffe describes how after September 2001 Washington policy makers viewed indigenous people as potential security threats and destabilizing influences on Latin American nation-states (Radcliffe 2007)

3. In the State Department's April 2008 country reports on terrorism, it is claimed that "Bolivia showed new potential as a possible site for terrorist activity." The report added that supporters and members of the National Liberation Army (ELN), the Fuerzas Armadas Revolucionarias de Colombia (FARC), and Peru's Movimiento Revolucionario Túpac Amaru (MRTA) might be present in Bolivia. However, no evidence was provided to support these allegations (Ledebur and Youngers 2008).

4. According to U.S. data, between 1997 and 2002, land under coca cultivation nationally declined from 45,800 to 18,900 hectares, with most of the reductions being driven by eradication in the Chapare (Jackson et al. 2003: iii).

5. The most significant contribution of USAID programs was the improvement in local road infrastructure (USAID 2005).

6. During the late 1990s and early 2000s, when the local economy was severely depressed (as a result of violent forced coca eradication), farmers would use their coca in barter exchanges known as *trueque* or *cambio* in order to secure highland goods that they could not produce in the tropics; this was beneficial, as it did away with profit-seeking intermediaries (for a discussion of how trueque functions in Peru, see Mayer 2001: 177).

7. Alternative development projects undertaken in the Yungas traditional region (located to the north of La Paz) faced similar challenges. In the late 1980s, the UN launched a crop substitution program known as Agro-Yungas, investing over $21 million. The coffee varieties introduced were more susceptible to disease than local varieties and, just as in the Chapare, market research was absent. After 2001, USAID-led coffee projects had more success, partly because of investments in processing plants, but also because of a growing international demand for specialty coffee. Still, the project was vulnerable to dramatic shifts in the price of coffee, leaving farmers at times in a vulnerable position (Farthing and Ledebur 2015: 18).

8. Since 2008, the official policy in relation to the Yungas of La Paz has been to differentiate between the "traditional" areas (protected under Law 1008) and new zones where coca growing has increased in recent years. In these so-called transitional areas, farmers have also been granted a "cato of coca." Given the steep slopes, the cato is larger, measuring 2,500 square meters. In the "traditional" Yungas area, there is no limit on coca growing (Farthing and Ledebur 2015: 19).

9. The national media and opposition politicians have been critical of investments directed at the Chapare. Commentators decry the lack of strategic planning and the preferential treatment the region seems to receive (Gómez 2013; *Los Tiempos* 2017b; *Pagina Siete* 2015a). One 2012 headline read "Rivers of State Money Flow to the Chapare" (*El Día* 2012b).

10. The government has committed to building a fish-processing plant in Chimore at a cost of $28 million (*El Deber* 2015).

11. In 2016, Bolivia signed drug control agreements with Peru, Brazil, Argentina, and Paraguay. The country also bought high-tech radar units to tackle illegal drug flights, and installed vehicle scanners on the border with Chile to strengthen controls (Yagoub 2016).

12. Clashes between coca growers and government troops have been reported in the media (*Los Tiempos* 2012).

13. Land titling was completed in 2010; as a result, it is no longer possible to subdivide plots.

14. Antistate attitudes can be traced back to the ways in which indigenous taxation was increased in the nineteenth century and was the basis of state revenues (Larson 1995; Platt 1984).

15. The process of making the Chapare legible can be traced further back to the creation of municipalities via the Law of Popular Participation in the mid-1990s (Kohl 2003).

CHAPTER 6. **The Unions and Local Government**

1. Union leaders acquire T-shirts with federation and MAS logos when they attend union meetings or rallies, and these are given out as gifts by aspiring union or political leaders. The T-shirts are much in demand and are highly prized.

2. The statutes of the women's federation reveal that they share the same demands as the mainstream (read: male) federation, including the protection of coca, territory, and loyalty to the political instrument, but they also include demands specific to women, including "the right to be leaders," "equality of rights," and "the right to have land as women" (Agreda, Rodriguez, and Conteras 1996: 40).

3. Day workers and sharecroppers are not allowed to assume leadership positions because they have no land, and therefore it is suspected that they lack commitment to the union. Full members (read: landowners) worry that they might run off with the sindicato's money.

4. Over the past five years, fusarium (a disease that effects coca) has taken hold, and is killing off the coca plants in the Shinahota municipality; by some accounts as much as two-thirds of the crop has been affected. There are many explanations for why fusarium is happening and why now. Locals muse that it might be a U.S. imperial strategy—a biological weapon released in order to destroy the coca crop. But most believe that "the plague" is a result of intensive farming practices. Since the launch of the cato accord, farmers have jacked up their use of fertilizer and pesticides in order to boost production on their legal 40 × 40 meter plots, and this seems to have had a deleterious impact. Morales and his team do not want the message to get out, as it undermines the notion that they are taking responsibility for the coca–cocaine issue. Thus, the state response to the fusarium has been minimal (Pearson 2016). Lidia's acknowledgment of this issue, and her demand that the government should act on it, therefore might have generated conflict with the executive branch.

5. A further twelve coca farmers faced less severe sanctions (including being banned from selling goods in the local markets) for the role they played.

6. Dissident coca growers, along with a handful of representatives from national-level social movements (including the former general secretary of the Bolivia Workers Central of El Alto, and the "Apu Mallku" (the leader of CONAMAQ), established the National Council for the Defense of Constitutional Rights (or the CNDDC by its Spanish acronym). At its first and only meeting, which was held in Shinahota, it was stated that the CNDCC's goal was to "end the fear of the MAS, and to face up and fight for our constitutional and political rights" (Zelada 2015).

7. **The Coca Union's Radio Station**

1. Here I refer to only one coca union, because Radio Aurora belongs to only one of the Six Federations (Federación Trópico).

2. Aware of the power of radio to mobilize the workers, the military dictator General Hugo Banzer (1971–78) arranged for televisions to be distributed free of charge in mining

communities, but still the radio exerted a strong influence over the miners (Barrios and Viezzer 1978: 182–85).

3. In 2003, as part of an effort to wean the coca growers off listening to Radio Aurora, the military (with funding from the U.S. embassy) established their own FM station in the Chapare. The station, which was called Radio Tricolor, drafted in professionals from La Paz and played the most up-to-date music. This strategy was not successful, as growers continued to listen to their own station and made several attempts to shut down the rival station, including surrounding it and laying siege on numerous occasions.

4. Over the period I conducted fieldwork, access to other communications devices became more widespread. Most significantly, since 2010 (when the state telecommunications company rolled out the mobile phone network in the region) farmers now have mobile phones, and some have access to the Internet (at cybercafes in towns or via their mobile phone network).

5. ERBOL is by no means the only institution that provides a platform for community radio stations to communicate with one another; it is, however, the largest and has the longest history in Bolivia.

6. Reporters from community-run stations provide updates to ERBOL's main office in La Paz via telephone. These are then compiled into the daily news program, which is transmitted via satellite, downloaded, and rebroadcast by all participating stations.

7. Since 2006 there have been six different vice ministers of coca, and each one is from the Yungas. Commentators have referred to the Yungas dominance in this area as a "quota"; put another way, Morales has given this post to the Yungas organizations to ensure their support for the MAS administration (Choque 2016).

CONCLUSION

1. Manfred Reyes Villa was the governor of Cochabamba between 2005 and 2008. He was a vocal opponent of Evo Morales and the MAS. He angered the coca growers by arguing for a departmental referendum on autonomy, only half a year after the previous one when the "no vote" won with 63 percent of the vote. This suggestion generated massive protests by the social movements aligned with MAS, including a strong presence of cocaleros in the streets of Cochabamba who called for Reyes Villa to resign (Albro 2007: 357).

2. The decriminalization of coca leaf might not actually work in the Chapare farmers' favor. If there were no controls on coca, then anyone could grow it anywhere. History tells us that when coca cultivation is extensive, as it was in the early 1990s, the price drops. Some farmers told me they were concerned about legalization of coca for exactly this reason.

3. The new constitution prevents presidents from serving more than two consecutive terms. The proposed 2019 election would be Morales's fourth term, but his third under the 2009 constitution.

REFERENCES

Abercrombie, Thomas. 1998. *Pathways of Memory and Power: Ethnography and History among an Andean People*. Madison: University of Wisconsin Press.

Abu-Lughod, Lila. 1993. "Finding a Place for Islam: Egyptian Television Serials and the National Interest." *Public Culture* 5 (3): 493–513.

Achtenberg, Emily. 2013. "Bolivia: USAID Out, Morales In for Re-Election Bid." Accessed November 23, 2016. http://nacla.org/blog/2013/5/11/bolivia-usaid-out-morales-re-election-bid.

Achtenberg, Emily. 2016. "After the Referendum, What's Next for Bolivia's Progressive Left?" https://nacla.org/blog/2016/04/15/after-referendum-what%E2%80%99s-next-bolivia%E2%80%99s-progressive-left.

Agreda, Evelin, Norma Rodriguez, and Alex Conteras. 1996. *Mujeres Cocaleras: Marchando por una vida sin violencia*. Cochabamba, Bolivia: CEDIB.

Aguilo, Federico. 1986. "Los Peones de la Cocaína." *Cuarto Intermedio* 1:44–57.

AIN. 2004. *Bolivia: Legacy of Coca*. http://ain-bolivia.org/2004/06/bolivia-legacy-of-coca/.

AIN. 2006. "Update on Drug Policy Issues in Bolivia." Accessed January 4, 2009. http://ain-bolivia.org/2006/11/update-on-drug-policy-issues-in-bolivia/.

AIN. 2008. "Bolivian Coca Growers Cut Ties with USAID." Accessed January 2, 2008. http://ain-bolivia.org/2008/06/bolivian-coca-growers-cut-ties-with-usaid/.

AIN. 2014. "Homicide Rates in Latin America." Accessed September 23, 2017. http://ain-bolivia.org/2014/07/homicide-rates-in-latin-america/.

AIN. 2017. "Nueva Ley de La Coca en Bolivia. " Accessed March 4, 2017. http://ain-bolivia.org/2017/03/nueva-ley-de-coca-en-bolivia/.

Albó, Xavier. 1977. *La Paradoja Aymara: Solidariedad y faccionalismo*. La Paz: CIPCA Cuaderno de Investigación 8.

Albó, Xavier. 1985. *Desafíos de la Solidaridad Aymara*. La Paz: CIPCA Cuaderno de Investigación 25.

Albó, Xavier. 1987. "From MNRistas to Kataristas to Katari." In *Resistance, Rebellion and Consciousness in the Andean Peasant World, 18th to 20th Centuries*, edited by S. Stern, 13–34. Madison: University of Wisconsin Press.

Albó, Xavier. 2000. "El Sector Campesino-Indígena, Actor Social Clave." In *Opiniones y Analisis: El Sindicalismo en Bolivia: Presente y Futuro*, 75–112. La Paz: Fundación Fundemos; Fundación Hanns-Seidel.

Albó, Xavier. 2002a. "Bolivia: From Indian and Campesino Leaders to Councillors and Parliamentary Deputies." In *Multiculturalism in Latin America: Indigenous Rights, Diversity and Democracy*, edited by Rachel Sieder. Basingstoke, UK: Palgrave Macmillan.

Albó, Xavier. 2002b. *Identidad etnica y politica*. La Paz: CIPCA Cuadernos de Investigación.

Albó, Xavier. 2002c. *Pueblos Indios en la política*. La Paz: CIPCA Cuadernos de Investigacion.

Albó, Xavier. 2007. "Bolivia: Avances y tropezones hacia un nuevo país plurinacional e intercultural." In *Pueblos Indígenas y Política en América Latina: El Reconocimiento de sus Derechos y el Impacto de sus Demandas a Inicios del Siglo XXI*, edited by Salvador Martí, 335–60. Barcelona: Fundació CIDOB.

Albó, Xavier. 2008a. "The Long Memory of Ethnicity and Some Temporary Oscillations." In *Unresolved Tensions: Bolivia Past and Present*, edited by John Crabtree and Laurence Whitehead, 13–34. Pittsburgh: University of Pittsburgh Press.

Albó, Xavier. 2008b. *Movimientos y poder indígena en Bolivia, Ecuador y Perú*. La Paz: CIPCA Cuadernos de Investigacion.

Albó, Xavier, and Victor Quispe. 2004. *Quienes son indígenas en los gobiernos municipales?* La Paz: CIPCA/Plural Editores.

Albro, Robert. 2005. "The Indigenous in the Plural in Bolivian Oppositional Politics." *Bulletin of Latin American Research* 24 (4): 433–53.

Albro, Robert. 2006. "The Culture of Democracy and Bolivia's Indigenous Movements." *Critique of Anthropology* 26 (4): 387–410.

Albro, Robert. 2007. "Indigenous Politics in Bolivia's Evo Era: Clientelism, Llunkerío, and the Problem of Stigma." *Urban Anthropology and Studies of Cultural Systems and World Economic Development* 36 (3): 281–320.

Allen, Catherine. 1981. "To Be Quechua: The Symbolism of Coca Chewing in Highland Peru." *American Ethnologist* 8 (1): 157–71.

Allen, Catherine. 1988. *The Hold Life Has: Coca and Cultural Identity in an Andean Community*. London: Smithsonian Institution Press.

Alvarez, Sonia, Evelina Dagnino, and Arturo Escobar. 1998. "Introduction: The Cultural and the Political in Latin American Social Movements." In *Cultures of Politics, Politics of Cultures: Revisioning Latin American Social Movements*, edited by Sonia Alvarez, Evelina Dagnino, and Arturo Escobar. Oxford: Westview.

Amnesty International. 2003. "Bolivia Country Profile." *Amnesty International Report 2003: Covering the Period January to December 2002*. http://www.amnesty.org.

ANB. 2014. *Cocaleros Expondrán Propiedades de la Hoja de Coca en el Aeropuerto de Santa Cruz Durante el G77 La Paz, Bolivia*. Accessed December 7, 2016. http://anbolivia.blogspot.co.uk/2014/06/cocaleros-expondran-propiedades-de-la.html.

Anderson, Benedict. 1991. *Imagined Communities: Reflections on the Origin and Spread of Nationalism*. London: Verso.

Anderson, Mark. 2007. "When Afro Becomes (like) Indigenous: Garifuna and Afro-Indigenous Politics in Honduras." *Journal of Latin American and Caribbean Anthropology* 12 (2): 384–413.

Andolina, Robert, Nina Laurie, and Sarah Radcliffe. 2009. *Indigenous Development in the Andes: Culture, Power and Transnationalism*. Durham, NC: Duke University Press.

ANF. 2001a. *Gobierno Asegura que Existe una "Dictadura Sindical" en el Chapare*. Agencia de Noticias Fides. Accessed June 2, 2017. https://http://www.noticiasfides.com/nacional /politica/gobierno-asegura-que-existe-una-dictadura-sindical-en-el-chapare-4960.

ANF. 2001b. *Ex cocaleros: dictadura sindical de Evo Morales impera en el Chapare*. Agencia de Noticias Fides. Accessed June 2, 2017. https://http://www.noticiasfides .com/nacional/politica/ex-cocaleros-dictadura-sindical-de-evo-morales-impera-en-el -chapare-63624.

Ang, Ien. 1996. *Living Room Wars: Rethinking Media Audiences for a Postmodern World*. London: Routledge.

Anria, Santiago. 2010. "Bolivia's MAS: Between Party and Movement." In *Latin America's Left Turns: Politics, Policies and Trajectories of Change*, edited by Maxwell Cameron and Eric Hershberg. Boulder, CO: Lynne Rienner.

Anria, Santiago. 2016a. "Democratizing Democracy? Civil Society and Party Organization in Bolivia." *Comparative Politics* 48 (4): 459–78.

Anria, Santiago. 2016b. "More Inclusion, Less Liberalism in Bolivia." *Journal of Democracy* 27 (3): 99–108.

Anria, Santiago, and Jennifer Cyr. 2017. "Inside Revolutionary Parties: Coalition-Building and Maintenance in Reformist Bolivia." *Comparative Political Studies* 50 (9): 1255–87.

Antezana, Mythyl. 2014. "Dirigentes del MAS detenidos van a la huelga por candidatura." *Opinion*, December 26.

Antezana, Tonchy. 2007. *Evo Pueblo*. La Paz: Ondamax Films.

Archondo, Rafael. 2003. *Incestos y Blindajes: Radiografía del Campo Político-Periodístico*. La Paz: Plural Editores.

Arias, Enrique Desmond. 2017. *Criminal Enterprises and Governance in Latin America and the Caribbean*. Cambridge: Cambridge University Press.

Arkonada, Katu. 2016. *De la derrota táctica a la victoria estratégica*. Accessed November 9, 2016. http://www.rebelion.org/noticia.php?id=209455.

Arnold, Denise, and Alison Spedding. 2005. *Mujeres en Los Movimientos Sociales en Boliva 2000–2003*. La Paz: CIDEM/ILCA.

Assies, Willem, and Ton Salman. 2003. "Crisis in Bolivia: The Elections of 2002 and Their Aftermath." *ISA Research Papers* 56. London: Institute of Latin American Studies.

Astuti, Rita. 1995. "The Vezo Are Not a Kind of People: Identity, Difference and 'Ethnicity' among a Fishing People of Western Madagascar." *American Ethnologist* 22 (3): 464–82.

Auyero, Javier. 2001. *Poor People's Politics: Peronist Survival Networks and the Legacy of Evita*. Durham, NC: Duke University Press.

Auyero, Javier, and Débora Swistun. 2009. *Flammable: Environmental Suffering in an Aregentine Shantytown*. New York: Oxford University Press.

Barrios, Domitila, and Moema Viezzer. 1978. *Let Me Speak! Testimony of Domitila, a Woman of the Bolivian Mines*. Translated by Victoria Ortiz. New York: Monthly Review Press.

Barrios Suvelza, Franz. 2017. "¿Qué tipo de régimen político impera en los países del Nuevo Constitucionalismo Latinoamericano? Indicaciones desde el caso boliviano." *Revista Latinoamericana de Política Comparada* 12:71–101.

Barth, Frederick. 1969. *Ethnic Groups and Boundaries: The Social Organization of Culture Difference*. Bergen, Norway: Universitetsforlaget.

Bebbington, Anthony, and Jeffrey Bury, eds. 2013. *Subterranean Struggles: New Dynamics of Mining, Oil, and Gas in Latin America*. Austin: University of Texas Press.

Beck, Ulrich, and Elisabeth Beck-Gernsheim. 2002. *Individualization: Institutionalized Individualism and Its Social and Political Consequences*. London: SAGE.

Becker, Constance D., and Rosario Leon. 2000. "Indigenous Forest Management in the Bolivian Amazon: Lessons from the Yuracaré People." In *People and Forests: Communities, Institutions and Governance*, edited by Clark Gibson, Margaret McKean, and Elinor Ostrom. Cambridge, MA: MIT Press.

Becket, Lois. 2017. "How Jeff Sessions and Donald Trump Have Restarted the War on Drugs." *The Guardian*, August 21.

Beltrán, Luis Ramiro. 1975. "Research Ideologies in Conflict." *Journal of Communication* 25:187–93.

Beltrán, Luis Ramiro. 1980. "A Farewell to Aristotle: Horizontal Communication." *Communication* 5 (1): 5–41.

Berezin, Mabel. 2009. *Illiberal Politics in Neoliberal Times: Culture, Security and Populism in the New Europe*. Cambridge: Cambridge University Press.

Bermeo, Nancy. 2016. "On Democratic Backsliding." *Journal of Democracy* 27 (1): 5–19.

Besnier, Niko. 2002. "Transgenderism, Locality, and the Miss Galaxy Beauty Pageant in Tonga." *American Ethnologist* 29 (3): 534–66.

BIF. 2016. *Bolivia Information Forum Bulletin* 34. Accessed March 13, 2016. http://ymlp.com/z1d898.

Bigenho, Michelle. 1998. "Coca as a Musical Trope of Bolivian Nation-Ness." *Political and Legal Anthropology Review* 21 (1): 114–22.

Bigenho, Michelle. 2006. "Embodied Matters: Bolivian Fantasy and Indigenismo." *Journal of Latin American Anthropology* 11 (2): 267–93.

Bjork-James, Carwil. 2013. "Claiming Space, Redefining Politics: Urban Protest and Grassroots Power in Bolivia." PhD diss., City University of New York.

Blanes, Jose. 1983. *De los Valles al Chapare*. Cochabamba: CERES.

Blanes, Jose. 1989. "Cocaine, Informality, and the Urban Economy in La Paz, Bolivia." In *The Informal Economy: Studies in Advanced and Less Developed Countries*, edited by Alejandro Portes, M. Castells, and L. Benton. Baltimore: Johns Hopkins University Press.

Bolton, Margaret. 2002. "Doing Waki in San Pablo de Lípez. Reciprocity between the Living and the Dead." *Anthropos* 97 (2): 379–96.

Bolton, Ralph. 1976. "Andean Coca Chewing: A Metabolic Perspective." *American Anthropologist* 78 (3): 630–34.

Bourgois, Philippe. 1995. *In Search of Respect: Selling Crack in El Barrio*. Cambridge: Cambridge University Press.

Brown, Wendy. 2009. *Edgework: Critical Essays on Knowledge and Politics*. Princeton, NJ: Princeton University Press.

Brown, Wendy. 2015. *Undoing the Demos: Neoliberalism's Stealth Revolution*. New York: Zone.

Bruzzone, Graciela, and Juan Clavijo. 1989. *Monografía del Trópico Departamento de Cochabamba*. Cochabamba: Estudios Regionales Centro de Investigación y Desarrollo Regional.

Brysk, Alison. 2000. *From Tribal Village to Global Village: Indian Rights and International Relations in Latin America*. Stanford, CA: Stanford University Press.

Bulmer-Thomas, Victor, and James Dunkerley, eds. 1999. *The United States and Latin America: The New Agenda*. London: Institute of Latin American Studies.

Burchard, Roderick. 1992. "Coca Chewing and Diet." *Current Anthropology* 33 (1): 1–24.

Burgos Gallardo, Christian. 2017. "La Polémica Ley General de la Coca y sus Efectos en Bolivia." Accessed April 16, 2017. https://lostiemposdigital.atavist.com/ley-coca-bolivia.

Cabieses, Hugo. 1997. "Enfoque Poblacional y de Organizaciones Sociales en Zonas de Cultivos con Fines Ilícitos de Bolivia, Colombia y Peru." In *Políticas y Estrategias Andinas Para el Desarrollo Alternativo*, edited by Martin Ramirez, 71–82. Lima: IICA; CReA; ACT.

Cajias, Lupe, and Guadalupe Lopez. 1999. *Ameneza o Fortaleza? Concentracion de Medios de Comunicacion en America Latina*. La Paz: Friedrich Ebert Stiftung/ILDIS.

Calcopietro, Carlos, Lida Rodríguez Ballesteros, Thomas Otter, Diego Giacoman, Javier Gómez, Rita Gutiérrez Agramont, and Moritz Lörcher. 2014. *Evaluation of EU Cooperation with Bolivia 2007–2013. Final Report*. Brussels: European Commission.

Caldeira, Teresa. 2000. *City of Walls: Crime, Segregation and Citizenship in São Paulo*. Berkeley: University of California Press.

Caldeira, Teresa, and James Holston. 1999. "Democracy and Violence in Brazil." *Comparative Studies in Society and History* 14 (4): 691–729.

Camacho, Adriana, and Daniel Mejía. 2015. "The Health Consequences of Aerial Spraying of Illicit Crops: The Case of Colombia." Working Paper 408, Center for Global Development. Accessed April 26, 2017. http://www.cgdev.org/publication/health-consequences-aerial-spraying-illicit-crops-case-colombia-working-paper-408.

Camacho, Carlos. 2001. *Las Radios Populares en la Construcción de Ciudadanía: Enseñazas de la Experiencia de ERBOL en Bolivia*. La Paz: Universidad Andina Simon Bolivar/ERBOL.

Camacho Balderrama, Natalia. 1999. "La marcha como táctica de concertación política (las marchas cocaleras de 1994 y 1995)." In *Empujando la concertación. Marchas campesinas, opinión pública y coca*, edited by Roberto Laserna, Natalia Camacho, and Eduardo Córdova. Cochabamba: CERES-PIEB.

Cameron, Maxwell. 2014. "The Myth of Competitive Authoritarianism in the Andes." University of British Columbia. http://documents.mx/documents/the-myth-of-competitive-authoritarianism-in-the-andes-jan14–1.html.

Canessa, Andrew. 2006. "'Todos Somos Indígenas': Towards a New Language of National Political Identity." *Bulletin of Latin American Research* 25 (2): 241–63.

Canessa, Andrew. 2008. "The Past Is Not Another Country: Exploring Indigenous Histories in Bolivia." *History and Anthropology* 19 (4): 353–69.

Canessa, Andrew. 2012a. "Conflict, Claim, and Contradiction in the New Indigenous State of Bolivia." Desigualidades Working Paper 22. Accessed June 3, 2016. http://www.desigualdades.net/Resources/Working_Paper/22_WP_Canessa_online.pdf.

Canessa, Andrew. 2012b. *Intimate Indigeneities: Race, Sex and History in the Small Spaces of Life*. Durham, NC: Duke University Press.

Canessa, Andrew. 2014. "Conflict, Claim and Contradiction in the New Indigenous State of Bolivia." *Critique of Anthropology* 34 (2): 151–71.

Cano, Marisol. 2007. *Media and Conflict in Bolivia: Fostering a Constructive Role for the Media in a Situation of Vulnerable Governability*. Copenhagen: International Media Support.

CAPHC. 1993. *Manifiesto de Macchu Picchu: Qosqo Perú*. La Paz, Bolivia: Consejo Permanente en Defensa de los Productores de Hoja de Coca en Los Paises Andinos.

Carey, James. 1989. *Communication as Culture: Essays on Media and Society*. London: Unwin Hyman.

Carter, William, ed. 1996. *Ensayos Científicos Sobre la Coca*. la Paz: Editorial Juventud.

Carter, William, and Mauricio Mamani. 1986. *Coca en Bolivia*. La Paz: Editorial Juventud.

Castellón, Juan René. 2013. "Un muerto y dos heridos de bala en un ataque a erradicadores de coca en Apolo." *La Razón*, October 19.

Castle, David. 1998. "Hearts, Minds and Radical Democracy." Accessed September 9, 2016. http://www.redpepper.org.uk/hearts-minds-and-radical-democracy/.

Caulkins, Jonathan, Beau Kilmer, Peter Reuter, and Gregory Midgette. 2015. "Cocaine's Fall and Marijuana's Rise: Questions and Estimates Based on New Estimates of Consumption and Expenditures in U.S. Drug Markets." *Addiction* 110 (5): 728–36.

Central Intelligence Agency. 2016. *Bolivia*. Accessed February 16, 2016. www.cia.gov/library/publications/the-world-factbook/geos/bl.html.

Choque, Franz. 2010. "Masistas aprueban una tabla para abrir era de dictadura sindical en instituciones." *La Patria*, March 2.

Choque, Marilyn. 2016. "Posesionan al sexto viceministro de la coca en 10 años." *La Razón*, June 16.

Clarin. 2008. "Vivimos una dictadura sindical." *Clarin Digital*, August 12.

Cody, Francis. 2011. "Publics and Politics." *Annual Review of Anthropology* 40:37–52.

Cohen, Abner. 1967. *Custom and Politics in Urban Africa: A Study of Hausa Migrants in Yoruba Towns*. London: Routledge.

Collins, Jennifer. 2004. "Linking Movements and Electoral Politics. Ecuador's Indigenous Movement and the Rise of Pachakutik." In *Politics in the Andes: Identity, Conflict, Reform*, edited by Jo-Marie Burt and Philip Mauceri, 38–57. Pittsburgh: University of Pittsburgh Press.

Collins, John, ed. 2014. *Ending the Drug Wars: Report of the LSE Expert Group on the Economics of Drug Policy*. London: London School of Economics.

Colloredo-Mansfeld, Rudi. 1998. "'Dirty Indians,' Radical Indígenas, and the Political Economy of Social Difference in Modern Ecuador." *Bulletin of Latin American Research* 17 (2): 185–205.

Colloredo-Mansfeld, Rudi. 2009. *Fighting like a Community: Andean Civil Society in an Era of Indian Uprisings*. Chicago: University of Chicago Press.

Comaroff, John, and Jean Comaroff. 1997. "Postcolonial Politics and Discourses of Democracy in Southern Africa: An Anthropological Reflection on African Political Modernities." *Journal of Anthropological Research* 53 (2): 123–46.

conaltid. 2013. *Gobierno presenta resultados del Estudio Integral de la Hoja de Coca*. La Paz: Secretaria de Coordinacion Consejo Nacional de Lucha Contra el Trafico Ilicito de Drogas (conaltid), Ministerio de Gobierno.

Conklin, Beth. 1997. "Body Paint, Feathers and vcrs: Aesthetics and Authenticity in Amazonian Activism." *American Ethnologist* 24 (4): 711–37.

Conzelman, Caroline. 2007. *Coca Leaf and Sindicato Democracy in the Bolivian Yungas: The Andeanization of Western Political Models and the Rise of the New Left*. Boulder: Department of Anthropology, University of Colorado.

Cook, Joanna, Nicholas Long, and Henrietta Moore, eds. 2016. *The State We're In: Reflecting on Democracy's Troubles*. London: Berghahn.

Corva, Dominic. 2007. "Neoliberal Globalization and the War on Drugs: Transnationalizing Illiberal Governance in the Americas." *Political Geography* 27 (2): 176–93.

cpdi. 2010. *Informe Final: Consultoria por Producto para Encuesta Socio Economica Tropico de Cochabamba y Yungas de La Paz*. La Paz: Consultores para el Desarrollo Integral.

Crabtree, John. 1987. *The Great Tin Crash: Bolivia and the World Market*. London: Latin American Bureau.

Crabtree, John, and Ann Chaplin. 2013. *Bolivia: Processes of Change*. London: Zed.

Crabtree, John, and Laurence Whitehead. 2008. "On Ethnicities." In *Unresolved Tensions: Bolivia Past and Present*, edited by John Crabtree and Laurence Whitehead, 9–12. Pittsburgh: University of Pittsburgh Press.

Crehan, Kate. 2002. *Gramsci, Culture and Anthropology*. London: Pluto.

Crouch, Colin. 2004. *Post-Democracy*. Cambridge: Polity.

Csete, Joanne, Adeeba Kamarulzaman, Michel Kazatchkine, Frederick Altice, Marek Balicki, Julia Buxton, Javier Cepeda, Megan Comfort, Eric Goosby, João Goulão, Carl Hart, Richard Horton, Thomas Kerr, Alejandro Madrazo Lajous, Stephen Lewis, Natasha Martin, Daniel Mejía, David Mathiesson, Isidore Obot, Adeolu Ogunrombi, Susan Sherman, Jack Stone, Nandini Vallath, Peter Vickerman, Tomáš Zábranský, and Chris Beyrer. 2016. "Public Health and International Drug Policy." *Lancet* 387 (10026): 1427–80.

D'Andrade, Roy Goodwin. 1995. "Moral Models in Anthropology: 1." *Current Anthropology* 36 (3): 399–408.

Dangl, Benjamin, and Kathryn Ledebur. 2003. "War on Terror Meets War on Drugs in Bolivia." Accessed January 3, 2008. http://upsidedownworld.org/main/content/view/34/31/.

De Franco, Mario, and Ricardo Godoy. 1992. "The Economic Consequences of Cocaine Production in Bolivia: Historical, Local, and Macroeconomic Perspectives." *Journal of Latin American Studies* 24 (2): 375–406.

de la Cadena, Marisol. 1995. "'Women Are More Indian': Ethnicity and Gender in a Community Near Cuzco." In *Ethnicity, Markets and Migration in the Andes: At the Crossroads of History and Anthropology*, edited by B. Larson and O. Harris, 329–48. Durham, NC: Duke University Press.

de la Cadena, Marisol. 1998. "'Silent Racism and Intellectual Superiority in Peru.'" *Bulletin of Latin American Research* 17 (2): 143–64.

de la Cadena, Marisol. 1999. *Indigenous Mestizos: The Politics of Race and Culture in Cuzco, Peru, 1919–1991*. Durham, NC: Duke University Press.

de la Cadena, Marisol. 2010. "Indigenous Cosmopolitics in the Andes: Conceptual Reflections beyond 'Politics.'" *Cultural Anthropology* 25 (2): 334–70.

de la Cadena, Marisol, and Orin Starn. 2007. "Introduction." In *Indigenous Experience Today*, edited by Marisol de la Cadena and Orin Starn, 1–31. Oxford: Berg.

de la Vega, Garcilaso. 1943. *Los Comentarios Reales de Los Incas—Primera Parte*. Buenos Aires: Biblioteca Ayacucho.

de los Santos, Germán. 2015. "Lucha contra los narcos en la selva." *La Nación*, Buenos Aires, November 29.

Derpic, Jorge, and Alex Ayala. 2016. *Bolivia: Los Linchados de El Alto*. Accessed February 12, 2017. http://www.revistaanfibia.com/cronica/bolivia-los-linchados-de-el-alto/.

Derpic, Jorge, and Alex Weinreb. 2014. "Undercounting Urban Residents in Bolivia: A Small-Area Study of Census-Driven Migration." *Population Research and Policy Review* 33 (6): 897–914.

Deschouwer, Kris. 2008. *New Parties in Government: In Power for the First Time*. London: Routledge.

Diamond, Larry. 1994. "Toward Democratic Consolidation." *Journal of Democracy* 5 (3): 4–17.

Diamond, Larry. 2015. "Facing Up to the Democratic Recession." *Journal of Democracy* 26 (1): 141–55.

Dion, Michelle, and Catherine Russler. 2008. "Eradication Efforts, the State, Displacement and Poverty: Explaining Coca Cultivation in Colombia during Plan Colombia." *Journal of Latin American Studies* 40 (3): 399–421. doi:10.1017/S0022216X08004380.

do Alto, Hervé, and Pablo Stefanoni. 2010. "El MAS: Las ambivalencias de la democracia corporativa." In *Mutaciones del campo político en Bolivia*, edited by Luis Alberto García Orellana and Fernando Luis García Yapur. La Paz: PNUD.

Downing, John. 2001. *Radical Media: Rebellious Communication and Social Movements*. Thousand Oaks, CA: SAGE.

Drake, Paul. 2006. "The Hegemony of US Economic Doctrines in Latin America." In *Latin America after Neoliberalism: Turning the Tide in the 21st Century?*, edited by Eric Hershberg and Fred Rosen. New York: New Press and NACLA.

Duke, James, David Aulik, and Timothy Plowman. 1975. "Nutritional Value of Coca." *Botanical Museum Leaflets, Harvard University* 24 (6): 113–19.

Dunkerley, James. 1984. *Rebellion in the Veins: Political Struggle in Bolivia, 1952–82*. London: Verso.

Dunkerley, James. 1990. *Political Transition and Economic Stabilisation: Bolivia, 1982–1989*. Research Paper 22. London: Institute of Latin American Studies.

Dunkerley, James. 2007a. *Bolivia: Revolution and the Power of History in the Present*. London: Institute for the Study of the Americas.

Dunkerley, James. 2007b. "Evo Morales, the 'Two Bolivias' and the Third Bolivian Revolution." *Journal of Latin American Studies* 39:133–66.

Dunkerley, James. 2013. "The Bolivian Revolution at 60: Politics and Historiography." *Journal of Latin American Studies* 45 (2): 325–50. doi:10.1017/S0022216X13000382.

Dunkerley, James, and Rolando Morales. 1986. "Crisis in Bolivia." *New Left Review* 155:86–106.

Durand Ochoa, Ursula. 2014. *The Political Empowerment of the Cocaleros of Bolivia and Peru, Studies of the Americas*. Basingstoke, UK: Palgrave Macmillan.

Eastwood, David, and Harry Pollard. 1986. "Colonisation and Coca in the Chapare, Bolivia: A Development Paradox for Colonisation Theory." *Tijdschrift voor Economische en Sociale Geografie* 77 (4): 258–68.

Economist. 2017. "Bolivia's President Chafes against Term Limits." *The Economist*, January 5.

Edelman, Marc. 2001. "Social Movements: Changing Paradigms and Forms of Politics." *Annual Review of Anthropology*, no. 30:285–317.

El Deber. 2015. "La mayor planta piscícola de Bolivia, en trópico cocalero de Cochabamba: Chimoré." *El Deberi*, September 8.

El Deber. 2016. "Chapare es la región con más privilegios impositivos." *El Deber*, January 1.

El Día. 2012a. "La marcha de la vergüenza." *El Día*, January 6.

El Día. 2012b. "Ríos de plata del Estado fluyen hacia el Chapare." *El Día*, October 15.

El Diario. 2001. "Evo Morales ya no es Interlocutor Valido." *El Diario*.

ERBOL. 2015a. "Denuncian 'terrorismo político-sindical' en el trópico de Cochabamba." Accessed April 1, 2016. http://www.erbol.com.bo/noticia/politica/28042015 /denuncian_terrorismo_politico_sindical_en_el_tropico_de_cochabamba.

ERBOL. 2015b. "Dirigente confirma que perderán sus catos los cocaleros que no postularon con el MAS." Accessed April 28, 2015. http://www.erbol.com.bo/noticia /politica/28042015/dirigente_confirma_que_perderan_sus_catos_los_cocaleros _que_no_postularon_con_el_mas.

Escárzaga, Fabiola. 2012a. "Comunidad indígena y revolución en Bolivia: El pensamiento indianista-katarista de Fausto Reinaga y Felipe Quispe." *Política y Cultura* 37: 185–210.

Escárzaga, Fabiola. 2012b. "El gobierno de los movimientos sociales." In *El Primer Gobierno de Evo Morales: Un Balance Retrospectivo*, edited by Tanja Ernst and Schmalz Stefan, 137–64. La Paz: Plural Editores.

Escobar, Arturo. 2010. "Latin America at a Crossroads: Alternative Modernizations, Post-Liberalism, or Post-Development?" *Cultural Studies* 24 (1): 1–65.

Escobar, Filemon. 1986. *La Mina Vista Desde la Guardajoto*. La Paz: Cuaderno de Investigacion 27.

Escobar, Filemon. 2008. *De la Revolución al Pachakuti: El Aprendizaje del Respecto Reciproco entre Blancos e Indianos*. La Paz: Garza Azul.

Estellano, Washington, and Kathryn Nava-Ragazzi. 1994. "From Populism to the Coca Economy." *Latin American Perspectives* 21 (4): 34–45.

EuropeAid. 2014. PRAEDAC: *Alternative Development in Bolivia*. European Commission. Accessed April 14, 2017. http://ec.europa.eu/europeaid/documents/case-studies /bolivia_praedac_en.pdf.

Evans Pritchard, Edward Evan. 1940. "The Nuer of the Southern Sudan." In *African Political Systems*, edited by Meyer Fortes and Edward Evan Evans-Pritchard, 272–96. London: Oxford University Press.

Fabricant, Nicole. 2009. "Performative Politics: The Camba Countermovement in Eastern Bolivia." *American Ethnologist* 36 (4): 768–83.

Fabricant, Nicole. 2011. "A Realigned Bolivian Right: New 'Democratic' Destabilizations." NACLA *Report on the Americas* 44 (1): 30–31.

Fabricant, Nicole. 2012. *Mobilizing Bolivia's Displaced: Indigenous Politics and the Struggle over Land*. Chapel Hill: University of North Carolina Press.

Fabricant, Nicole, and Bret Gustafson, eds. 2011. *Remapping Bolivia: Resources, Territory and Indigeneity in a Plurinational State*. Santa Fe, NM: SAR Press.

Faguet, Jean-Paul. 2003. "Decentralization and Local Government in Bolivia: An Overview from the Bottom Up." Working Paper 29. DESTIN, London School of Economics, LSE Crisis States.

Fanon, Frantz. 1967. "The Voice of Fighting Algeria." In *Studies in a Dying Colonialism*. Harmondsworth, UK: Penguin.

Farah, Douglas. 2009. *Into the Abyss: Bolivia under Evo Morales and the MAS*. Alexandria, VA: International Assessment and Strategy Center.

Farfán, Williams. 2013. "El consumo habitual de coca se da en tres de cada diez personas." *La Razón*, November 14.

Farthing, Linda. 2016. "'We Are in Shock': Historic Bolivia Drought Hammers Homes and Crops." *The Guardian*, November 25.

Farthing, Linda. 2017. "Negotiating with Growers, Bolivia Forges Its Own Approach to Coca Production." *World Politics Review*, April 11. Accessed April 14, 2017. http://www.worldpoliticsreview.com/articles/21803/negotiating-with-growers-bolivia-forges-its-own-approach-to-coca-production.

Farthing, Linda, and Benjamin Kohl. 2005. "Conflicting Agendas: The Politics of Development Aid in Drug-Producing Areas." *Development Policy Review* 23 (2): 183–98. doi:10.1111/j.1467-7679.2005.00282.x.

Farthing, Linda, and Benjamin Kohl. 2012. "Supply-Side Harm Reduction Strategies: Bolivia's Experiment with Social Control." *International Journal of Drug Policy* 23 (6): 488–94.

Farthing, Linda, and Benjamin Kohl. 2014. *Evo's Bolivia: Continuity and Change*. Austin: University of Texas Press.

Farthing, Linda, and Kathryn Ledebur. 2004. "The Beat Goes On: The U.S. War on Coca." NACLA *Report on the Americas* 38 (3): 34–39.

Farthing, Linda, and Kathryn Ledebur. 2015. *Habeas Coca: Bolivia's Community Coca Control*. New York: Open Society Foundations.

FELCN. 2017. *Resultados Obtenidos en la Lucha Contra el Narcotráfico*. Accessed August 2, 2017. http://www.felcn.gob.bo/R-Est-2016.aspx.

Ferguson, James. 2013. "Declarations of Dependence: Labour, Personhood, and Welfare in Southern Africa." *Journal of the Royal Anthropological Institute* 19 (2): 223–42.

Fernández, Roberto. 2004. FMI, *Banco Mundial y Estado Neocolonial: Poder Supranacional en Bolivia*. La Paz: Plural Editores.

FETCTC. 2012. "Resoluciones y Estatutos." In *XXIII Congreso Ordinario*. Cochabamba: Federacion Especial de Trabajadores Campesinos del Tropico Cochabambino.

Feuchtwang, Stephan. 2003. "Peasants, Democracy and Anthropology." *Critique of Anthropology* 23 (1): 93–120.

Feuchtwang, Stephan, and Alpa Shah, eds. 2015. *Emancipatory Politics: A Critique.* London: Open Anthropology Co-Operative Press.

Fides. 2015. "Erradican cato de coca de excandidato a la alcaldía de Shinahota por el frente UNICO." *Grupo Fides*, May 8.

Field, Thomas. 2016. *Minas, balas y gringos: Bolivia y la Alianza para el Progreso en la era de Kennedy.* La Paz: Centro de Investigaciones Sociales.

Fifer, Valerie. 1967. "Bolivia's Pioneer Fringe." *Geographical Review* 57 (1): 1–23.

Fifer, Valerie. 1982. "The Search for a Series of Small Successes: Frontiers of Settlement in Eastern Bolivia." *Journal of Latin American Studies* 14 (2): 407–32.

Flores, Gonzalo, and Jose Blanes. 1984. *¿Donde va el Chapare?* Cochabamba: Centro de Estudios de la Realidad Económica y Social.

Flores-Galindo, Alberto. 1987. "In Search of an Inca." In *Resistance, Rebellion and Consciousness in the Andean Peasant World, 18th to 20th Centuries,* edited by Steve Stern, 193–210. Madison: University of Wisconsin Press.

Foa, Roberto, and Yascha Mounk. 2016. "The Danger of Deconsolidation: The Democratic Disconnect." *Journal of Democracy* 27 (3): 5–17.

Foster, George. 1965. "Peasant Society and the Image of the Limited Good." *American Anthropologist* 67 (2): 293–315.

Fraser, Nancy. 1992. "Rethinking the Public Sphere: A Contribution to the Critique of Actually Existing Democracy." In *Habermas and the Public Sphere,* edited by Craig Calhoun, 109–39. Cambridge, MA: MIT Press.

Freedom House. 1999. *Democracy's Century: A Survey of Global Political Change in the 20th Century.* New York: Freedom House.

Freud, Sigmund. 1984. "Über Coca." *Journal of Substance Abuse Treatment* 1 (3): 206–17.

Fuentes, Cesar. 2006. "Evo Morales Se Declara Victima de los Medios." *El Juguete Rabioso*, October 1.

Fuentes, Federico. 2011. "Government, Social Movements, and Revolution in Bolivia Today: An Exchange." *International Socialist Review* 76.

Gagliano, Joseph. 1994. *Coca Prohibition in Peru: The Historical Debate.* Tucson: University of Arizona Press.

Gamarra, Eduardo. 1994. *Entre la Droga y la Democracia: La Cooperación entre Estados Unidos-Bolivia y la Lucha Contra el Narcotráfico.* La Paz: ILDIS.

Gamarra, Eduardo. 2007. *Bolivia on the Brink.* Special Report 24. New York: Council on Foreign Relations.

Gamson, William, and Gadi Wolfsfeld. 1993. "Movements and Media as Interacting Systems." *Annals of the American Academy of Political and Social Science* 528 (July): 114–25.

GAO. 2002. *Report to Congressional Requesters: Drug Control. Efforts to Develop Alternatives to Cultivating Illicit Crops in Colombia Have Made Little Progress and Face Serious Obstacles.* Washington, DC: U.S. General Accounting Office.

García, Alberto, and Fernando García. 2012. *Atlas electoral de Bolivia.* La Paz: Sopocachi Tribunal Supremo Electoral; PNUD Bolivia.

García Linera, Álvaro. 2004. "The 'Multitude.'" In *Cochabamba! Water War in Bolivia*, edited by Oscar Olivera and Tom Lewis, 65–86. Cambridge, MA: Southend.

García Linera, Álvaro. 2006. "El Evismo: Lo nacional-popular en acción." *Revista OSAL: Observatorio Social de América Latina* 6 (19).

García Linera, Álvaro. 2014. *Plebeian Power: Collective Action and Indigenous, Working-Class and Popular Identities in Bolivia*. Leiden: Brill.

García Linera, Álvaro, Marxa Chávez, and Patricia Costas. 2004. *Sociología de los movimientos sociales en Bolivia: Estructuras de movilización, repertorios culturales y acción política*. La Paz: Diakonia, Oxfam.

García Linera, Álvaro, Raquel Gutierrez, Raul Prada, and Luis Tapia. 2007a. *El Retorno de la Bolivia Plebeya*. La Paz: Muela del Diablo Editores.

García Linera, Álvaro, and Mariana Ortega Breña. 2010. "The State in Transition: Power Bloc and Point of Bifurcation." *Latin American Perspectives* 37 (4): 34–47.

García Linera, Álvaro, Luis Tapia, and Raul Prada, eds. 2007b. *La Transformacion Pluralista del Estado*. La Paz: Muela del Diablo.

Gay, Robert. 2010. *Popular Organization and Democracy in Rio de Janeiro: A Tale of Two Favelas*. Philadelphia: Temple University Press.

GCDP. 2016. *Advancing Drug Policy Reform: A New Approach to Decriminalization*. Geneva: Global Commission on Drug Policy.

Geschiere, Peter. 2009. *The Perils of Belonging: Autochthony, Citizenship, and Exclusion in Africa and Europe*. Chicago: University of Chicago Press.

Geschiere, Peter. 2013. *Witchcraft, Intimacy, and Trust: Africa in Comparison*. Chicago: University of Chicago Press.

Giacoman Aramayo, Diego. 2011. "Drug Policy and the Prison Situation in Bolivia." In *Systems Overload: Drug Laws and Prisons in Latin America*, edited by Pien Metaal and Coletta Youngers, 21–30. Amsterdam: Transnational Institute and Washington Office on Latin America.

Gilbert, Alan. 2002. "On the Mystery of Capital and the Myths of Hernando de Soto: What Difference Does Legal Title Make?" *International Development Planning Review* 24 (1): 1–19.

Gill, Lesley. 1987. *Peasants, Entrepreneurs, and Social Change: Frontier Development in Lowland Bolivia*. Boulder, CO: Westview.

Gill, Lesley. 2000. *Teetering on the Rim: Global Restructuring, Daily Life and the Armed Retreat of the Bolivian State*. New York: Columbia University Press.

Gill, Lesley. 2004. *School of the Americas: Military Training and Political Violence in the Americas*. Durham, NC: Duke University Press.

Gillies, Allan. Forthcoming. "Contesting the 'War on Drugs' in the Andes: US-Bolivian Relations of Power and Control (1989–1993)." *Journal of Latin American Studies*.

Ginsburg, Faye, Lila Abu-Lughod, and Brian Larkin. 2002. "Introduction." In *Media Worlds: Anthropology on New Terrain*, edited by Faye Ginsburg, Lila Abu-Lughod, and Brian Larkin, 1–36. Berkeley: University of California Press.

Gledhill, John. 1997. "Liberalism, Socio-Economic Rights and the Politics of Identity: From Moral Economy to Indigenous Rights." In *Human Rights, Culture and Context: Anthropological Approaches*, edited by Richard Wilson. London: Pluto.

Gledhill, John. 2000. *Power and Its Disguises: Anthropological Perspectives on Politics, Anthropology, Culture and Society*. London: Pluto.

Gledhill, John. 2004. "Beyond Speaking Truth to Power: Anthropological Entanglements with Multicultural and Indigenous Rights Politics." *Manchester Anthropology Working Papers*. Manchester, UK: University of Manchester Press.

Goldstein, Daniel. 2003. "'In Our Own Hands': Lynching, Justice, and the Law in Bolivia." *American Ethnologist* 30 (1): 22–43.

Goldstein, Daniel. 2004. *Spectacular City: Violence and Performance in Urban Bolivia*. Durham, NC: Duke University Press.

Goldstein, Daniel. 2005. "Flexible Justice: Neoliberal Violence and 'Self-Help' Security in Bolivia." *Critique of Anthropology* 25 (4): 389–411.

Goldstein, Daniel. 2012. *Outlawed: Between Security and Rights in a Bolivian City*. Durham, NC: Duke University Press.

Goldstein, Daniel, and Fatimah Castro. 2006. "Creative Violence: How Marginal People Make News in Bolivia." *Journal of Latin American Anthropology* 11 (2): 380–407.

Gómez, Andrés. 2006a. "Dictadura Mediatica." *El Juguete Rabioso*.

Gómez, Andrés. 2006b. *Mediopoder: Libertad de Expresión y Derecho a la Comunicación en la Democracia de la Sociedad de la Información*. La Paz: Gente Común.

Gómez, Andrés. 2013. "Kawsachun Bolivia, Wanuchun Cocaleros." *Pagina Siete*, October 27.

Gomis, Benoît. 2017. "What Does the Trump Era Mean for Drug Policy in Latin America?" *World Politics Review*, March 28.

Goodale, Mark. 2006. "Reclaiming Modernity: Indigenous Cosmopolitanism and the Coming of the Second Revolution in Bolivia." *American Ethnologist* 33 (4): 634–50.

Gootenberg, Paul. 2004. "Secret Ingredients: The Politics of Coca in US–Peruvian Relations, 1915–65." *Journal of Latin American Studies* 36 (2): 233–65.

Gootenberg, Paul. 2008. *Andean Cocaine: The Making of a Global Drug*. Chapel Hill: University of North Carolina Press.

Gootenberg, Paul. 2012. "Cocaine's Long March North, 1900–2010." *Latin American Politics and Society* 54 (1): 159–80.

Gootenberg, Paul. 2014. "Peruvian Cocaine and the Boomerang of History." *North American Congress on Latin America* 47 (3): 48–49.

Gootenberg, Paul. 2016. "Shifting South: Cocaine's Diverging Histories and Drug Politics in Bolivia, Colombia, and Peru." Paper presented at the meeting of the Latin American Studies Association, New York.

Gordillo, José María. 2000. *Campesinos revolucionarios en Bolivia: Identidades, territorio y sexualidad en el Valle Alto de Cochabamba, 1952–1964*. La Paz: PROMEC-Universidad de la Cordillera-Plural Editores-CEP.

Gossen, Gary. 1999. *Telling Maya Tales: Tzotzil Identities in Modern Mexico*. New York: Routledge.

Gotkowitz, Laura. 2007. *A Revolution for Our Rights: Indigenous Struggles for Land and Justice in Bolivia, 1880–1952*. Durham, NC: Duke University Press.

Graeber, David. 2014. *The Democracy Project: A History, a Crisis, a Movement*. London: Penguin.

Grandin, Greg. 2006. *Empire's Workshop: Latin America, the United States and the Rise of the New Imperialism*. New York: Metropolitan.

Green, Emily, and William Gallery. 2016. "Measuring Democracy." In *In Search of Democracy*, edited by Larry Diamond, 46–75. London: Routledge.

Gregory, James, Peter Bertocci, H. Claessen, Matthew Cooper, Peter Coy, Alain Dessaint, Ronald Duncan, George Foster, Charles Lave, Grant McCall, Thomas Maloney, Manning Nash, Claude Robineau, Richard Salisbury, H. Schneider, and Sharon Tiffany. 1975. "Image of Limited Good, or Expectation of Reciprocity? [and Comments and Reply]." *Current Anthropology* 16 (1): 73–92.

Grisaffi, Thomas. 2010. "We Are *Originarios* . . . 'We Just Aren't from Here': Coca Leaf and Identity Politics in the Chapare, Bolivia." *Bulletin of Latin American Research* 29 (4): 425–39.

Grisaffi, Thomas. 2013. "All of Us Are Presidents: Radical Democracy and Citizenship in the Chapare Province, Bolivia." *Critique of Anthropology* 33 (1): 47–65.

Grisaffi, Thomas. 2014. *Can You Get Rich from the Bolivian Cocaine Trade? Cocaine Paste Production in the Chapare*. Accessed April 1, 2014. http://ain-bolivia.org/2014/03/can-you-get-rich-from-the-bolivian-cocaine-trade-cocaine-paste-production-in-the-chapare/.

Grisaffi, Thomas. 2016. "Social Control in Bolivia: A Humane Alternative to the Forced Eradication of Coca Crops." In *Drug Policies and the Politics of Drugs in the Americas*, edited by Bia Labate, Clancy Cavnar, and Thiago Rodrigues. Cham, Switzerland: Springer.

Grisaffi, Thomas, Linda Farthing, and Kathryn Ledebur. 2017. "Integrated Development with Coca in the Plurinational State of Bolivia: Shifting the Focus from Eradication to Poverty Alleviation." *Bulletin on Narcotics*. 61:131–57.

Grisaffi, Thomas, and Kathryn Ledebur. 2016. "Citizenship or Repression? Coca, Eradication and Development in the Andes." *Stability: International Journal of Security and Development* 5 (1): 1–19.

Gudynas, Eduardo. 2011. "El nuevo Extractivismo progresista en America del Sur: Tesis sobre un viejo problema bajo nuevas expresiones." In *Colonialismos del Siglo XXI: Negocios extractivos y defensa del territorio en América Latina*, edited by A. Acosta, Eduardo Gudynas, F. Houtart, L. Macas, J. Martinez Alier, H. Ramirez Soler, and E. Siliprandi, 75–92. Barcelona: Icaria Editorial.

Guimarães, Alice. 2009. "Fronteras Borrosas: La Nueva Relacion Entre Sociedad Civil y Estado en la Region del Chapare, Bolivia." Paper presented at the XXVIII International Congress of the Latin American Studies Association (LASA), Pontificia Universidade Catolica do Rio de Janeiro.

Gumucio Dagron, Alfonso, and Lupe Cajias. 1989. *Las Radios Mineras de Bolivia*. La Paz: CIMCA, UNESCO.

Gupta, Akhil. 1995. "Blurred Boundaries: The Discourse of Corruption, the Culture of Politics, and the Imagined State." *American Ethnologist* 22 (2): 375–402.

Gustafson, Bret. 2006. "Spectacles of Autonomy and Crisis: Or, What Bulls and Beauty Queens Have to Do with Regionalism in Eastern Bolivia." *Journal of Latin American Anthropology* 11 (2): 351–80.

Gustafson, Bret. 2009. *New Languages of the State: Indigenous Resurgence and the Politics of Knowledge in Bolivia*. Durham, NC: Duke University Press.

Gustafson, Bret. 2016. *Bolivia after the "No" Vote*. Accessed March 22, 2016. https://nacla.org/news/2016/03/07/bolivia-after-no-vote.

Gutierrez Aguilar, Raquel. 2014. *Rhythms of Pachakuti: Indigenous Uprising and State Power in Bolivia*. Durham, NC: Duke University Press.

Habermas, Jürgen. 1989. *The Structural Transformation of the Public Sphere: An Inquiry into a Category of Bourgeois Society*. Translated by T. Burger and F. Lawrence. Cambridge: Polity.

Hagopian, Frances, and Scott Mainwaring, eds. 2005. *The Third Wave of Democratization in Latin America: Advances and Setbacks*. Cambridge: Cambridge University Press.

Hale, Charles. 1994. "Between Che Guevara and the Pachamama: Mestizos, Indians, and Identity Politics in the Anti-Quincentenary Campaign." *Critique of Anthropology* 14 (2): 9–39.

Hale, Charles. 2002. "Does Multiculturalism Menace? Governance, Cultural Rights, and the Politics of Identity in Guatemala." *Journal of Latin American Studies* 34:485–524.

Hall, Gillette, and Harry Patrinos. 2005. *Indigenous Peoples, Poverty and Human Development in Latin America: 1994–2004*. Washington, DC: World Bank.

Hall, Stuart. 1977. "Culture, the Media and the 'Ideological Effect.'" In *Mass Communication and Society*, edited by James Curran, M. Gurevitch, and Janet Woolacott. London: Edward Arnold.

Hall, Stuart. 1991. "The Local and the Global: Globalisation and Ethnicity." In *Culture, Globalisation and the World System: Contemporary Conditions for the Representation of Identity*, edited by A. King, 19–39. London: Macmillan.

Hammond, John. 2004. "The MST and the Media: Competing Images of the Brazilian Landless Farm Workers Movement." *Latin American Politics and Society* 46 (4): 61–90.

Hammond, John. 2011. "Indigenous Community Justice in the Bolivian Constitution of 2009." *Human Rights Quarterly* 33 (3): 649–81.

Harris, Olivia. 2000a. "Complementarity and Conflict: An Andean View of Women and Men." In *To Make the Earth Bear Fruit: Essays on Fertility, Work and Gender in Highland Bolivia*, edited by O. Harris. London: Institute for Latin American Studies.

Harris, Olivia. 2000b. *To Make the Earth Bear Fruit: Essays on Fertility, Work and Gender in Highland Bolivia*. London: Institute of Latin American Studies.

Harris, Olivia, and Xavier Albó. 1976. *Monteras y Guardatojos: Campesinos y Mineros en el Norte de Potosí*. La Paz: Centro de Investigación y Promoción del Campesinado.

Harten, Sven. 2011. *The Rise of Evo Morales and the MAS*. London: Zed.

Harvey, David. 2004. "The 'New' Imperialism: Accumulation by Dispossession." *Socialist Register* 40:63–87.

Harvey, David. 2005. *A Brief History of Neoliberalism*. Oxford: Oxford University Press.

Harvey, Neil. 1998. *The Chiapas Rebellion: The Struggle for Land and Democracy*. Durham, NC: Duke University Press.

Harvey, Penelope. 2002. "Elites on the Margins: *Mestizo* Traders in the Southern Peruvian Andes." In *Elite Cultures: Anthropological Perspectives*, edited by Chris Shore and Stephen Nugent, 74–90. London: Routledge.

Harvey, Penelope, and Hannah Knox. 2015. *Roads: An Anthropology of Infrastructure and Expertise*. Ithaca, NY: Cornell University Press.

Harvey, Penny. 1994. "Gender, Community and Confrontation: Power Relations in Drunkenness in Ocongate (Southern Peru)." In *Gender, Drink and Drugs*, edited by Maryon McDonald, 209–33. Oxford: Berg.

Healy, Kevin. 1986. "The Boom within the Crisis: Some Recent Effects of Foreign Cocaine Markets on Bolivian Rural Society and Economy." In *Coca and Cocaine Effects on People and Policy in Latin America*, edited by D. Pacini and C. Franquemont. Peterborough, NH: Cultural Survival, Inc. LASP.

Healy, Kevin. 1997. "The Coca Cocaine Issue in Bolivia: A Political Resource for All Seasons." In *Coca, Cocaine, and the Bolivian Reality*, edited by B. Léons and H. Sanabria. Albany: State University of New York Press.

Henkel, Ray. 1986. "The Bolivian Cocaine Industry." In *Drugs in Latin America: Studies in Third World Societies*, edited by Edmundo Morales, 53–80. Williamsburg, VA: Studies in Third World Societies.

Henman, Anthony. 1992. *Mama Coca*. La Paz: Hisbol.

Henman, Anthony, and Pien Metaal. 2009. "Coca Myths." *Drugs and Conflict* 17 (June).

Herrera, Karina, and Juan Ramos. 2013. "Comunicación, red y lucha social: Hacia la reactivación de las radiosmineras de Bolivia." *Quórum, Académico* 10 (1): 11–28.

Hickel, Jason. 2015. *Democracy as Death: The Moral Order of Anti-Liberal Politics in South Africa*. Berkeley: University of California Press.

Himpele, Jeff. 2008. *Circuits of Culture: Media, Politics and Indigenous Identity in the Andes*. Minneapolis: University of Minnesota Press.

Hindery, Derrick. 2013. *From Enron to Evo: Pipeline Politics, Global Environmentalism, and Indigenous Rights in Bolivia*. Tucson: University of Arizona Press.

Hobsbawm, Eric. 1995. "Inventing Traditions." In *The Invention of Tradition*, edited by Eric Hobsbawm and Terence Ranger, 1–14. Cambridge: Cambridge University Press.

Holston, James. 2008. *Insurgent Citizenship: Disjunctions of Democracy and Modernity in Brazil*. Princeton, NJ: Princeton University Press.

Hooker, Juliet. 2005. "Indigenous Inclusion/Black Exclusion: Race, Ethnicity and Multicultural Citizenship in Latin America." *Journal of Latin American Studies* 37:285–310.

Horkheimer, Max, and Theodor Adorno. 1997. "The Culture Industry: Enlightenment as Mass Deception." In *Dialectic of Enlightenment: Philosophical Fragments*, edited by Gunzelin Noeer, 120–67. London: Verso.

Howard, Philip, and Muzammil Hussain. 2013. *Democracy's Fourth Wave? Digital Media and the Arab Spring*. Oxford: Oxford University Press.

Huesca, Robert, and Brenda Dervin. 1994. "Theory and Practice in Latin American Alternative Communication Research." *Journal of Communication*. 44 (4): 53–73.

Hunter, Wendy. 2010. *The Transformation of the Workers' Party in Brazil, 1989–2009*. Cambridge: Cambridge University Press.

Huntington, Samuel. 1993. *The Third Wave: Democratization in the Late Twentieth Century*. Norman: University of Oklahoma Press.

Hylton, Forrest. 2011. "Old Wine, New Bottles: In Search of Dialectics." *Dialectical Anthropology* 35:243–47. doi:10.1007/s10624-011-9250-x.

Hylton, Forrest, and Sinclair Thomson. 2007. *Revolutionary Horizons: Popular Struggle in Bolivia*. London: Verso.

Ibáñez, Carlos, and Eduardo Vélez. 2008. "Civil Conflict and Forced Migration: The Micro Determinants and Welfare Losses of Displacement in Colombia." *World Development* 36 (4): 659–76. doi:10.1016/j.worlddev.2007.04.013.

INE. 2003. *Bolivia: Características Sociodemográficas de la Población*. La Paz: Instituto Nacional de Estadísticas de Bolívia/UMPA.

INE. 2014. *Instituto Nacional de Estadistica: Nota de Prensa*. Accessed September 3, 2015. http://www.ine.gob.bo/pdf/boletin/np_2014_4.pdf.

Ingraham, Christopher. 2017. "In Trump's 'Ruthless' Vow, Experts See a Return to the Days of the Drug War." *Washington Post*, February 10.

Isacson, Adam. 2005. "Closing the 'Seams': U.S. Security Policy in the Americas." *NACLA: Report on the Americas* 38 (6): 13–19.

Isbell, Billie Jean. 1978. *To Defend Ourselves: Ecology and Ritual in an Andean Village*. Austin: University of Texas Press.

Jabin, David. 2014. "Nómadas en la ciudad. La apropiación yuqui del espacio urbano." *Amazonía, política indígena y ciudad: La dimensión urbana de la política indígena en la Amazonía. Seminario del GRDI APOCAMO*. Pontificia Universidad Católica, Lima, Perú, April 10.

Jackson, Donald, David Bathrick, Patricia Martin, and Danielle Rodriguez-Schneider. 2003. *Assessment of the USAID/Bolivia Alternative Development Strategy*. Arlington, VA: USAID; Development Associates, Inc.

Jackson, Jean, and Kay Warren. 2005. "Indigenous Movements in Latin America, 1992–2004: Controversies, Ironies, New Directions." *Annual Review of Anthropology* 34:549–73.

Jaffe, Rivke. 2015. "Between Ballots and Bullets: Elections and Citizenship in and beyond the Nation-State." *Citizenship Studies* 19 (2): 128–40.

Jelsma, Martin. 2016. "UNGASS 2016: Prospects for Treaty Reform and UN System-Wide Coherence on Drug Policy." Washington, DC: Brookings Institution, Center for 21st Century Security and Intelligence Latin America Initiative.

Jones, Jeffrey. 2015. *Confidence in U.S. Institutions Still Below Historical Norms*. Gallup. Accessed December 5, 2016. http://www.gallup.com/poll/183593/confidence-institutions-below-historical-norms.aspx.

Joyce, Elizabeth. 1999. "Packaging Drugs: Certification and the Acquisition of Leverage." In *The United States and Latin America: The New Agenda*, edited by Victor Bulmer-Thomas and James Dunkerley. Cambridge, MA: Institute of Latin American Studies, University of London; Center for Latin American Studies, Harvard University.

Juris, Jeffrey. 2012. "Reflections on Occupy Everywhere: Social Media, Public Space, and Emerging Logics of Aggregation." *American Ethnologist* 39 (2): 259–79.

Kalb, Don. 2009. "Conversations with a Polish Populist: Tracing Hidden Histories of Globalization, Class and Dispossession in Post-Socialism (and Beyond)." *American Ethnologist* 36 (2): 207–23.

Karandinos, George, Laurie Hart, Fernando Montero Castrillo, and Philippe Bourgois. 2014. "The Moral Economy of Violence in the US Inner City." *Current Anthropology* 55 (1): 1–22.

Kaup, Brent. 2010. "A Neoliberal Nationalization? The Constraints on Natural-Gas-Led Development in Bolivia." *Latin American Perspectives* 37 (3): 123–38.

Kilmer, Beau, Susan Everingham, Jonathan Caulkins, Gregory Midgette, Rosalie Pacula, Peter Reuter, Rachel Burns, Bing Han, and Russell Lundberg. 2014. *What America's Users Spend on Illegal Drugs: 2000–2010*. Washington, DC: Office of National Drug Control Policy.

Klein, Herbert. 1986. "Coca Production in the Bolivian Yungas in the Colonial and Early National Periods." In *Coca and Cocaine: Effects on People and Policy in Latin America*, edited by D. Pacini and C. Franquemont. Peterborough, NH: Cultural Survival Inc.

Klein, Herbert. 2011. *A Concise History of Bolivia*. Cambridge: Cambridge University Press.

Koch, Insa. 2015. "'The State Has Replaced the Man': Women, Family Homes, and the Benefit System on a Council Estate in England." *Focaal* 73:84–96.

Koch, Insa. 2016. "Bread-and-Butter Politics: Democratic Disenchantment and Everyday Politics on an English Council Estate." *American Ethnologist* 43 (2): 282–94.

Koch, Insa. 2017a. "Moving beyond Punitivism: Punishment, State Failure and Democracy at the Margins." *Punishment and Society* 19 (2): 203–20.

Koch, Insa. 2017b. "What's in a Vote? Brexit beyond Culture Wars." *American Ethnologist* 44 (2): 225–30.

Koch, Insa. 2017c. "When Politicians Fail: Zombie Democracy and the Anthropology of Actually Existing Politics." *Sociological Review* 65 (1): 105–20.

Koch, Insa. 2018. *Personalising the State: An Anthropology of Law, Welfare, and Politics in Austerity Britain*. Oxford: Oxford University Press.

Kohl, Benjamin. 2002. "Stabilizing Neoliberalism in Bolivia: Popular Participation and Privatization." *Political Geography* 21 (4): 449–72.

Kohl, Benjamin. 2003. "Democratizing Decentralization in Bolivia: The Law of Popular Participation." *Journal of Planning Education and Research* 23 (2): 153–64.

Kohl, Benjamin, and Rosalind Bresnahan. 2010. "National Agenda, Regional Challenges, and the Struggle for Hegemony." *Latin American Perspectives* 37 (4): 5–20.

Kohl, Benjamin, and Linda Farthing. 2006. *Impasse in Bolivia: Neoliberal Hegemony and Popular Resistance*. London: Zed.

Kohl, Benjamin, Linda Farthing, and Félix Muruchi. 2011. *From the Mines to the Streets: A Bolivian Activist's Life*. Austin: University of Texas Press.

Kuncar Camacho, Gridvia. 1989. *Comunicación Alternativa y Sindicalismo en Bolivia: La Experiencia de las Radios Mineras (1950 a 1980)*. La Paz: Centro Boliviano de Investigacion y Accion Educativa.

Kuper, Adam. 2003. "The Return of the Native." *Current Anthropology* 44 (3): 389–402.

Labate, Beatriz, Clancy Cavnar, and Thiago Rodrigues, eds. 2016. *Drug Policies and the Politics of Drugs in the Americas*. Cham, Switzerland: Springer International.

Laclau, Ernesto. 2005. *On Populist Reason*. London: Verso.

La Patria. 2001. "El Narcotráfico (del Chapare) Quiere Fomentar el Terrorismo." *La Patria*, November 28.

La Patria. 2011. "Video: Cocaleros acusaron de ejercer 'dictadura sindical' a Evo Morales." *La Patria*, July 20.

Lapegna, Pablo, and Javier Auyero. 2012. "Democratic Processes, Patronage Politics, and Contentious Collective Action in El Alto, Bolivia." In *Clientelism in Everyday Latin American Politics*, edited by Hilgers Tina, 63–80. New York: Palgrave Macmillan.

La Prensa. 2006. "Dos muertos y tres heridos en erradicación de coca ilegal." *La Prensa*, September 30.

La Razón. 2011. "El 93,5% de Coca del Chapare No Pasa por el Mercado Legal." *La Razón*, September 14.

La Razón. 2013. "Incautación de cocaína creció en 234% sin participación de la DEA." *La Razón*, January 20.

Larson, Brooke. 1988. *Colonialism and Agrarian Transformation in Bolivia: Cochabamba 1550–1900*. Princeton, NJ: Princeton University Press.

Larson, Brooke. 1995. "Andean Communities, Political Cultures and Markets: The Changing Contours of a Field." In *Ethnicity, Markets, and Migration in the Andes: At the Crossroads of History and Anthropology*, edited by Brooke Larson and Olivia Harris, 5–54. Durham, NC: Duke University Press.

Larson, Brooke, and Olivia Harris, eds. 1995. *Ethnicity, Markets and Migration in the Andes: At the Crossroads of History and Anthropology*. Durham, NC: Duke University Press.

Laserna, Roberto, ed. 1999. *Empujando la Concertación: Marchas Campesinas, Opinión Pública y Coca*. La Paz: PIEB-CERES.

Laserna, Roberto. 2000. "Desarrollo alternativo en Bolivia: Análisis preliminar de una experiencia inconclusa." *Seminario Internacional*. Bogotá, Colombia: Pontificia Universidad Javeriana.

Laserna, Roberto. 2007. "El caudillismo fragmentado." *Nueva Sociedad* 209 (May–June): 100–117.

Laserna, Roberto. 2010. "Mire, La Democracia Boliviana, en los Hechos. . . ." *Latin American Resarch Review* 45:27–58.

Laurie, Nina, Robert Andolina, and Sarah Radcliffe. 2002. "The Excluded 'Indigenous'? The Implications of Multi-Ethnic Policies for Water Reform in Bolivia." In *Multiculturalism in Latin America: Indigenous Rights, Diversity and Democracy*, edited by R. Sieder. Basingstoke, UK: Palgrave Macmillan.

Lazar, Sian. 2004. "Personalist Politics, Clientelism and Citizenship: Local Elections in El Alto, Bolivia." *Bulletin of Latin American Research* 23 (2): 228–43.

Lazar, Sian. 2008. *El Alto, Rebel City: Self and Citizenship in Andean Bolivia*. Durham, NC: Duke University Press.

Lazar, Sian. 2013. "Group Belonging in Trade Unions: Idioms of Sociality in Bolivia and Argentina." In *Sociality: New Directions*, edited by Nicholas Long and Henrietta Moore. Oxford: Berghahn.

Lazar, Sian. 2015. "'This Is Not a Parade, It's a Protest March': Intertextuality, Citation, and Political Action on the Streets of Bolivia and Argentina." *American Anthropologist* 117 (2): 242–56.

Lazar, Sian. 2017a. *The Social Life of Politics: Ethics, Kinship, and Union Activism in Argentina.* Stanford, CA: Stanford University Press.

Lazar, Sian, ed. 2017b. *Where Are the Unions? Workers and Social Movements in Latin America, the Middle East and Europe.* London: Zed.

Lazar, Sian, and John-Andrew McNeish. 2006. "The Millions Return? Democracy in Bolivia at the Start of the Twenty-first Century." *Bulletin of Latin American Research* 25 (2): 157–62.

Ledebur, Kathryn. 2003. *Drug War Monitor: Coca and Conflict in the Chapare.* WOLA Briefing Series. Washington, DC: Washington Office on Latin America.

Ledebur, Kathryn. 2004. "Bolivian Police Arrest Colombian and Coca Growers: U.S. Suggests FARC and ELN Presence." Accessed November 13, 2004. http://www.wola .org/andes/Bolivia/bolivia_ain_updates 2003.

Ledebur, Kathryn. 2005. "Bolivia: Clear Consequences." In *Drugs and Democracy in Latin America: The Impact of U.S. Policy,* edited by Coletta Youngers and Eileen Rosin, 143–84. Boulder, CO: Lynne Rienner.

Ledebur, Kathryn. 2016. "Some Are More Equal Than Others: US 'Decertification' of Bolivia's Drug Control Efforts." Accessed August 16, 2016. http://ain-bolivia.org/2016/09 /some-are-more-equal-than-others-u-s-decertification-of-bolivias-drug-control-efforts/.

Ledebur, Kathryn, and Coletta Youngers. 2008. "Balancing Act: Bolivia's Drug Control Advances and Challenges." Accesssed June 4, 2008. http://www.ain-bolivia.org /AINWOLABalancingAct52308.pdf 2008.

León, Rosario, Patricia Uberhuaga, Jean-Paul Benavides, and Krister Andersson. 2012. "Public Policy Reforms and Indigenous Forest Governance: The Case of the Yuracaré People in Bolivia." *Conservation and Society* 10 (2): 195–207.

Leons, Barbara, and William Leons. 1971. "Land Reform and Economic Change in the Yungas." In *Beyond the Revoloution: Bolivia since 1952,* edited by James Malloy and R. Thorn. Pittsburgh: University of Pittsburgh Press.

Leons, Barbara, and Harry Sanabria. 1997. "Coca and Cocaine in Bolivia: Reality and Policy Illusion." In *Coca, Cocaine, and the Bolivian Reality,* edited by Barbara Leons and Harry Sanabria. Albany: State University of New York Press.

Levitsky, Steven, and James Loxton. 2013. "Populism and Competitive Authoritarianism in the Andes." *Democratization* 20 (1): 107–36.

Linz, Juan J., and Alfred C. Stepan. 1996. "Toward Consolidated Democracies." *Journal of Democracy* 7 (2): 14–33.

Los Tiempos. 2002. "El embajador rocha pide a los electores que no voten por Evo." *Los Tiempos,* June 27.

Los Tiempos. 2003. "Mesa admite que hay terrorismo en Chapare y promete erradicarlo." *Los Tiempos,* December 1.

Los Tiempos. 2012. "Cocaleros y erradicadores se enfrentan en Bulo Bulo." *Los Tiempos,* May 10.

Los Tiempos. 2014a. "Analizan traspaso de Ebo Coca; funciona a medias." Los Tiempos, March 17.

Los Tiempos. 2014b. "Envían a la cárcel a masistas de Shinahota y despejan vía." Los Tiempos, December 26.

Los Tiempos. 2015a. "'Dictadura' masista en Chapare: Denuncian acoso del oficialismo a 30 cocaleros 'disidentes.'" Los Tiempos, May 12.

Los Tiempos. 2015b. "MAS reafirma su poder en alcaldías del tropico." Los Tiempos, April 2.

Los Tiempos. 2016. "Morales: Guerra por la coca fue la más intensa." Los Tiempos, May 28.

Los Tiempos. 2017a. "Actividad piscícola ya es otro rubro productivo en Chapare." Los Tiempos, April 12.

Los Tiempos. 2017b. "Editorial: Planta de urea en Bulo Bulo." Los Tiempos, March 14.

Los Tiempos. 2017c. "Evo entrega ley de coca en una masiva concentración en Chapare." Los Tiempos, March 18.

Lucero, Jose Antonio. 2008. Struggles of Voice: The Politics of Indigenous Representation in the Andes. Pittsburgh: University of Pittsburgh Press.

Lupu, Noam. 2004. "Towards a New Articulation of Alternative Development: Lessons from Coca Supply Reduction in Bolivia." Development Policy Review 22 (4): 405–21.

MacWilliams, Matthew. 2016. "Who Decides When the Party Doesn't? Authoritarian Voters and the Rise of Donald Trump." PS: Political Science and Politics 49 (4): 716–21. doi:10.1017/S1049096516001463.

Madrid, Raul. 2008. "The Rise of Ethnopopulism in Latin America." World Politics 60:475–508.

Madrid, Raul. 2011. "Bolivia: Origins and Policies of the Movimiento al Socialismo." In The Resurgence of the Left in Latin America, edited by Steven Levitsky and Kenneth Roberts, 239–59. Baltimore: Johns Hopkins University Press.

Madrid, Raul. 2012. The Rise of Ethnic Politics in Latin America. Cambridge: Cambridge University Press.

Maeckelbergh, Marianne. 2009. The Will of the Many: How the Alterglobalisation Movement Is Changing the Face of Democracy. London: Pluto.

Mainwaring, Scott, Ana Maria Bejarano, and Eduardo Leongomez. 2006. "The Crisis of Democratic Representation in the Andes: An Overview." In The Crisis of Democratic Representation in the Andes, edited by Scott Mainwaring, Ana Maria Bejarano, and Eduardo Leongomez, 1–44. Stanford, CA: Stanford University Press.

Mainwaring, Scott, and Aníbal Pérez-Liñán. 2015. "Cross-Currents in Latin America." Journal of Democracy 26 (1): 114–27.

Mair, Peter. 2013. Ruling the Void: The Hollowing of Western Democracy. London: Verso.

Makaran, Gaya. 2016. "La Figura del Llunk'u y el Clientelismo en la Bolivia de Evo Morales." Revista Antropologías del Sur 5:33–47.

Mallon, Florencia E. 1992. "Indian Communities, Political Cultures, and the State in Latin America, 1780–1990." Journal of Latin American Studies 24 (S1): 35–53.

Malloy, James. 1970. Bolivia: The Uncompleted Revolution. Pittsburgh: University of Pittsburgh Press.

Malloy, James, and Richard Thorn. 1971. *Beyond the Revolution: Bolivia since 1952*. Pittsburgh: University of Pittsburgh Press.

Manin, Bernard. 1997. *The Principles of Representative Government*. Cambridge: Cambridge University Press.

Mansfield, David. 2011. "Assessing Supply-Side Policy and Practice: Eradication and Alternative Development." Working Paper for the first meeting of the Global Commission on Drug Policy, Geneva, January 24–25.

Mathieu, Hans, and Catalina Niño Guarnizo, eds. 2013. *From Repression to Regulation: Proposals for Drug Policy Reform*. Bogotá: Friedrich-Ebert-Stiftung.

Mattelart, Armand. 1979. "Communication Ideology and Class Practice." In *Communication and Class Struggle*, Vol. 1: *Capitalism, Imperialism*, edited by A. Mattelart and S. Siegelaub, 115–23. New York: IG/IMMRC.

Mauss, Marcel. [1954] 1990. *The Gift: Forms and Functions of Exchange in Archaic Societies*. London: Routledge.

Mayer, Enrique. 2001. *The Articulated Peasant: Household Economies in the Andes*. Oxford: Westview.

Mayorga, Fernando. 2011. *Dilemas: Ensayos Sobre Democracia Intercultural y Estado Plurinacional*. La Paz: Plural Editores.

Mayorga, René. 2009. "Bolivia Sociedad civil y Estado bajo un populismo plebiscitario y autoritario." In *La "Nueva Izquierda" en America Latina: Derechos Humanos, Participacion Politica, y Sociedad Civil*, edited by Cynthia Arnson, Ariel Armony, Catalina Smulovitz, Gastón Chillier, Enrique Peruzzotti, and Giselle Cohen, 106–14. Washington, DC: Woodrow Wilson Center.

Mayorga, René. 2017. "Populismo autoritario y transición regresiva: La dictadura plebiscitaria en la región andina." *Revista Latinoamericana de Política Comparada* 12 (39–69): 39–69.

Mazzarella, William. 2004. "Culture, Globalization, Mediation." *Annual Review of Anthropology* 33:345–67.

McCarthy, John, Jackie Smith, and Mayer Zald. 1996. "Accessing Public, Media, Electoral, and Governmental Agendas." In *Comparative Perspectives on Social Movements: Political Opportunities, Mobilizing Structures and Cultural Framings*, edited by Doug McAdam, John McCarthy, and Mayer Zald. Cambridge: Cambridge University Press.

Medrano, Elisa. 2017. "Ley 1008, guerra a la coca antes que contra el narcotráfico." *La Razón*, March 12.

Mejía, Daniel. 2010. "Evaluating Plan Colombia." In *Innocent Bystanders: Developing Countries and the War on Drugs*, edited by Philip Keefer and Norman Loayza. New York: World Bank and Palgrave Macmillan.

Mejía, Daniel. 2015. "Plan Colombia: An Analysis of Effectiveness and Costs." Improving Global Drug Policy Series. Washington, DC: Brookings Institution.

Mejía, Daniel. 2017. "Anti-Drug Policies under Plan Colombia: Costs, Effectiveness, and Efficiency." In *Anti-Drug Policies in Colombia: Successes, Failures, and Wrong Turns*, edited by Alejandro Gaviria and Daniel Mejía. Nashville, TN: Vanderbilt University Press.

Mendez, Cecilia. 1996. "Incas si, Indios no: Notes on Peruvian Creole Nationalism and Its Contemporary Crisis." *Journal of Latin American Studies* 28 (1): 197–226.

Menzel, Sewall. 1996. *Fire in the Andes: U.S. Foreign Policy and Cocaine Politics in Bolivia and Peru.* New York: University Press of America.

Mercille, Julien. 2011. "Violent Narco-Cartels or US Hegemony? The Political Economy of the 'War on Drugs' in Mexico." *Third World Quarterly* 32 (9): 1637–53.

Meruvia, Fanor. 2000. *Historia de la coca: Los Yungas de Pocona y Totora.* La Paz: Plural/CERES.

Mesa, Jose, Teresa Gisbert, and Carlos Mesa. 2003. *Historia de Bolivia.* La Paz: Editorial Gisbert.

Metaal, Pien. 2014. "Coca in Debate: The Contradiction and Conflict between the UN Drug Conventions and the Real World." In *Prohibition, Religious Freedom, and Human Rights: Regulating Traditional Drug Use,* edited by Beatriz Labate and Clancy Cavnar, 25–44. Berlin: Springer.

Metaal, Pien, Martin Jelsma, Mario Argandona, Ricardo Soberon, Anthony Henman, and Ximera Echeverria. 2006. "Coca Yes, Cocaine, No? Legal Options for the Coca Leaf." TNI Briefing Series. Amsterdam: Transnational Institute.

Mezza, Victor, and Isabel Quisbert. 2004. *Cochabamba: Indicadores Sociodemográficos por Provincia y Secciones de Provincia 1992–2001.* La Paz: Instituto Nacional de Estadística.

Michaels, Eric. 2002. "Hollywood Iconography: A Warlpiri Reading." In *The Anthropology of Globalisation: A Reader,* edited by John Inda and Renato Rosaldo. Oxford: Blackwell.

Michelutti, Lucia. 2008. *The Vernacularisation of Democracy: Politics, Caste and Religion in India.* Delhi: Routledge.

Ministerio de Gobierno. 1997. *Por La Dignidad! Estrategia Boliviana de lucha contra el narcotrafico. Republica de Bolivia—1998–2002.* La Paz: Ministerio de Gobierno.

Mintz, Sidney. 1986. *Sweetness and Power: The Place of Sugar in Modern History.* Harmondsworth, UK: Penguin.

Mitchell, Timothy. 2005. "The Work of Economics: How a Discipline Makes Its World." *European Journal of Sociology* 46:297–320.

Molina, Fernando. 2013. "¿Por qué Evo Morales sigue siendo popular? Las fortalezas del mas en la construcción de un nuevo orden." *Nueva Sociedad* 245 (May–June): 4–14.

Molina, George Gray. 2010. "The Challenge of Progressive Change under Evo Morales." In *Leftist Governments in Latin America: Successes and Shortcomings,* edited by Kurt Weyland, Raúl Madrid, and Wendy Hunter, 57–76. Cambridge: Cambridge University Press.

Morales, Cristina. 2001. "Tuto: El Narcotráfico se Cobija Detrás de Demandas Sociales." *La Prensa,* C2.

Morales, Evo. 2003. *Evo Morales habla para PF: "Queremos recuperar el Gas para Bolivia."* Accessed May 1, 2017. http://www.puntofinal.cl/537/bolivia.htm.

Morales, Evo. 2006. *La Revolucion Democratica y Cultural: Diez discursos de Evo Morales.* La Paz: Malatesta.

Morales, Juan Antonio, and Jeffrey Sachs. 1988. *Bolivia's Economic Crisis*. Cambridge, MA: National Bureau of Economic Research.

Mouffe, Chantal. 2005. *On the Political*. Milton Park, UK: Routledge.

Murra, John. 1986. "Notes on Pre-Colombian Cultivation of Coca Leaf." In *Coca and Cocaine: Effects on People and Policy in Latin America*, edited by Deborah Pacini and Christine Franquemont. Peterborough, NH: Cultural Survival, Inc. LASP.

Murra, John. 1995. "Did Tribute and Markets Prevail in the Andes before the European Invasion?" In *Ethnicity, Markets and Migration in the Andes: At the Crossroads of History and Anthropology*, edited by Brooke Larson and Olivia Harris. Durham, NC: Duke University Press.

Murray Li, Tania. 2000. "Articulating Indigenous Identity in Indonesia: Resource Politics and the Tribal Slot." *Comparative Studies in Society and History* 42 (1): 149–79.

Nader, Laura. 1990. *Harmony Ideology: Justice and Control in a Zapotec Mountain Village*. Stanford, CA: Stanford University Press.

Nash, June. 1979. *We Eat the Mines and the Mines Eat Us: Dependency and Exploitation in Bolivian Tin Mines*. New York: Columbia University Press.

Nash, June. 1995. "The Reassertion of Indigenous Identity: Mayan Responses to State Intervention in Chiapas." *Latin American Research Review* 30 (3): 7–41.

Nash, June. 1997a. "The Fiesta of the Word: The Zapatista Uprising and Radical Democracy in Mexico." *American Anthropologist* 99 (2): 261–74.

Nash, June. 1997b. "Press Reports on the Chiapas Uprising: Towards a Transnationalized Communication." *Journal of Latin American Anthropology* 2 (2): 42–75.

Negri, Toni, Michael Hardt, Giuseppe Cocco, Judith Revel, Alvaro García Linera, and Luís Tapia. 2008. *Imperio, multitud, y sociedad abigarrada*. La Paz: Muela del Diablo Editores.

New York Times. 2016. "How Bolivia Fights the Drug Scourge." *New York Times*, September 14.

Ng'weno, Bettina. 2007. "Can Ethnicity Replace Race? Afro-Colombians, Indigeneity and the Colombian Multicultural State." *Journal of Latin American and Caribbean Anthropology* 12 (2): 414–40.

Nixon, Richard. 1973. "Message to Congress Establishing the Drug Enforcement Administration. March 28, 1973." Accessed September 23, 2017. http://www.presidency.ucsb.edu/ws/index.php?pid=4159—axzz1PCJydj15.

Nugent, David. 2008. "Democracy Otherwise: Struggles over Popular Rule in the Northern Peruvian Andes." In *Democracy: Anthropological Approaches*, edited by Julia Paley, 21–62. Santa Fe, NM: SAR Press.

Nugent, David. 2010. "States, Secrecy, Subversives: APRA and Political Fantasy in Mid-20th-Century Peru." *American Ethnologist* 37 (4): 681–702.

Nugent, David. 2012. "Commentary: Democracy, Temporalities of Capitalism, and Dilemmas of Inclusion in Occupy Movements." *American Ethnologist* 39 (2): 280–83.

OAS. 2013. *The Drug Problem in the Americas: The Economics of Drug Trafficking*. Washington, DC: Organization of American States.

O'Phelan, Godoy Scarlett. 1995. *La gran rebelión en Los Andes: De Túpac Amaru a Túpac Catari*. Cusco: PetroPerú—CBC Centro de Estudios Regionales Andinos Bartolomé de las Casas.

Opinión. 2006a. "Gobierno sospecha que 'narcos' Colombianos operan en Carrasco." *Opinión*, October 3.

Opinión. 2006b. "Policias de Umopar Reciben Bono Mensual de la Embajada de EEUU." *Opinión*, October 16.

Opinión. 2014. "Unos 800 cocaleros perdieron cultivos por infringir los límite del 'cato' de coca." *Opinion*, July 25.

Orduna, Victor, and Gabriella Guzman. 2001. "Prohibido Cantar 'Coca-Cero': Advertencias de un Zar." *Pulso*, November 2–8.

Orlove, Ben. 1998. "Down to Earth: Race and Substance in the Andes." *Bulletin of Latin American Research* 17 (2): 207–22.

O'Shaughnessy, Hugh. 2007. "Media Wars in Latin America." *British Journalism Review* 18 (3): 66–72.

Pagina Doce. 2006. "Los discursos de Evo." *Pagina Doce*, February 1.

Pagina Siete. 2015a. "Chimoré y su aeropuerto." *Pagina Siete*, October 24.

Pagina Siete. 2015b. "Excandidato opositor denuncia dice que agentes destruyen sus cocales por razón política." *Pagina Siete*, May 9.

Pagina Siete. 2017. "Bolivia se prepara para exportar coca a 2 países." *Pagina Siete*, January 14.

Painter, James. 1994. *Bolivia and Coca: A Study in Dependency*. Boulder, CO: Lynne Rienner.

Painter, Michael. 1998. "Economic Development and the Origins of the Bolivian Cocaine Industry." In *The Third Wave of Modernization in Latin America*, edited by Lynne Phillips. Wilmington, DE: Scholarly Resources.

Paley, Dawn. 2014. *Drug War Capitalism*. Oakland, CA: AK Press.

Paley, Julia. 2001. *Marketing Democracy: Power and Social Movements in Post-Dictatorship Chile*. Berkeley: University of California Press.

Paley, Julia, ed. 2008. *Democracy: Anthropological Approaches, Democracy*. Santa Fe, NM: SAR Press.

Paulovich. 2013. "¿La coca es sagrada?" *Los Tiempos*, October 22.

Pearson, Zoe. 2016. "'Coca Got Us Here and Now It's Our Weakness': *Fusarium Oxysporum* and the Political Ecology of a Drug War Policy Alternative in Bolivia." *International Journal of Drug Policy* 33 (July): 88–95.

Peck, Jamie, and Adam Tickell. 2002. "Neoliberalizing Space." *Antipode* 34 (3): 380–404.

Pellegrini, Alessandra. 2016. *Beyond Indigeneity: Coca Growing and the Emergence of a New Middle Class in Bolivia*. Tucson: University of Arizona Press.

Penny, Mary, A. Zavaleta, M. Lemay, M. Liria, M. Huaylinas, and M. Alminger. 2009. "Can Coca Leaves Contribute to Improving the Nutritional Status of the Andean Population?" *Food and Nutrition Bulletin* 30 (3): 205–16.

Perez, Carlos. 1992. "Tendencias migratorias en las areas de producción de coca en Cochabamba, Bolivia." In *Drogas y sociedad: Síntesis del seminario de Cochabamba del grupo CLACSO narcotráfico y sociedad*, edited by Monica Roa, 26–34. Cochabamba: CERES/CLACSO.

Perreault, Thomas. 2006. "From the Guerra Del Agua to the Guerra Del Gas: Re-source Governance, Neoliberalism and Popular Protest in Bolivia." *Antipode* 38 (1): 150–72.

Perreault, Tom. 2015. "Performing Participation: Mining, Power, and the Limits of Public Consultation in Bolivia." *Journal of Latin American and Caribbean Anthropology* 20 (3): 433–51.

Piot, Charles. 1999. *Remotely Global: Village Modernity in West Africa*. Chicago: University of Chicago Press.

Platt, Tristan. 1983. "Conciencia Andina y Conciencia Proletaria: Qhuyaruna y Ayllu en el Norte de Potosi." *Revista Latino Americana de Histórica Económica* 2:47–73.

Platt, Tristan. 1984. "Liberalism and Ethnocide in the Southern Andes." *History Workshop Journal* 17:3–18.

Plowman, Timothy. 1986. "Coca Chewing and the Botanical Origins of Coca in South America." In *Coca and Cocaine: Effects on People and Policy in Latin America*, edited by Deborah Pacini and Christine Franquemont, 5–34. Peterborough, NH: Cultural Survival, Inc. LASP.

PNUD. 2005. *Bolivia: Atlas Estadístico de Municipios*. La Paz: Programa de las Naciones Unidas para el Desarrollo; El Instituto Nacional de Estadística.

PNUD. 2007. *El Estado del Estado en Bolivia: Informe nacional sobre Desarrollo Humano*. La Paz: Programa de las Naciones Unidas para el Desarrollo.

Poole, Deborah. 2004. "Between Threat and Guarantee: Justice and Community in the Margins of the Peruvian State." In *Anthropology in the Margins of the State*, edited by Veena Das and Deborah Poole. Santa Fe, NM: SAR Press.

Postero, Nancy. 2007. *Now We Are Citizens: Indigenous Politics in Post-Multicultural Bolivia*. Stanford, CA: Stanford University Press.

Postero, Nancy. 2010. "The Struggle to Create a Radical Democracy in Bolivia." *Latin American Research Review* 45:59–78.

Postero, Nancy. 2017. *The Indigenous State: Race, Politics, and Performance in Plurinational Bolivia*. Berkeley: University of California Press.

Quijano, Aníbal. 2007. "Coloniality and Modernity/Rationality." *Cultural Studies* 21 (2–3): 168–78.

Quiroga, Carlos. 2008. *Bolivia's Morales Bars "Spying" U.S. DEA Agents*. Accessed November 23, 2016. http://www.reuters.com/article/us-bolivia-usa-dea-idUSTRE4A01IW20081101.

Radcliffe, Sarah. 2007. "Latin American Indigenous Geographies of Fear: Living in the Shadow of Racism, Lack of Development, and Anti-Terror Measures." *Annals of the Association of American Geographers* 97 (2): 385–97.

Ramirez, Maria Clemencia. 2010. "Maintaining Democracy in Colombia through Political Exclusion, States of Exception and Dirty War." In *Violent Democracies in Latin America*, edited by Enrique Desmond Arias and Daniel Goldstein, 84–107. Durham, NC: Duke University Press.

Ramirez, Maria Clemencia. 2011. *Between the Guerrillas and the State: The Cocalero Movement, Citizenship and Identity in the Colombian Amazon*. Durham, NC: Duke University Press.

Ramos, Alcida Rita. 1998. *Indigenism: Ethnic Politics in Brazil*. Madison: University of Wisconsin Press.

Rancière, Jacques. 1995. *On the Shores of Politics*. New York: Verso.

Rappaport, Joanne. 2005. *Intercultural Utopias: Public Intellectuals, Cultural Experimentation and Ethnic Pluralism in Colombia*. Durham, NC: Duke University Press.

Ravindran, Tathagatan. 2016. "From Populist to Institutionalist Politics: Political Cultures of Protest in Contemporary Andean Bolivia." *Critical Sociology* 44 (1): 61–74.

Rayner, J. 2014. "When Participation Begins with a 'NO': How Some Costa Ricans Realized Direct Democracy by Contesting Free Trade." *Etnofoor* 26 (2): 11–32.

Razsa, Maple, and Andrej Kurnik. 2012. "The Occupy Movement in Žižek's Hometown: Direct Democracy and a Politics of Becoming." *American Ethnologist* 39 (2): 238–58.

Regalsky, Pablo. 2010. "Political Processes and the Reconfiguration of the State in Bolivia." *Latin American Perspectives* 37 (172): 35–50.

Reinaga, Fausto. 1969. *La Revolucion India*. La Paz: Ediciones Fundacion Amautica "Fausto Reinaga."

Rivera, Alberto. 1991. *¿Qué Sabemos Sobre el Chapare?* Cochabamba: CERES/CLACSO.

Rivera, Silvia. 1987. *Oppressed but Not Defeated: Peasant Struggles among the Aymara and Quechua in Bolivia, 1900–1980*. Geneva: UN Research Institute for Social Development.

Rivera, Silvia. 1990. "Liberal Democracy and Ayllu Democracy in Bolivia." *Journal of Development Studies* 26 (4): 97–121.

Rivera, Silvia. 2003. *Las fronteras de la coca*. La Paz: Aruwiyiri IDIS-UMSA.

Rivera Cusicanqui, Silvia. 2010. *Ch'ixinakax utxiwa: Una reflexión sobre prácticas y discursos descolonizadores*. Buenos Aires: Tinta Limón.

Robinson, Matthew, and Renee Scherlen. 2007. *Lies, Damned Lies, and Drug War Statistics: A Critical Analysis of Claims Made by the Office of National Drug Control Policy*. Albany: State University of New York Press.

Rockefeller, Stuart. 2007. "Dual Power in Bolivia: Movement and Government since the Election of 2005." *Urban Anthropology* 36 (3): 161–93.

Rodríguez, Roberto. 1996. *A la Sombra de la Coca: Relatos del Chapare Boliviano*. Cochabamba: Accion Andina.

Rodriguez Ostria, Gustavo. 1991. *El socavon y el sindicato: Ensayos historicos sobre los trabajadores mineros, siglos XIX–XX*. La Paz: ILDIS.

Roseberry, William. 1994. "Hegemony and the Language of Contention." In *Everyday Forms of State Formation: Revolution and the Negotiation of Rule in Modern Mexico*, edited by Gilbert Joseph and Daniel Nugent. Durham, NC: Duke University Press.

Rossell Arce, Pablo. 2012. "2011: ¿El parteaguas del evismo? Bolivia después del conflicto del Tipnis." *Nueva Sociedad* 237 (January–February): 4–16.

Rousseau, Stéphanie. 2011. "Indigenous and Feminist Movements at the Constituent Assembly in Bolivia: Locating the Representation of Indigenous Women." *Latin American Research Review* 46 (2): 5–28.

Rowe, William, and Vivian Schelling. 1991. *Memory and Modernity: Popular Culture in Latin America*. Critical Studies in Latin American Culture. London: Verso.

Sahlins, Marshall. 1999. "What Is Anthropological Enlightenment? Some Lessons of the Twentieth Century." *Annual Review of Anthropology* 28:i–xxiii.

Salman, Ton. 2006. "The Jammed Democracy: Bolivia's Troubled Political Learning Process." *Bulletin of Latin American Research* 25 (2): 163–82.

Sanabria, Harry. 1993. *The Coca Boom and Rural Social Change in Bolivia*. Ann Arbor: University of Michigan Press.

Sanabria, Harry. 1999. "Consolidating States, Restructuring Economies, and Confronting Workers and Peasants: The Antinomies of Bolivian Neoliberalism." *Comparative Studies in Society and History* 41 (3): 535–61.

Sanchez, Darynka. 2011. "Hallan fábrica gigante de cristalización en Isiboro y mueren 2 personas." *Opinión*, October 21.

Schedler, Andreas. 1998. "What Is Democratic Consolidation?" *Journal of Democracy* 9 (2): 91–107.

Scheper-Hughes, Nancy. 1995. "The Primacy of the Ethical: Propositions for a Militant Anthropology." *Current Anthropology* 36 (3): 409–40.

Schipani, Andres. 2010. *Cocaine Production Rise Spells Trouble for Bolivia*. BBC Online, June 16. Accessed July 3, 2010. http://www.bbc.co.uk/news/10231343.

Schultze-Kraft, Markus. 2016. *Evolution of Estimated Coca Cultivation and Cocaine Production in South America (Bolivia, Colombia and Peru) and of the Actors, Modalities and Routes of Cocaine*. Lisbon: European Monitoring Centre for Drugs and Drug Addiction.

Scott, James. 1998. *Seeing Like a State: How Certain Schemes to Improve the Human Condition Have Failed*. New Haven, CT: Yale University Press.

Seligson, Mitchell, and Daniel Moreno. 2006. *La cultura política de los bolivianos: Aproximaciones cuantitativas*. Cochabamba: Ciudadania, LAPOP.

Sen, Amartya Kumar. 1999. "Democracy as a Universal Value." *Journal of Democracy* 10 (3): 3–17.

Shah, Alpa. 2010. *In the Shadows of the State: Indigenous Politics, Environmentalism, and Insurgency in Jharkhand, India*. Durham, NC: Duke University Press.

Shah, Alpa. 2014. "'The Muck of the Past': Revolution, Social Transformation, and the Maoists in India." *Journal of the Royal Anthropological Institute* 20 (2): 337–56.

Shakow, Miriam. 2014. *Along the Bolivian Highway: Social Mobility and Political Culture in a New Middle Class*. Philadelphia: University of Pennsylvania Press.

Sieder, Rachel. 2002. "Introduction." In *Multiculturalism in Latin America: Indigenous Rights, Diversity and Democracy*, edited by Rachel Sieder. Basingstoke, UK: Palgrave Macmillan.

Sivak, Martín. 2010. *Evo Morales: The Extraordinary Rise of the First Indigenous President of Bolivia*. Basingstoke, UK: Palgrave Macmillan.

Skarbek, David. 2014. *The Social Order of the Underworld: How Prison Gangs Govern the American Penal System*. Oxford: Oxford University Press.

Solway, Jacqueline. 2009. "Human Rights and NGO 'Wrongs': Conflict Diamonds, Culture Wars and the 'Bushman Question.'" *Africa* 79 (3): 321–46.

Soux, Maria Luisa. 1993. *La coca liberal: Producción y circulación a principios del siglo XIX*. La Paz: CID.

Spedding, Alison. 1994. *Wachu wachu: Cultivo de coca e identidad en los Yunkas de La Paz*. La Paz: Hisbol.

Spedding, Alison. 1997. "The Coca Field as a Total Social Fact." In *Coca, Cocaine, and the Bolivian Reality*, edited by B. Leons and H. Sanabria, 47–70. Albany: State University of New York Press.

Spedding, Alison. 1998. "Contra-afinidad: Algunos comentarios sobre el compadrazgo andino." In *Gente de Carne y Hueso: Las Tramas de Parentesco en los Andes*, edited by Denise Arnold and Juan de dios Yapita. La Paz: CLASE/ILCA.

Spencer, Jonathan. 1997. "Post-Colonialism and the Political Imagination." *Journal of the Royal Anthropological Institute* 3 (1): 1–19.

Spencer, Jonathan. 2007. *Anthropology, Politics, and the State: Democracy and Violence in South Asia*. Cambridge: Cambridge University Press.

Spronk, Susan. 2007. "Roots of Resistance to Urban Water Privatization in Bolivia: The 'New Working Class,' the Crisis of Neoliberalism, and Public Services." *International Labor and Working-Class History* 71 (spring): 8–28.

Starn, Orin. 1992. "'I Dreamed of Foxes and Hawks': Reflections on Peasant Protest, New Social Movements and the Rondas Campesinas of Northern Peru." In *The Making of Social Movements in Latin America: Identity, Strategy and Democracy*, edited by A. Escobar and S. Alvarez. Boulder, CO: Westview.

Starn, Orin. 1999. *Nightwatch: The Politics of Protest in the Andes*. Durham, NC: Duke University Press.

Stearman, Allyn MacLean. 1996. "Los Yuqui de la Amazonía boliviana: Estrategias de subsistencia, prestigio y liderazgo en una sociedad en proceso de aculturación." In *Globalización y cambio en la Amazonía indígena*, edited by Fernando Santos-Granero, 89–129. Quito: Abya-Yala/FLACSO.

Stefanoni, Pablo. 2003. *El nacionalismo índigena como identidad política: La emergencia del MAS-IPSP (1995–2003)*. Accesssed October 30, 2014. http://bibliotecavirtual .clacso.org.ar/ar/libros/becas/2002/mov/stefanoni.pdf.

Stefanoni, Pablo. 2007. "Bolivia, Bajo el Signo del Nacionalismo Indigena." In *Reinventando la Nacion en Bolivia: Movimientos Sociales, Estado y Poscolonialidad*, edited by Karin Monasterios, Pablo Stefanoni, and Herve Do Alto. La Paz: CLACSO/Plural Editores.

Stefanoni, Pablo. 2010. *Qué hacer con los indios: Y otros traumas irresueltos de la colonialidad*. La Paz: Plural Editores.

Stefanoni, Pablo. 2016. *Bolivia: A Referendum Decided by Penalty Shootout*. Open Democracy. Accessed November 9, 2016. https://http://www.opendemocracy.net /democraciaabierta/pablo-stefanoni/bolivia-referendum-decided-by-penalty-shootout.

Stephenson, Marcia. 2002. "Forging an Indigenous Counterpublic Sphere: The Taller De Historia Oral Andina in Bolivia." *Latin American Research Review* 37 (2): 99–118.

Steur, Luisa. 2009. "Adivasi Mobilization: 'Identity' versus 'Class' after the Kerala Model of Development?" *Journal of South Asian Development* 4 (1): 25–44.

Stocks, Anthony. 2005. "Too Much for Too Few? Problems of Indigenous Land Rights in Latin America." *Annual Reivew of Anthropology* 34:85–104.

Sturtevant, Chuck. 2015. "'Some Time from Now They'll Be Good Farmers': Rethinking Perceptions of Social Evolution in an Area of Interethnic Contact in Lowland Bolivia." *Latin American and Caribbean Ethnic Studies* 10 (2): 180–98.

Svampa, Maristella, and Pablo Stefanoni. 2007. "Entrevista a Álvaro García Linera: 'Evo simboliza el quiebre de un imaginario restringido a la subalternidad de los indígenas.'" OSAL 8 (22): 143–64.

Tate, Winifred. 2015. Drugs, Thugs, and Diplomats: U.S. Policymaking in Colombia. Stanford, CA: Stanford University Press.

Thompson, Edward P. 1971. "The Moral Economy of the English Crowd in the Eighteenth Century." Past and Present 50:76–136.

Thomson, Sinclair. 2009. "Bull Horns and Dynamite: Echoes of Revolution in Bolivia." NACLA Report on the Americas (March/April), 21–27.

Thoumi, Francisco. 2002. "Illegal Drugs in Colombia: From Illegal Economic Boom to Social Crisis." Annals of the American Academy of Political and Social Science 582:102–16. doi:10.1177/000271620258200108.

Ticona, Alejo. 2003. "El Thaki entre los Aymara y Quechua o la democracia de los gobiernos comunales." In Los Andes desde los Andes, edited by Alejo Ticona, 125–46. La Paz: Ediciones Yachaywasi.

Ticona, Esteban, Gonzalo Rojas, and Xavier Albó, eds. 1995. Votos y Wiphalas: Campesinos y pueblos originarios en democracia. La Paz: CIPCA; Fundación Milenio.

Tokatlian, Juan Gabriel. 2010. "La 'guerra antidrogas' y el Comando Sur." Foreign Affairs Latinoamérica 10 (1): 43–50.

Toranzo, Carlos. 1997. "Informal and Illicit Economies and the Role of Narco Trafficking." In Coca, Cocaine, and the Bolivian Reality, edited by B. Leons and H. Sanabria. Albany: State University of New York Press.

Toranzo Roca, Carlos, ed. 1990. Debate Regional: El Chapare actual' sindicatos y ONG's en la Region. Cochabamba: CERES.

Torrico, Erick. 2008. "The Media in Bolivia: The Market-Driven Economy, 'Shock Therapy' and the Democracy That Ended." In The Media in Latin America, edited by Jairo Lugo-Ocando. Glasgow: Open University Press.

Torrico, Erick R., and Sandra Villegas. 2016. Análisis del Desarrollo Mediático en Bolivia. La Paz: UNESCO; PIDC.

Tsing, Anna. 2007. "Indigenous Voice." In Indigenous Experience Today, edited by Marisol de la Cadena and Orin Starn, 33–68. New York: Berg.

Turner, Terence. 1995. "An Indigenous People's Struggle for Socially Equitable and Ecologically Sustainable Production: The Kayapó Revolt against Extractivism." Journal of Latin American Anthropology 1 (1): 98–121.

UNDP. 2016. "Reflections on Drug Policy and Its Impact on Human Development: Innovative Approaches." HIV, Health and Development. Vienna: UN Development Programme.

UNODC. 2007. Coca Cultivation in the Andean Region: A Survey of Bolivia, Colombia, Ecuador and Peru. Vienna: UN Office on Drugs and Crime.

UNODC. 2015. Estado Plurinacional de Bolivia: Monitoreo de Cultivos de Coca 2014. La Paz: Oficina de las Naciones Unidas Contra la Droga y el Delito.

UNODC. 2016a. Colombia: Monitoreo de territorios afectados por cultivos ilicitos 2015. Vienna: UN Office on Drugs and Crime.

UNODC. 2016b. *Estado Plurinacional de Bolivia: Monitoreo de Cultivos de Coca 2015*. La Paz: Oficina de las Naciones Unidas Contra la Droga y el Delito.

UNODC. 2016c. *Peru: Monitoreo de Cultivos de Coca 2015*. Vienna: UN Office on Drugs and Crime.

UNODC. 2016d. *World Drug Report*. Vienna: UN Office on Drugs and Crime.

UNODC. 2017a. *Colombia: Monitoreo de territories afectados por cultivos ilicitos 2016*. Bogotá: UN Office on Drugs and Crime.

UNODC. 2017b. *Estado Plurinacional de Bolivia: Monitoreo de Cultivos de Coca 2015*. La Paz: Oficina de las Naciones Unidas Contra la Droga y el Delito.

Urioste, Miguel. 1989. *Resistencia campesina: Efectos de la politica econmica neo-liberal del Decreto Supremo 21060*. La Paz: CEDLA.

USAID. 2005. *Bolivia Program Description and Activity Data Sheets*. U.S. Agency for International Development, July 13. Accessed September 16, 2016. http://2001–2009 .state.gov/p/inl/rls/fs/49024.htm.

Valenzuela, Arturo. 2004. "Latin American Presidencies Interrupted." *Journal of Democracy* 15 (4): 5–19.

Van Cott, Donna Lee. 2003. "From Exclusion to Inclusion: Bolivia's 2002 Elections." *Journal of Latin American Studies* 35 (4): 751–75.

Van Cott, Donna Lee. 2005. *From Movements to Parties in Latin America: The Evolution of Ethnic Politics*. Cambridge: Cambridge University Press.

Van Cott, Donna Lee. 2007. "Latin America's Indigenous Peoples." *Journal of Democracy* 18 (4): 127–41.

Van Cott, Donna Lee. 2008. *Radical Democracy in the Andes*. New York: Cambridge University Press.

Van Vleet, Krista. 2008. *Performing Kinship: Narrative, Gender and the Intimacies of Power in the Andes*. Austin: University of Texas Press.

Vargas, Gonzalo. 2014. "Identidad en el Chapare: De cocaleros a indígenas originarios campesinos." *Nueva Crónica y Buen Gobierno* 142 (April 16).

Vargas, Jose, and Santiago Garriga. 2015. "Explaining Inequality and Poverty Reduction in Bolivia." IMF Working Paper. Washington, DC: International Monetary Fund.

Vásquez, Katiuska. 2013. "Linchamientos, un problema sin fin." *Los Tiempos*, October 6.

Vazualdo, Diego Mattos. 2014. "Coca y representación: La hoja de coca en la constitución de la nación Boliviana en la época neoliberal." *Latin American Research Review* 49 (1): 23–38.

Vegas, Luis. 2002. "Gobierno Tiene Agenda de Evo con Direcciones de las FARC y ELN." *El Deber*.

Velasco, Susan, and Marco Fernandez. 2007. "Monasterio, Anez y Kuljis Tienen el Control de la Carne." *La Prensa*, November 19.

Veltmeyer, Henry. 1997. "Decentralisation as the Institutional Basis for Community-Based Participatory Development: The Latin American Experience." *Canadian Journal of Development Studies* 18 (2): 303–25.

Vincent, Susan. 2017. "Transformations of Collectivism and Individualism in the Peruvian Central Andes: A Comunidad over Three Decades." *Ethnography* 19 (1): 63–83.

Viola, Andreu. 2001. *Viva La Coca, Mueran Los Gringos: Movilizaciones Campesinas y Etnicidad en el Chapare (Bolivia)*. Estuis d'Antropologia Social i Cultural 6. Barcelona: Publicacions de la Universitat de Barcelona.

Wacquant, Loic. 2012. "Three Steps to a Historical Anthropology of Actually Existing Neoliberalism." *Social Anthropology* 20 (1): 66–79.

Wacquant, Loic. 2014. "The Global Firestorm of Law and Order: On Punishment and Neoliberalism." *Thesis Eleven* 122 (1): 72–88.

Wade, Peter. 1993. *Blackness and Race Mixture: The Dynamics of Racial Identity in Colombia*. Baltimore: Johns Hopkins University Press.

Wade, Peter. 2007. *Race and Ethnicity in Latin America*. London: Pluto.

Wallace, Gregory. 2016. "Voter Turnout at 20-Year Low in 2016." Accessed November 30, 2016. http://edition.cnn.com/2016/11/11/politics/popular-vote-turnout-2016/.

Walsh, Catherine. 2010. "Development as *buen vivir*: Institutional Arrangements and (De)Colonial Entanglement." *Development* 53 (1): 15–21.

Webber, Jeffrey. 2005. "Left-Indigenous Struggles in Bolivia: Searching for Revolutionary Democracy." *Monthly Review* 57 (4): 34–48.

Webber, Jeffrey. 2010a. *From Rebellion to Reform in Bolivia: Class Struggle, Indigenous Liberation, and the Politics of Evo Morales*. Chicago: Haymarket.

Webber, Jeffrey. 2010b. "From Rebellion to Reform: Image and Reality in the Bolivia of Evo Morales." *International Socialist Review* 73. http://isreview.org/issue/73/rebellion-reform.

Webber, Jeffrey. 2011. *Red October: Left-Indigenous Struggles in Modern Bolivia*. Leiden: Brill.

Webber, Jeffrey. 2012. "Revolution against 'Progress': The TIPNIS Struggle and Class Contradictions in Bolivia." *International Socialism Quarterly Journal*. http://www.isj.org.uk/?id=780.

Webber, Jeffrey. 2016. "Evo Morales and the Political Economy of Passive Revolution in Bolivia, 2006–15." *Third World Quarterly* 37 (10): 1855–76.

Webber, Jeffrey. 2017. "Evo Morales, Transformismo, and the Consolidation of Agrarian Capitalism in Bolivia." *Journal of Agrarian Change* 17 (2): 330–47.

Weismantel, Mary. 2001. *Cholas and Pishtacos: Stories of Race and Sex in the Andes*. Chicago: University of Chicago Press.

Weismantel, Mary. 2006. "Ayllu: Real and Imagined Communities in the Andes." In *The Seductions of Community: Emancipations, Oppressions, Quandaries*, edited by G. W. Creed. Santa Fe, NM: SAR Press.

Wennergren, Boyd, and Morris Whitaker. 1976. "Investment in Access Roads and Spontaneous Colonization: Additional Evidence from Bolivia." *Land Economics* 52 (1): 88–95.

Weyland, Kurt. 2013. "The Threat from the Populist Left." *Journal of Democracy* 24 (3): 18–32.

Whitehead, Laurence. 2003. "The Bolivian National Revolution: A Comparison." In *Proclaiming Revolution: Bolivia in Comparative Perspective*, edited by Merilee Grindle and Pilar Domingo. London: Institute of Latin American Studies and David Rockefeller Center for Latin American Studies.

Wiel, Connie. 1983. "Migration among Landholdings by Bolivian Campesinos." *Geographical Review* 73 (2): 182–97.

Wilson, Pamela, and Michelle Stewart. 2008. "Indigeneity and Indigenous Media on the Global Stage." In *Global Indigenous Media: Cultures, Poetics and Politics*, edited by Pamela Wilson and Michelle Stewart. Durham, NC: Duke University Press.

Wolf, Eric. 2001. *Pathways of Power: Building an Anthropology of the Modern World*. Berkeley: University of California Press.

Wolf, Eric, and Edward Hansen. 1967. "Caudillo Politics: A Structural Analysis." *Comparative Studies in Society and History* 9 (2): 168–79.

Wolff, Jonas. 2013. "Towards Post-Liberal Democracy in Latin America? A Conceptual Framework Applied to Bolivia." *Journal of Latin American Studies* 45 (1): 31–59.

World Bank. 2016a. "Bolivia Data." Accessed October 10, 2016. http://data.worldbank.org/country/bolivia.

World Bank. 2016b. "Proportion of Seats Held by Women in National Parliaments (%)." Accessed November 19, 2016. http://data.worldbank.org/indicator/SG.GEN.PARL.ZS?locations=BO.

World Bank. 2017. "GDP per Capita (Current US$)." http://data.worldbank.org/indicator/NY.GDP.PCAP.CD.

Yagoub, Mimi. 2016. *Challenging the Cocaine Figures, Part I: Bolivia*. Accessed April 16, 2017. http://www.insightcrime.org/news-analysis/challenging-the-cocaine-figures-part-1-bolivia.

Yashar, Deborah. 2005. *Contesting Citizenship in Latin America: The Rise of Indigenous Movements and the Postliberal Challenge*. Cambridge: Cambridge University Press.

Youngers, Coletta. 2003. *The U.S. and Latin America after 9–11 and Iraq*. http://fpif.org/the_us_and_latin_america_after_9–11_and_iraq/.

Youngers, Coletta, and Kathryn Ledebur. 2015. *Building on Progress: Bolivia Consolidates Achievements in Reducing Coca and Looks to Reform Decades-Old Drug Law*. Washington, DC: Washington Office on Latin America.

Youngers, Coletta, and Eileen Rosin, eds. 2005a. *Drugs and Democracy in Latin America: The Impact of U.S. Policy*. Boulder, CO: Lynne Rienner.

Youngers, Coletta, and Eileen Rosin. 2005b. "The U.S. 'War on Drugs': Its Impact in Latin America and the Caribbean." In *Drugs and Democracy in Latin America*, edited by Coletta Youngers and Eileen Rosin. Boulder: Lynne Rienner.

Youngers, Coletta, and John Walsh. 2010. *Development First: A More Humane and Promising Approach to Reducing Cultivation of Crops for Illicit Markets*. Washington, DC: Washington Office on Latin America.

Zabalaga, Carmen. 2004. *La Organización de las Mujeres del Chapare: El camino recorrido, sus luchas y liderazgos*. Coordinadora De Mujeres Campesinas Del Trópico De Cochabamba. Accessed November 4, 2016. http://www.cepalforja.org/sistem/documentos/organizacion_de_mujeres_del_chapare.pdf.

Zegada, Teresa, Yuri Torrez, and Gloria Camara. 2008. *Movimientos Sociales en Tiempos de Poder: Articulaciones y Campos de Conflicto en el Gobierno del MAS*. La Paz: Centro Cuarto Intermedio, Plural.

Zeiderman, Austin. 2016. *Endangered City: The Politics of Security and Risk in Bogotá*. Durham, NC: Duke University Press.

Zelada, Michel. 2015. "Grupo de cocaleros en Chapare desafía a Evo." *Los Tiempos*, May 23.

Zibechi, Raúl. 2010. *Dispersing Power: Social Movements as Anti-State Forces*. Oakland, CA: AK Press.

Zibechi, Raúl. 2015. "Se acelera el fin del ciclo progresista sudaméricano." *La Jornada*, October 30.

Žižek, Slavoj. 1997. "Multiculturalism or, The Cultural Logic of Multinational Capitalism." *New Left Review* 1 (225): 28–51.

Zuazo, Moira. 2010. "¿Los movimientos sociales en el poder? El gobierno del mas en Bolivia." *Nueva Sociedad* 227 (May–June): 120–35.

Index

Page numbers followed by *f* indicate illustrations.

Bolivia, 27–29, ixf; economics of, 52, 140–42, 208n23, 212n9; indigenous movements in, 115–19; LPP (Ley de Participación Popular), 44–45, 206nn9,10. *See also* coca headings (e.g., coca growers); MAS (Movimiento al Socialismo); Morales, Evo; *sindicatos*; unions

Bolivian Syndical Confederation of Intercultural First Peoples Communities of Bolivia. *See* CSCIOB (Confederación Sindical de Comunidades Interculturales Originarios de Bolivia)

Bolivian Workers Union. *See* COB (Central Obrera Boliviana)

Bono Juancito Pinto (cash transfer plan), 207n16

Bourgois, Philippe, 58

Brazil, 75, 207n12

Brysk, Allison, 113

Bureau of International Narcotics and Law Enforcement Affairs, 131

Bustamante, Apolonia, 43

cable car system, 51

Caceres, Felipe, 207n13

caducaciones (repossession of land), 91

Cajias, Freddy, 168, 169

Caldeira, Teresa, 10

cambio, 212n6

Campero, Jose Carlos, 59

campesinos, 17, 19, 116, 117, 120

Campos, Matilde, 169

Canal Siete (television), 188

Canessa, Andrew, 113, 118–19, 126

CAPHC (Consejo Andino de Productores de Hoja de Coca), 41, 120

Caranavi (province), 138

cash transfer programs, 50, 207n16

cato policy: as alternative to eradication, 21, 139, 148; community oversight of, 128–29, 137–41; confiscations by sindicatos, 91, 102; economic impact of, 141–44; eligibility under, 138–39, 143–44, 146; environmental impact of, 213n4; in Isiboro Secure, 143–44; limitations of, 22, 104, 142–48; regional allocations, 138, 212n8; subversions of, 138, 145

catos fantasmas (ghost catos), 145

caudillismo, 7, 204n9

Cayo, Sergio, 54, 114, 189

cell phones, 180, 214n4

centrals, 37f

Chaco War, 29, 69, 88

Chapare, 18f, 53f, 59; anti-government protests, 130–31; author's research in, 52–57; demographics of, 17, 19; expansion of telecommunications services to, 188; government investments in, 50–52, 140–42, 212n9; human rights violations in, 38, 132–33; indigenous peoples of, 69–70; legibility of, 147, 198, 212n15; migrations to, 38, 68–69, 70–72; peasant movements' control of municipal government, 206; as red zone, 41–43; settlement of, 35–36, 68–69; sheriffs in, 209n5. *See also* coca growers; MAS (Movimiento al Socialismo); sindicatos; unions

Chavez, Emiliana, 165, 166

Chavez, Gualberto, 145

chewing of coca leaf, 19, 60–62, 61f, 67–68, 70, 72–75, 98, 112, 125, 142, 181, 192, 208n3

Chiapas (Mexico), 91

Choque, Emilio, 133

CIDOB, 118

citizenship, 12, 35, 86, 115, 116–17, 194–95

CNMCIOB-BS (Confederación Nacional de Mujeres Campesinas Indígenas Originarias de Bolivia "Bartolina Sisa"), 31, 36, 207n11

COB (Central Obrera Boliviana), 29, 30, 31, 39, 115, 206n2

coca, 21; in barter exchanges, 212n6; chemical composition of, 2, 65, 67; criminalization of, 111; cultivation of, 133, 134f; defense of, 196; international community on cultivation of, 13, 21–22, 31–33, 65–68, 141, 148, 198–200, 208n6, 208n23; legal uses of, 2, 16, 19, 65–68, 141, 198–99, 208n5; medicinal uses of, 19, 64–65, 205n24; revenues, 16, 59, 72, 132, 138, 144–45; sales of, 65–67, 71, 75–76, 198–99, 209n11; state monitoring of, 128; Supreme Decree 26415, 130–31; in traditional rituals and healing practices, 59. See also *cato* policy

Coca, Oscar, 184

coca chakas, 75–76

Mercille, Julian, 31

Mesa administration (Carlos Mesa), 21, 128, 137–38

migrations, 30–31, 38, 69–72, 130, 211n1

military: arrests of union members, 43; attacks on radio station, 177–78; Chapare, 41, 42f; deployments against population, 33–34, 38; drug trafficking by, 71; growers' self-defense committees, 40–41; repression of coca farmers, 41, 42f; seizures of cocaine by, 141; suspension of civil rights, 30, 41, 206n8; UMOPAR (Rural Mobile Unit), 38, 41, 43; union control of, 106; violence of, 19–20, 30–31, 38, 41–42, 132, 137–38, 177–78

miners: COB (Central Obrera Boliviana), 29, 30, 31, 39, 115, 206n2; as coca growers, 49, 72, 162, 177; coca use by, 62; on indigenous groups, 113, 210n5; migrations of, 38, 72, 88; mine closures (Decree 21060), 31, 32, 72, 88, 178; political activism of, 30, 34, 38; radio station, 177

minifundio, 72

Mitchell, Timothy, 145

MNR (Movimiento Nacionalista Revolucionario), 29, 52, 68, 88, 116, 169

mobile phone networks, 180, 214n4

Monasterio, Osvaldo, 175

Montero, Pablo, 112, 113

Moore, Henrietta, 10

moral aspects of drug trade, 80–81

Morales, Evo, 1, 6f; background of, 7, 38–39, 87; on coca cultivation, 1, 2, 21–23, 67–68, 143–48, 196; criticism of, 7, 8, 22, 51, 84–85, 143–44, 170–71, 175, 184–85; drug policy of, 21, 77–78, 123–24, 128–29, 141, 143–44, 196–97, 213n4; economic growth under, 50–52; election of, 4–5, 45, 52, 200, 208nn21,22, 214n3; Epifano Condori's confrontation with, 185–86; indigenous rights in agenda of, 119–20; intervention in Shinahota mayoral election, 168–70; media criticized by, 185–88; nominations for government ministers, 184–85, 214n7; opposition to, 45, 51, 52, 207n19, 208n21; patronage distributed by, 7, 160, 164, 214n7; personal accounts of, 1, 168–71, 175, 184–85, 192–94; political style of, 4, 6, 34, 54, 119–20, 188; relations with unions, 6, 7, 22–23, 44–45,

87, 168–69, 184–85, 203nn5,6; sanctions against UNICO, 169–70, 213n5; telecommunications legislation (Supreme Decree 29174), 188; union activism of, 6, 39, 41, 45, 158, 206n7; United States, relations with, 2, 45, 128, 137, 141, 204n11, 207n19. *See also* MAS (Movimiento al Socialismo)

Moreno, Marcelo, 41, 43, 45, 48–49

Mouffe, Chantal, 151, 155, 172

Movement toward Socialism. *See* MAS (Movimiento al Socialismo)

MST (Movimiento sin Terra), 88

multicultural reforms, 115–16

Munachi, Grover, 1, 54, 91–92, 109, 178, 184

municipal government: allies in leadership positions, 164; author's presence at, 55; citizens' personal relationships with, 160–61, 164, 167; *comités de vigilancia* (oversight committees), 44, 163, 206n9; elections, 150–52, 163–65, 168–72; federation representation in, 165–66; *gestion compartida* (shared administration), 165; as locus of union activity, 54–55, 116; popular participation in, 44–45, 206nn9,10; rotating representation in, 165; sanctions against sindicatos, 104; union candidates for public office, 163–64. *See also* Shinahota municipal election

Murray Li, Tania, 115

Nash, June, 62

National Agrarian Reform Institute. *See* INRA (Instituto Nacional de Reforma Agraria)

National Colonization Institute, 69

National Coordination for Change. *See* CONALCAM (Coordinadora Nacional por el Cambio)

National Radio (miners' station), 177–78, 179

National Radio System of the First Peoples (Sistema Nacional de Radios de los Pueblos Originarios), 188

National Revolution (1952), 29–30, 52, 68, 116

National Revolutionary Movement. *See* MNR (Movimiento Nacionalista Revolucionario)

Negri, Antonio, 34

Negron, Arturo, 175

neoliberalism: cocaine trade as antidote to, 71–72; decentralization, 44–45, 163,

206nn9,10, 207n11; decline of workers' unions, 117–18; models of economic development, 35; privatization, 28, 31, 32; war on drugs, 43
neoliberal reforms, 31–32, 33
1952 revolution, 29–30, 52, 68, 116
Nugent, David, 11
Nuñez, Gaston, 189

October Agenda, 35
Operation Blast Force, 129
organic intellectuals (Gramsci), 159
organic life, 85, 97, 98, 100–101
Ortiz, Porfilio, 165, 210n7
OTB (Territorial Base Organization), 206n9
oversight committees (*comités de vigilancia*), 44, 163, 206n9

Pachamama, 62, 64, 65, 120, 209n7
Pacheco, Franco, 41
la palabra (the word), 154
Paracas, Tito, 84–85
Paraguay, 29, 69
patronage, 7, 160, 164, 214n7
Paz Zamora, Jamie, 67, 130
peasants/peasantry: after National Revolution, 29–30; campesinos, 116, 117, 120; Chaco War, 29; collective action of, 41; dependence on coca, 22; government pacts with, 30–31, 50; migrations to Chapare, 72; militias, 206n3; political activism of, 29–31, 34, 44–45; revolution of, 29–30; social mobility, 29; tensions with miners, 30–31, 206n3; unions of, 31, 36, 37f, 39, 116–17, 206n5, 207n11; violence against, 51
personal accounts on: anti-coca legislation, 129–30; anti-drug policies (U.S.), 43; behavior at meetings, 154–55; on bottom-up control, 171; cato policy, 142–44; challenges of maintaining bottom-up control, 192–93; coca industry, 39–40, 45–46, 60, 64–65, 72, 74, 124–25, 128, 132–33, 139; confrontations between workers, 82; credibility of, 57; directed colonization, 69; dismissal of Epifanio Condori, 185–86; drug trafficking, 75, 81; economic boom in Chapare, 72; of eradication programs, 140, 180–81; fear of surveillance, 169; federation representa-

tion in federal government, 167; formation of political parties, 43, 44–45, 169–70; hierarchy of decision-making, 157, 162; illegal drug trade, 58, 64–65, 72, 74–75, 79; on indigeneity, 114; leadership responsibilities, 161–62; limits of coca cultivations, 143–45; MAS, 43, 45–46, 48–50, 93–94, 144, 150, 152, 207n14; member participation in unions, 97–98; migrations to Chapare, 72; Morales government, 1, 48, 168–71, 175, 184–85, 186, 192–94; municipal government, 165–66; plaintiffs in property disputes, 93–95; radio stations, 140, 173, 177–79, 180–81, 183–86, 188–89; relations with UDESTRO, 139; selection of candidates, 163–64, 184–85; self-defense committees, 40–41; sindicato authority, 90–94, 96–97, 104–5; sponsorship of community events, 81, 101; threats against members, 169–70; tropical fruit markets, 135–36, 143; union authority, 41–42, 84–85, 105–6, 155, 159–60, 194–95; unions' political activism, 43–44, 165–66; violence against coca growers, 38, 123–25, 132–33, 211n11; women's political activism, 157–58
Peru, 13, 16, 75, 205n18
PIB (Bolivian Indian Party), 121
pichicateros (drug workers), 77–78, 81
pitillos, 71, 82
Plan Colombia, 14–15, 204n17
Plan Dignidad (Dignity Plan), 130, 132, 211n1
POA (Plan Operativo Anual), 206n9
police, 42, 79–82, 92–93, 105–6, 156–57, 156f
political instrument, 44–46, 48, 153, 170, 207n11, 213n2
political Instrument for the Sovereignty of the People. *See* IPSP (Instrumento Político por la Soberanía de los Pueblos)
Poma, Lidia, 168
Popular Participation Law (Ley de Participación Popular; LPP). *See* LPP (Ley de Participación Popular)
Postero, Nancy, 49, 119
Pozo, Ricardo, 177–78, 179
Pozo, Samuel, 143–44
practice voting, 164, 165
PRAEDAC (municipal strengthening program), 137